IN OUR BLOOD

IN OUR BLOOD

CONVERSATIONS WITH PLAYERS, HEROES AND FANS ON WIGAN WARRIORS

TOM McCOOEY

Officially Endorsed
by Wigan Warriors

For my dad

First Published in Great Britain in 2018 by DB Publishing,
an imprint of JMD Media Ltd

© Tom McCooey, 2018

ISBN 9781780915791

Printed and bound in Great Britain by Marston Book Services Ltd, Oxfordshire

INTRODUCTION

There are times I profess not to care; it's only a game and there are more important things in life. But the expression I wore and the manner I slumped at the kitchen table earlier this year while on a family holiday after a tense defeat to St Helens is just one instance that proves otherwise. I'm a terrible poker player.

Two hours before this game that I didn't care about was due to start, I was frantically bashing an ageing laptop while sacrificing a month's worth of mobile data to stream said match, and spent the afternoon perched six inches away from the pixelated display on the screen shouting at it. This reveals the truth that actually I do care, and I care more than I think is healthy – but then again so do many others.

And a lot of it has to do with Dad.

My infliction in some ways has a very traditional beginning and in other ways it's unconventional. The traditional part is that I was taken to my first rugby league match nine days after my eighth birthday by my dad. 11 October 1995. England demolished Fiji 46-0 in the World Cup in front of 26,000 people at Central Park, and by 1998 we were making the trip to watch Wigan every home game.

But, unlike the majority, I wasn't born into a rugby league-mad house and I wasn't presented with no choice in where my allegiance would lie. My parents are actually from St Helens (gulp), and, despite that town's affinity with rugby league, neither, unusually, were particularly drawn to the sport.

That left me free to choose when I joined a school friend at Orrell St James when I was seven, a request Dad was happy to help with, though he would become my rugby transport. And this being a Wigan team there was one real option – so really I didn't choose at all.

But you can't choose really can you? Not if you're doing it properly, otherwise you'd change your mind all the time. Who wants to be in a mood for weeks, months, sometimes whole seasons when the going is tough?

I've never really been able to be indifferent to anything, so a liking for anything – in this case rugby league – develops into a fascination that involves reading and watching everything on said subject enough to get you a respectable score on Mastermind. And as rugby league was the first love of my life, I had more than a decade to read, watch, write and collect enough knowledge and memorabilia for it to define me.

In 2002 Dad and I went to the Challenge Cup Final together, just us on a coach, no mum or brothers and sisters. The Challenge Cup in particular was one of my fascinations, and as a youngster I could reel off chronological lists of winners, scores and quirky facts going back more than 100 years – it was an obsession started by a book, *The Rugby League Challenge Cup, an illustrated history by Les Hoole,* and a video, *The People's Final*, which meant I needed to go to the final at Murrayfield.

So, my dad left my mum at home, who was expecting my little brother at the time, to take me to a final Wigan were not expected to win. Everyone remembers Radlinski's foot, his man-of-the-match performance, that Wiganer Sean Long failed to kick a single goal for Saints, and the fact Wigan won the cup.

My dad was by then as staunch a Wigan fan as I am, despite the small matter of being from the place he'd just seen Wigan beat, and my overriding memory of that game is him standing on his chair with the rest of the Warriors fans celebrating the win to DJ Otzi's terrible cover of 'Hey Baby'.

From world club challenges, grand finals and the last match at Central Park, after which I pulled a crumbling piece of the wall I used to sit on and put it in my pocket, that day in Edinburgh with my dad is why Wigan and rugby league will always, in some way, define me.

Dad spent years freezing on muddy touchlines as I flung myself about on a pitch with no real hope of becoming more than a name on a team sheet in junior rugby league matches, often as a substitute, and a lot of money on Epson ink cartridges when making my own Wigan Warriors magazines became my preferred way to spend weekends in the late 1990s.

There has been programme collecting, ill-judged tattoos, putting rugby before a social life and planning holidays around fixtures. When I've not been to games, waiting for Ceefax to flick over morphed into scrolling, scrolling and scrolling on a phone to get score updates, and eventually that magazine making childhood hobby led to my season ticket being swapped for a press pass. I was never going to be asked to lace-up my boots, but rugby league was still going to be the foundation of my life.

It's difficult to answer the question when you think about what Wigan and rugby league means to us.

Hopefully the conversations recorded with players, supporters and those involved with the club in the pages ahead go some way to putting the answer into words.

PART ONE

LOOKING BACK
IN CONVERSATION WITH WIGAN'S PAST PLAYERS

BILLY BOSTON

Wigan debut: 21 November 1953 at home to Barrow (won 27-15)
Last Wigan match: 27 April 1968 away to Wakefield, championship play-off semi-final (lost 29-6)
Appearances: 487
Tries: 479
Goals: 7
Points: 1,448

Central Park had been standing for 51 years and the Riversiders won the championship in two of the previous three seasons. The year was 1953 and Wigan were in the midst of an indifferent start to the rugby league season. Ten wins had been accompanied by six losses and a 19-all draw away to Bramley, but something special was about to happen to Wigan. A 19-year-old winger from Tiger Bay was set to make his first-team debut as a legendary 15-year stay at Central Park dawned.

But Billy Boston was, at first, reluctant to move to the town he still calls home more than 60 years on. Playing for the Royal Signals rugby union team in the Army Cup Final at Aldershot in March 1953, Boston rattled up six tries against the Welsh Guards, prompting the Wigan directors to raid the bank.

'They (club directors) used to come down to South Wales, but as soon as I saw any fancy cars I used to go home,' Boston recalled. 'One day they caught me up and they put so much money on the table.'

Billy Boston won the Challenge Cup three times and a League Championship during his time with Wigan.

Billy Boston was honoured with a statue in Wigan town centre in 2016.

The middle child in a household of six boys and five girls, born to an Irish mother and a father from Sierra Leone, he had made an impression wherever he went. And Wigan wanted him at any cost.

Boston continued: 'They put £1,500 on the table and I said, "get rid of them mum, I want to stop here." So she said put £3,000 on the table and he'll sign, so they did.'

Wigan tried to suppress the news of their new signing until Boston's release from the army but came clean after Eddie Waring broke the story in his Sunday pictorial column. 'I was in the army and I went home on leave,' he explained. 'I signed while I was in the army and they kept it quiet. Considering I hadn't seen a rugby league game it was fantastic from the start,' Boston added. 'It was the best thing I ever did.'

Fantastic it certainly was. Boston crossed the whitewash in his first-team debut on 21 November in a 27-15 win over Barrow. He was gradually fed into the side, having come from rugby's amateur code, but still returned 14 tries from nine starts in his first season.

Wigan finished seventh as Warrington claimed the League Championship, but Boston had already done enough to earn his Great Britain call-up. He was on his way to Australia where he began an international career that saw him play for his country 31 times.

But Boston was still learning the game he was making a name for himself in. 'They had me learning how to play the ball in corridors at the hotel,' he laughed. 'Everybody wanted to see me at their club. Everything got shoved on you straight away.'

Boston appeared in the 1960 World Cup and the Great Britain 1962 tour, following which he needed a knee operation which he says could have ended his career. Pulling his trouser leg up to expose scarred legs, Boston explained: 'It was always wet and muddy but the ground in Australia was jagged and rough. I never wore knee bandages so every time I went down I was cut to ribbons. I always had to have an operation when I came back.'

Away from the field, Boston met wife Joan on a blind date in 1955 at the old Hippodrome theatre.

'A team mate of mine, Roy Williams, was courting with a friend of Joan's and organised a date. We used to go every Friday night,' said Boston.

Joan remembers being star-struck for much of that first night, and she feared not everyone would approve of her dating Wigan's new superstar.

'My first impression was my mother will kill me,' laughed Joan. 'We hardly spoke that night.'

With games taking place mainly on Saturdays, the town's rugby league players had time for socialising - leaving Boston scratching his head as to how little training these so called professional players did.

'We only trained twice a week, on Tuesdays and Thursdays, and I couldn't believe it,' he said. 'I was in the army and used to do physical training and was in the gym all the time. I ran and played rugby but when I came to Wigan, which is a professional club, they only trained twice a week.'

Post-game get-togethers usually took place in the Royal Oak on Standishgate, handy for its close proximity to Central Park. During the day, Boston worked for one of the directors who signed him, Joe Taylor, making furniture at Pemberton's.

Settled in Wigan, Boston never left once his playing days were over. Before retiring he had a variety of jobs, including running the Griffin pub at the bottom of Standishgate. Boston explained: 'I never learned a trade – now players are looked after but in those days that was it. At first I was a linesman at the post office and I really enjoyed that. But then I was offered a pub and Joan worked in Marks and Spencer – she didn't want to know but we needed something and we went there and stayed 16 years – it was a good life and my daughter Angela took over after us.'

In Boston's fifth season at Central Park, he started a relationship with a very special place and sentimental piece of silverware for rugby league people. On 10 May 1958, the Welsh wizard lined-up in the 13-9 Challenge Cup Final win over Workington, having helped the Riversiders to the final with a try in the 8-0 win over Oldham in the quarter-final.

Boston went on to appear at Wembley six times, winning three, and has mixed emotions of his experience at the national stadium: 'Wembley – it's fabulous,' he said with a smile. 'Six times isn't bad out of 15 years.'

His second appearance came a year later in the 30-13 win over Hull, before losses to St Helens in 1961 and 1966 sandwiched the classic 20-16 victory over Hunslet in 1965. The win over Hull produced his only two tries at Wembley, a stat that Boston gives the sense he wishes was different: 'I never saved my best for Wembley. I was never outstanding,' he explained. But playing before crowds of between 66,000 and 98,000 didn't touch the nerves of Wigan's top all-time try-scorer. 'I never got nervous at Wembley but Dave Bolton and Eric Ashton did,' he said. 'Some lads would have a cigarette in the tunnel and David used to be sick.'

When Boston's days at Wigan were up, after three Challenge Cups, a League Championship in 1960, a Lancashire Cup and a BBC Floodlit Trophy – the now legend finished his playing career at Blackpool – after having initially announced his retirement.

He played 11 games for the seaside club, bowing out against Huyton on 25 August 1970 but his memories of Blackpool – and his wife's – are not exactly glittering. 'It was only for a few months and I was over the hill,' he said. 'I used to work and then go to training but I never got paid! At Wigan you got your kit hung up for you and your boots shone.'

Joan also shared less-than-fond memories of the year, where Blackpool finished bottom with six wins from 34 games. She said, 'At Blackpool he brought his kit home for washing and I said he must be joking!'

Boston continued: 'The first week I went in for my wages and another lad said, "we haven't had ours for the past month," at Wigan it was there every week – right on time. I got more injuries there in a few months than in 15 years at Wigan.'

Boston's career, which returned 478 tries from 488 appearances in Wigan colours, took its toll on his body. 'I had to have two new knees when I finished – had cartilage and a foreign body out,' he said. 'The foreign body nearly finished my career. They never told us what it was and I had to go to Leeds to have it out.'

Since washing his kit for the final time, Boston has never felt the desire to leave the town he calls home. Joan admits she would have been happy to go with him if he had chosen to return to Cardiff, but Boston's heart is in the town that loves him.

'I class myself as a Wiganer. I have no intentions of leaving,' he said, having lived there now for more than 60 years. 'Wigan is a small place and I've been treated like a Lord. I even found a Wigan girl.'

Boston is a regular at both Wigan Athletic and Wigan Warriors games at the DW Stadium, insisting he will support any team bearing the town's name. As much as Wigan has cast its spell on the great man, Boston's influence spreads much further.

In 2012 he was named in Sporting Equals' top 10 black athletes of all time, though he is passionately adamant his achievements are not just his own doing. 'For me, for rugby league, to get into that, especially when you talk about the runners and great sportsmen,' Boston reflected with a sigh of disbelief when speaking about the list. 'It's not what I have done for the sport, it's what the sport has done for me.'

In 1996, Boston was awarded the MBE, though he points out it was for his charity work and not for services to rugby league, and he features in the rugby league statue at Wembley.

One statue he is also part of, which he wishes was better looked after, is the bronze rugby ball at the Central Park Tesco, roughly placed on the spot where the Hilton Street turnstile to the Popular Stand used to be.

'Tesco – it is awful what they've done with that. It's already wearing away,' he said, wishing the statue had been placed away from the elements. 'It should've been covered up.'

But across town, at the DW Stadium, where its biggest stand is named after him, Boston has watched on with admiration at the current crop of stars. Joan states former Warrior and current Warrington Wolves star Josh Charnley reminds her of how her husband used to play, and Boston shares her appraisal of the 2013 Super League top try scorer.

Billy Boston scored his first Wigan try on his debut in a 27-15 win over Barrow, and went on to cross the line 479 times for the club.

'I met him and I only shook his hand and he started shaking,' Boston laughed. 'I like to watch him. I like Josh and Sam Tomkins. I told Sam when he first came to Wigan he would be great. I don't know how he does his step – he can go either way – have you ever seen anyone who can sidestep both ways? I could do right to left but never left to right, he looks really slim but he has a lot of upper body strength – he's rubbery.'

And he is also wary of top rugby league talent leaving the sport to play rugby union.

'The difference between rugby union and rugby league is money,' he explained, before sharing the opinion that the 15-man code was not always a fully amateur game before turning professional in 1995. 'It's a load of rubbish – even when I was playing rugby union I used to get travelling money,' he said. 'Cardiff to Neath cost me three and four in old money and they used to give me a fiver. I couldn't spend it though – it was for my mum.'

But regardless of which players move on, Boston is assured the notorious production line will ensure success for years to come: 'Shaun Wane has done well and the Wigan team – the top rugby players are all from Wigan. The greatest of all I've seen, Brian McTigue, born and bred in Wigan. The Tomkins brothers, Andy Gregory, Shaun Edwards, Joe Lydon, John Barton, Frank Collier – all Wiganers.'

Such is Boston's admiration for Wigan's ability to develop talent at home, the man many regard as Wigan's greatest-ever player insists they didn't need him.

He continued: 'Where do they find them from? They didn't need to sign me. Maybe they think it brings people in, people might get complacent so they will watch people from somewhere else. But they don't need to. Look at them now, there is no need for them to go out and buy anybody. This is such a small place with so much talent – and it's in all kinds of sports – not just rugby league.'

Boston's 60 years-plus in Wigan have provided him, and countless others, with the kind of memories people share, making him a recognisable figure to even the youngest and most novice followers of rugby league.

There were some bad times, such as his suspension in April 1956, following a refused transfer request after a Challenge Cup semi-final loss to Halifax and his transfer listing of £10,000 in 1963, which was resolved in time for the new season.

But these are overshadowed by a haze of euphoric images of try celebrations and adoring fans. He was loved by the young fans who talk about him as adults and Boston remembers running out at Central Park fondly. 'There were kids leaning over the top when we were coming out of the tunnel – I think I lost my hair from them stroking my head,' he said.

But Boston's happiest day came years after he played his final game. He marks Wigan's 27-0 victory over St Helens in the 1989 Challenge Cup Final as 'the happiest day ever,' after he took more than he thinks is his fair share of beatings from Wigan's arch-rivals in his playing days.

'They beat us more than we beat them,' he said with a shake of the head, which is a sure symptom of being a bona-fide Wiganer. 'They beat us twice at Wembley but [in 1989] we went and it was the happiest day ever! We had the photograph in the pub and I used to have to take it down before the Saints fans came in. We used to get all the fans and there were never any problems.'

Beating St Helens by any margin is important for Boston, though for Joan the quality of the game is more important. She said: 'I'd rather have a game where it's close – it's good to watch – but Billy just wants Wigan to win!'

Boston has since seen his beloved Cherry and Whites smash records, sweep all before them, fall from grace and rise to the top again.

His playing career is just a small part of his effect on the town and the club where he is a member of the hall of fame.

'It's short and sweet,' he reflected. 'I've been here 60 years now and you only play for 15 of those. Wigan is unbelievable and I've never regretted a minute.'

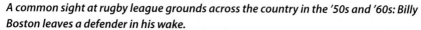

A common sight at rugby league grounds across the country in the '50s and '60s: Billy Boston leaves a defender in his wake.

1957-58

Elvis was top of the charts with 'All Shook Up' when Wigan kicked off their season at Station Road, but Doris Day's number one of 12 months before would have been more apt for the Cherry and Whites. The 1957-58 season ended with a trip to Wembley – after a seven-year wait – and it was the first time a certain Billy Boston would play there.

It was a season of no other honours for The Riversiders, finishing fifth in the league, but 'que sera sera' – there would be an open-top bus parade through Wallgate for the first time since the start of the decade.

The Beatles met later in 1957 and you could fill up your new Vauxhall Victor to the brim thanks to the end of the petrol rationing brought on by the Suez oil crisis. Prime Minister Harold Macmillan said, 'most of our people have never had it so good,' and as Boston scored a hat-trick on that 28-5 opening day win over Swinton on 17 August, things were certainly bright up here in Wigan.

AUGUST

Wigan, in fact, started the season at a pace more suitable for the first section of motorway, the Preston bypass, which wasn't to open for another year. August went without a hitch, with Joe Egan's side beating Workington, Huddersfield and Widnes before a rematch with Swinton in the first round of the Challenge Cup on 31 August. Terry O'Grady and Norman Cherrington scored two tries each as Wigan had no problems reaching the second round with an 18-10 win.

SEPTEMBER

Autumn arrived and with it Wigan's first loss of the season, despite scoring four tries at Wakefield. But the 23-16 defeat on 7 September was short-lived in the memory as the Cherry and Whites went on another winning streak. Leigh were cast aside 12-2 in the second Lancashire Cup round on Wednesday, 11 September, before wins over Leigh, Whitehaven and Barrow – with Boston scoring a hat-trick – on 28 September.

OCTOBER

Boston scored his second treble in as many games with the 52-0 demolition of Rochdale in the Lancashire Cup semi-final on 1 October. That set-up a date in the final with Oldham, but before then big wins over Liverpool City, 39-11, and Hull, 56-8, would have made for a confident mood around Central Park. Wigan's wait for silverware would go on though, as all they could manage in the 19 October final were tries from Brian McTigue and O'Grady in a 13-8 defeat.

Back in the league, Wigan suffered a second loss of the season, this time to Leigh by 9-7 on 26 October.

NOVEMBER

A third loss in a row for the only time this season followed at Warrington on 2 November before Wigan made amends with a 44-5 win over Liverpool City on 5 November, with Eric Ashton scoring five tries. But losses away to Leeds and Hunslet on 16 and 23 November followed before Wigan closed the month on 30 November with a 23-10 home win over Wakefield.

DECEMBER

Wigan lost 8-3 on 7 December at Workington Town before a win/loss pattern emerged through the month, starting with victory over Widnes the following Saturday. A 37-5 defeat to Hull followed on 21 December before Wigan met Salford for their penultimate Christmas Day match. The Riversiders won 14-8 at the Willows thanks to tries from Ashton and Bernard McGurrin.

Wigan hosted St Helens the following day with only three changes to their side – and lost 12-9. Signing off from 1957 in style though, Cherrington and O'Grady both scored twice as Wigan beat Blackpool Borough 30-13 at Central Park on Saturday 28 December.

JANUARY

Boston scored a double in the 22-12 New Year's Day win over Warrington, and Wigan followed that up with wins over Halifax and Rochdale before the first of only two postponements that season. A frozen pitch claimed the home match against Whitehaven on 25 January.

FEBRUARY

Three Jack Cunliffe goals were all Wigan had to offer in a 9-6 loss to Oldham on 1 February before their Challenge Cup campaign began on 8 February at home to Whitehaven. But there were no problems here as Mick Sullivan scored three in a 39-10 success.

A 24-0 home win over Hunslet followed on 15 February before the second round of the cup brought with it a trip to Wakefield. Ernie Ashcroft, Ashton and Boston all found the whitewash in an 11-5 win at Belle Vue.

MARCH

The trip to Rochdale on Saturday 1 March was called off due to snow before an 8-0 Challenge Cup quarter-final win over Oldham a week later. A league double over Blackpool was achieved on 15 March, thanks to a 13-2 win, before league wins followed over Whitehaven and Halifax, both at Central Park.

Wigan were at Station Road again on 29 March for the Challenge Cup semi-final, where 29,597 watched Wigan beat Rochdale 5-3 thanks to a Mick Sullivan try. A heavy pitch made for an armwrestle in which McTigue had a try disallowed in the closing stages.

APRIL

Wigan suffered the indignity of failing to beat St Helens this season when they lost 32-7 at Knowsley Road on Good Friday, 4 April, and lost 19-7 at Oldham on Easter Monday. But that would be the last time the Wigan supporters would see their side lose for the rest of the season in a busy schedule until cup final day.

Swinton and Salford were both beaten in the last home games of the season, with Sullivan scoring three and four tries respectively, before a trip to Huddersfield on Wednesday 16 April resulted in a 31-11 win.

The trips to Barrow, Leigh and Rochdale between 19 and 26 April also produced wins, but they weren't enough for fifth-placed Wigan to secure a top-four play-off place, and they finished two points behind fourth-placed, and eventual champions, Hull.

MAY

But the focus that year was on Wembley.

Wakefield were Wigan's opponents for their sixth appearance at the national stadium on 10 May and the match was joined for live coverage by BBC Television midway through the first half (they'd been showing horse racing at Kempton when the match kicked-off).

After going behind to an Ike Southward try and goal, Wigan hit back through Sullivan, John Barton and McTigue to record a 13-9 win and end a five-year wait for a trophy.

RAY ASHBY

Wigan debut: 13 April 1964 away at Hunslet (won 33-11).
Last Wigan match: 11 November 1967 at home to Rochdale (won 30-0).
Appearances: 124
Tries: 10
Goals: 1
Points: 32

Ray Ashby with former teammate Billy Boston as a statue to Boston is unveiled in Wigan in 2016.

When great Wembley tries are debated, the players hurtling towards the line through the mind's eye always seem to be wearing Cherry and White. Joel Tomkins, Henderson Gill, Martin Offiah. And in 1965, Trevor Lake.

Considering Wigan's 20-16 win over Hunslet at Wembley was played before Super League, full-time athletes and modern training methods, the evidence of the match video suggests the pace was anything other than old fashioned. End-to-end action and a nail-biting comeback from Hunslet provided the foundation for one Wigan star to take centre stage – Ray Ashby, who shared the Lance Todd Trophy with Hunslet's Ryan Gabbitas.

The hallmark of the final came in the 59th minute, when Ashby sent Lake on his way into folklore. He takes up the story: 'There were only two men involved, me and Trevor,' Ashby said, filling with the warmth of memories only a privileged few ever get to keep. 'The pass to me was high actually – I was coming through the gap and I had to pull it down and in doing that they caught up on me.

'I managed to beat three men because they were all coming at me at once and I managed to step around them, and I put the foot down and went through to meet the wingman and full-back. And I know Trevor Lake's outside me and he could catch pigeons. He could fly.

'Obviously my point was to keep it straight to occupy the full-back, move left slightly to occupy the wingman, and as soon as he did that, out went the ball, in he goes.'

Ashby's performance, along with the efforts of Hunslet's Gabbitas saw the man-of-the-match award shared at a Challenge Cup Final for the first time. For a man who had signed from Liverpool City the year before, it was a proud moment for a humble family from Haresfinch in St Helens, especially for his dad Les, who had coached and supported Ray as he grew as a player.

'It's very humbling and very flattering for a lad who just loved going out playing rugby,' Ashby explained. 'To play for the greatest club team to have ever put jerseys on to be honest is a massive honour. Mother fainted – sort of collapsed into my dad's arms when they found out I'd won the Lance Todd Trophy.

'He never saw my interview with the BBC's David Coleman because mother was that excited she flopped and they had to leave their seats to get some first aid for her. He missed the presentation and my interview. But I can't put into words the emotion. On that Monday when I got home and went in, my dad wept. What a feeling. Humble me could go and do that.'

The trip to Wembley was no new experience for some of the Wigan ranks. Legendary forward Brian McTigue was on his third visit and had some calming words of inspiration for Ashby.

'We go back to the day before and the mighty Brian McTigue, one of the greatest I've ever watched or been privileged to play with, goes onto the pitch with me,' he said. 'We go onto the pitch the day before and have a look round and look at things like where your wife will sit, where your mum and dad's going to sit. All those little things that add to the build-up to the day. He says to me, "Ray does the stadium look

Ray Ashby was man of the match at the Challenge Cup Final in 1965 – and he had a hand in this moment for Trevor Lake, the try of the match.

big?" and I said, "Brian it's huge." He said, "Wait 'til you get on it tomorrow pal, it looks 10 times bigger!' That filled me full of confidence but that was him!'

Playing at Wembley is something the vast majority of us can only dream of. And winning a Challenge Cup for Wigan alongside the likes of Billy Boston and Eric Ashton is something a lot of fans will wonder what it would be like.

Ashby said, 'On the day it was just marvellous. To walk out and the roar go up. It was tremendous. The wind round that bowl – it didn't just come at you. It was as though it was coming straight through your body, straight through your head. Eric won the toss so they kick off, and what do they do? They put the ball straight out of play. I've since spoken to people from Hunslet as I thought it was a deliberate ploy, that if they lose the toss, don't give Wigan first chance at the ball. But they all say it wasn't.

'Nobody expected us to put the ball down in the middle of the pitch and Laurie Gilfedder's going to kick for goal. People showed it but never voiced their nerves before the final and everyone was completely relaxed after that.

'Before anyone else had touched the ball other than Eric Ashton, the kid who kicked it off, and Laurie Gilfedder, Wigan were two points up.'

It proved to be the last time Wigan would win the Challenge Cup until 1985 – making the match even more precious for the players. But even after a downpour of

Wembley visits for the club, and Ashby as a spectator since then, the final he made history in takes pride of place in his mind.

'It was a wonderful experience because you could see all the Cherry and White,' he said. 'The pity was you can't hear the effect of the crowd noise from the recording, the individual chants, because it was all in the background then. But we got it full blast and it was coming at us. It was a feeling, believe you me, you feel like a million dollars.'

BILL ASHURST

Wigan debut: 31 August 1968, at home to Huyton (won 43-7).
Last Wigan match: 11 March 1978, Challenge Cup round two at home to Bradford (lost 22-10)
Appearances: 186
Tries: 74
Goals: 146
Drop goals: 6
Points: 520

Each weekend, players across the country take to the field and throw themselves into each collision, attacking move and chase every kick with no reward other than the chance to play the game they love. Amateur rugby league is a mix of some players hoping to catch the eye of a professional club, some who have known nothing else

Wigan forward Bill Ashurst on the attack against Rochdale with support from Bill Francis and Geoff Lyon at Central Park in 1968.

Bill Ashurst is also well known for his time playing for Penrith in Australia.

for years and just love the sport and some who find it the best way to enjoy the craic with mates. The ingredients often make for a good way to spend an afternoon, and on the sidelines one ex-professional in particular takes his spot to enjoy the humble spectacle.

Rugby league has been a constant heartbeat in Bill Ashurst's life since he was 10 years old, and despite having scaled the heights of international rugby and Australia's top competition, he is drawn back to the playing fields to absorb the atmosphere provided by those at grassroots level.

'I just love amateur rugby league – it's the best game in the world,' said Ashurst. 'I mostly go to St Pat's. I was a Rose Bridge lad but I will watch anything – the excitement of rugby league is better than anything. You see a lot of kids play exciting rugby, off the cuff rugby, and they try something different.'

Ashurst is regarded by many as Wigan's outstanding talent of the 1970s. In an otherwise barren period for the famous Central Park club, his unusual handling skills and knack for tactical kicking for a big player complimented his strength and no-nonsense style of play.

His Wigan debut came in August 1968 in a straightforward 43-7 win over Huyton and his first medal came the following December when Wigan beat St Helens 7-4 in the Floodlit Trophy Final.

'Playing St Helens was always a highlight,' explained Ashcroft. 'I was only 18 when I made my Wigan debut and I was very fortunate to have been able to get into the team. I did five years the first time and then I went to Penrith for four years and did a year when I came back in 1977.'

Before the high-profile move to Penrith in July 1973, for a then Australian record of £15,000, Ashurst had played in Wigan's Challenge Cup Final loss to Castleford in 1970 and a losing Championship Final in 1971. Wigan had finished top of the table, but Ashurst's try in the final couldn't prevent a 16-12 defeat to St Helens.

At Penrith, Ashurst played alongside former Sky pundit Mike Stephenson, and although they reportedly did not get on, Stephenson couldn't hide his admiration for the Ince man. 'Ashurst is the best second row forward I have played with or against,' he wrote. 'He is magnificently equipped with just about every attribute a footballer could have.'

Bill Ashurst had two stints at Wigan, scoring his last try against Castleford in January 1978.

Ashurst has fond memories of his time in Australia. 'I loved it at Penrith and I loved challenging myself against great players,' he said.

He moved back to Wigan in 1977 for a more modest £6,250, and he managed 21 games before making his final appearance in a 22-10 loss to Bradford in 1978's Challenge Cup second round.

Edging towards the end of his career, he moved to Wakefield. 'Wakefield came for me and I went there to stay in the top division,' Ashurst explained. 'I started getting bad knee injuries and then had to pack it in.'

But finishing as a player couldn't keep Ashurst away from the game, and he coached at Wakefield before moving back to Wigan to work alongside Alex Murphy in 1981.

'I did a year coaching at Wigan with Alex Murphy – it was the year we won our first trophy for a long time – the John Player Trophy in '82 [a 15-4 win over Leeds] – before I moved on to Runcorn Highfield [where a players' strike forced him out of retirement for a game against Wigan at the age of 40 – he was sent off] and then retired,' he said.

But his influence would still be felt, as he took-up coaching at Ince Rose Bridge to see through future generations of players before moving on to a new chapter.

'I concentrated on coaching young people for a while,' he said. 'Now I do a lot of work with churches, speaking at churches and sportsman's dinners.'

Bill Ashurst probably deserved more success as a Wigan player. He won the BBC Two Floodlit Trophy in his first year with Wigan and the Lancashire Cup in the 1971-72 season.

Despite keeping tabs on all levels of the sport from amateur to NRL, Ashurst admits he is always drawn back to watch Wigan. 'Once a Wiganer, always a Wiganer, rugby has been my life since I was 10,' he said. 'That was when I fell in love with Wigan and I was fortunate enough to one day play for the most famous club in the world.'

GEORGE FAIRBAIRN

Wigan debut: 17 November 1974, away at Dewsbury (lost 14-5).
Last Wigan match: 20 April 1981 away at Blackpool (won 23-8).
Appearances: 178
Tries: 30
Goals: 551
Drop goals: 9
Points: 1,201

When legendary full-backs are remembered, thoughts turn to glory: Kris Radlinski's hat-trick in a Premiership Final mauling of Leeds in 1995; Sam Tomkins lifting the Super League Trophy in his final game before a temporary stint in the NRL.

George Fairbairn takes on Billy Benyon and Harry Pinner at Knowsley Road in a Premiership first-round tie in 1977.

Read the history books and it's impossible to ignore newspaper clippings of Jim Sullivan's points scoring exploits in a 24-year Wigan career. But what about those who have shone in the dark times?

He didn't grace Wembley while at Wigan. He didn't decorate an intoxicatingly successful side by smashing records. What George Fairbairn did do was arguably much more important.

'The team at the time was struggling, but it was full of lads who wanted to do well. It was just one of those things,' said the Scot on what was Wigan's lowest point in history as far as matters on the field were concerned.

Wigan were, of course, relegated from rugby league's top flight at the end of the 1979-80 campaign, after finishing 13th out of a 16-team division. But Fairbairn, though the modesty of him suggests he would disagree, proved to be the foundation that made a swift return possible.

Despite Wigan's lowly league status, Fairbairn won the Man of Steel award that season, and was the only Riversiders' player in the 1979 Great Britain touring side.

The following season, the former Kelso RU player became Wigan's player coach. 'I stuck with Wigan as player coach and got them back to the First Division,' he remembers. 'I enjoyed it but it was hard work at the time. We had players to pick and players to drop and they were lads I was friends with.'

Fairbairn got Wigan promoted back to the First Division at the first time of asking, thanks to a second-place finish behind York, and his last Wigan match came as a substitute in the 23-8 win over Blackpool on the final day of the season.

His Wigan career lasted seven years, having been signed for a reported £8,000 from Scottish rugby union. Despite moving on to Hull KR the following season – for a then rugby league record of £72,500 – Fairbairn has special memories of playing at Central Park. 'It was superb. I'd come from playing rugby union in front of 800 people in Scotland to playing in front of 16,000 at Central Park and it was tremendous,' he said. 'The opportunity to become player coach was great and when Wigan offered me the player coach's job I thought I'd give it a go. I was young but I enjoyed it and learned a lot from it.'

Fairbairn's time at the Robins in later years brought him winner's medals in the Championship, John Player Trophy, Premiership and Yorkshire Cup, before a Wembley appearance against Castleford in 1986, just as the sleeping giant Wigan was waking up. 'It was a big difference because Hull KR were top of the league and reaching finals and all the rest of it,' he reflected.

Fairbairn went into coaching, first at Hull KR before spending the 1994-95 season at Huddersfield. He also coached Scotland in 1996 and remembers watching the 2013 World Cup with a smile on his face. 'We all thought we might get New Zealand

George Fairbairn models some stylish knitwear in 1974, seen here with Wigan chairman Norman Bibby.

The Wigan dressing room at Central Park around 1975-76 with, left to right, Bob Blackwood, Colin Clarke, Green Vigo, John Martindale (kitman), Keith Mills (long-serving physio), Jimmy Nulty, Tony Korelias, Brian Gregory, Bernard Coyle, Bill Francis and George Fairbairn.

in that quarter-final at Leeds for a moment. It was a great match but they edged us out,' he laughed about the 40-4 defeat, though Scotland did perform well for much of the match.

A match commissioner at the RFL years later, Fairbairn's involvement in the sport has enabled him to see it develop past what he knew as a player, and he cites his old full-back role as one which has changed the most. 'It's still a defensive role and because the game it that fast you have to cover side to side more than we used to do,' he said. 'Attacking wise, you see some of them, they are changing the role from beyond what we used to do.'

And Fairbairn was also pleased to see Shaun Wane at the helm during much happier times on the field than when he was at the club. Although Wane came into the first team the season after Fairbairn left, the two know each other well, and Fairbairn says Wane's role as coach is the right reward for his dedication to the club. 'I've known Shaun for a long time and he deserves it,' he said. 'He works hard and gets them motivated. It's great to see a British coach doing really well.'

1959-60

As Eric Ashton lifted the Championship Trophy in the sun on 19 May 1960, the scene couldn't be more far removed from the opening day of the season against the same opponents. Two tries from Ashton, Billy Boston, and one from Bill Sayer had helped Wigan to a 27-3 win over Wakefield Trinity and their ninth championship while 83,000 fans watched on.

But it wasn't a season of plain sailing, and Joe Egan's men had only made it into the play-offs thanks to Leeds beating Featherstone on the last day of the regular season.

And the season didn't start too well.

AUGUST

Tries from Boston and Mick Sullivan were not enough to help Wigan as they lost 21-14 away at Wakefield on Saturday 15 August 1959, but they did manage to get off the mark the following Wednesday with a 16-12 win over Widnes before Boston scored a hat-trick at Central Park in a 37-6 win over Swinton.

On Wednesday 26 August, Wigan travelled to Hilton Park, where Frank Collier was sent off during the second half of a 22-22 draw. Ashton, Boston and Mick Sullivan scored two tries each the following Saturday as Wigan went through to the second round of the Lancashire Cup with a 39-20 win over Rochdale.

SEPTEMBER

Dave Bolton scored a treble, while Ashton and Boston each helped themselves to doubles in the second round of the Lancashire Cup on 7 September as Wigan beat Salford 39-15.

A rare week off between games was followed by the Lancashire Cup semi-final against Warrington at Central Park. Wigan looked to have the game under control after building a 10-0 lead inside the opening 10 minutes thanks to tries from Jack Cunliffe and Ashton. But Warrington hit back and eventually won 15-13 to book their place in the final against St Helens, which they won 5-4. Bolton and Boston each scored twice, while Sullivan, Ashton and Keith Holden added one each in a 29-13 win over Leeds on 19 September, but the wheels fell off with an awful 18-8 loss to Rochdale on 26 September.

OCTOBER

Warrington inflicted a 16-6 loss on Wigan on 3 October, which was the Riversiders' second game in a row without scoring a try, but Boston was back on form the following week with a hat-trick in a 31-12 win over Whitehaven. That sparked a six-match winning run, with Liverpool City brushed aside 17-6 at Central Park before a 35-7 win at Dewsbury, helped by a hat-trick from Frank Halliwell.

NOVEMBER

The points-scoring frenzy Wigan were on continued with a 38-3 win at Hunslet, the team who had knocked them out of the championship play-offs the year before. Ashton and Boston were on form again on 14 November by scoring a try each in front of 24,466 as Wigan beat the touring Australians 16-9.

Boston was at it again with a double in Hull on 21 November with Syd Fenton and Geoff Lyon also scoring. Wigan were lucky to have Boston in the side, as Great Britain were in action on the same day at Headingley, with Dave Bolton and Brian McTigue helping the Lions square the Test Series at 1-1 with an 11-10 win.

Wigan travelled to Thrum Hall on 28 November where their run came to an end in a 21-20 loss.

DECEMBER

The month started with three wins against Oldham, Workington and Blackpool Borough, but the result went the wrong way in the match of the month that really counted. St Helens came to Central Park on Boxing Day, as well as a crowd of 33,197, and Ashton's try had the scores locked at 7-7 at the break, but Wigan fell away in the second half and lost 19-7.

On 28 December Wigan beat Salford 20-13.

JANUARY

Wigan made light work of Warrington on New Year's Day, winning 34-5 with a Brian Bevan converted try being Wire's only answer to a rampant display. But a poor month followed. A 15-10 loss to Hunslet was followed by a loss to Workington and a

7-7 draw against Whitehaven, before Wigan got back on track with a 12-10 win over Leigh, thanks to two Sullivan tries.

The trip to Blackpool on 30 January was called-off due to snow.

FEBRUARY

Wigan scored 11 tries in a 43-3 thumping of Barrow on 6 February before Boston scored a try in the first round of the Challenge Cup on 13 February – a 9-5 win away to Hunslet. A home double-header against Leeds followed, with two tries from Boston and one from Holden, helping them to a 9-0 win before the cup game was won 14-11 by the Riversiders on 27 February.

MARCH

Wigan won trips to Rochdale and Oldham before facing a trip to Hull on 19 March for a place in the Challenge Cup semi-finals. After having beaten Workington and Hull in the previous two finals, Wigan were aiming to become the first team to win the Challenge Cup three times on the bounce, but the Black and Whites got revenge for their defeat in the previous year's final by winning 12-8. They went on to face Wakefield in the final but lost 38-5, famously having to wait until 2016 to win at Wembley.

The league campaign resumed on 26 March and a Fenton double ensured an 18-12 win over Halifax.

APRIL

A packed April campaign saw Wigan make a dash for the final play-off spot, starting with a 42-9 win over Widnes on 2 April in which Boston scored six tries.

The following Saturday, Boston helped himself to another six tries in a 58-16 win over Dewsbury prior to an 11-0 win at Barrow before Easter weekend, with Boston adding another try to his season tally. Wigan failed to beat St Helens on Good Friday, losing 12-4 in front of 33,000 – can you imagine what that would have felt like on those terraces?

A trip to Liverpool the following day, with only one change, Jim McCormack for Keith Holden, was won 39-20. The last home game of the season on 18 April saw Wigan win 38-13 before the penultimate game against Swinton, which The Riversiders scraped through 16-14.

The re-arranged trip to Blackpool Borough took place on 30 April, with Wigan winning 30-7 against the team that finished 28th in the 30-strong division.

Featherstone, who finished fifth, were pushing for the final play-off spot but lost 15-11 to Leeds, meaning Wigan would face St Helens in the play-offs. Having not beaten Saints all year, it was a relief for the Wigan supporters to witness a 19-9 win to book their place in the final, again in front of 33,000.

In the final at Bradford, Wakefield went 3-0 ahead before two Fred Griffiths goals put Wigan 4-2 in front, and Boston's converted try gave them a 9-3 lead the at the break. Ashton with two, Sayer and Boston all crossed in the second half to ensure Wigan would be crowned champions.

HENDERSON GILL

Wigan debut: 11 October 1981 away at home to Barrow (lost 20-15).
Last Wigan match: 16 December 1989 Regal Trophy quarter-final away at Leeds (drew 10-10).
Appearances: 232
Tries: 145
Goals: 106
Points: 762

Mike Ford sends the ball to Brett Kenny, a looping pass from the Australian finds David Stephenson and then Henderson Gill is away. He shrugs off Hull's Peter Sterling in his own half before slipping through a desperate tackle attempt from Gary Kemble, uncomfortably close to the touchline – no one will catch him.

It is the 1985 Challenge Cup Final between Wigan and Hull, and Gill's try before half-time has given his side a 16-8 lead.

Recalling one of the most exciting tries Wembley had ever seen, Gill said, 'I felt on top of the world – it was one of the greatest feelings I've ever had. It made it even better because it was in a Challenge Cup Final.'

Shaun Edwards runs to congratulate Henderson Gill after 'that' try in the 1985 Challenge Cup Final.

Henderson Gill wasted no time in getting on the scoresheet for Wigan, crossing for a try on his debut against Barrow in 1981. He kept the habit up, scoring his last try for the club in his last match.

Gill had moved to Wigan in 1981 from Rochdale Hornets and had played in the 1984, 19-6 Wembley loss to Widnes. But the mood in the camp the following year was different, and Gill had a feeling the outcome this time would be better.

'We set off to Wembley about three or four days before the final,' he said. 'The feeling in the camp was just of excitement. We went through our training procedures and did all the ball handling skills. It was pretty much a similar build-up to what we'd had for any other game we'd played because we always trained with an early morning session the day before a match as well. I remember Wigan started those a long time ago so the day before the game we always had a light session.

'Everything was going well, we were looking good in training. I think what made it even better was the fact we'd been the year before and failed so it wasn't like it was new to us. We knew what it was going to be like down there and we knew what we had to do to get it right.'

Gill had a hard upbringing in Huddersfield during the '60s when racial tension was rife. 'There were bars and clubs in Huddersfield which we couldn't go to,' he said. 'They just wouldn't let us in! We'd have regular fights against the skinheads. We'd come out of clubs and have to walk home in groups of two or three, to keep safe.'

But the upbringing moulded him so that even in his early days he was never a bread-and-butter rugby player. His gift for shimmying out of tackles and instinctive reading of a split-second situation got him noticed by the Wigan directors while he was playing for Rochdale Hornets. But even before then his career very nearly withered away.

Gill takes up the story: 'I started at Bradford and I left there after my first knee injury. I didn't think I was getting the chance I deserved at Bradford and as a young lad you start to lose faith. I think it was when the great Australia side came over in 1979, I'd always heard about Ian Schubert, this great Australian winger, and I was looking forward to playing against him at Odsal. But I got dropped to 16th man for that game and after that my days at Bradford were numbered really. I had the operation on my knee and I got fed up really. I cut the bandage off myself, I took the stitches out myself and I thought, well, I'll build my leg back up my way. Then I just didn't go back to Bradford. I was about to quit the game and Rochdale Hornets came. They encouraged me to come back into the game.'

Gill only needed a season at second-division Rochdale before Wigan, a club that had just been promoted back to the top flight itself, took note of the obvious talents at his disposal. He made a try-scoring debut on 11 October 1981, in a 20-15 loss to Barrow, but Gill knew his career was about to take an upward curve because he had the word of the club that had treated him so well.

'Wigan had seen me and I'd scored a couple of tries against a Wigan A team and I must have demoralised them,' said Gill. 'I knew a player called Alan Hodgkinson who used to be at Rochdale Hornets. He had played for GB back in the day and because he was around there he told them I was a good player. He also told them I was one of the jack the lads,' Gill joked. 'He was telling them I was a good player but they wouldn't get their own way with me. I thought that was funny at the time but they signed me anyway.'

But the move wasn't easy for Gill, as his experiences at the Hornets were so different to the bitter fall-out he experienced at Odsal.

Gill continued: 'I have a lot to thank Rochdale Hornets for because they revitalised my career. I was about to turn my back on the game but they took me in, looked after me, and the whole club and directors treated me like a son. At that time, it was something that was needed. It brought me round and I paid them back while I played there. I didn't want to leave the club, but it was the chairman at the time, [Jack Grindrod] he persuaded me to leave. He told me Rochdale Hornets had done as much as they could for me and he told me this move could change my career. As much as he didn't want me to leave he said, "This is a career move for you Henderson," God rest his soul that's exactly happened! It was helping the club as well because what Wigan were offering was a lot of money for a second-division side like Rochdale who were struggling.'

Gill's time at Central Park was unquestionably fruitful. He scored 145 in 232 appearances for Wigan, lifting two Challenge Cups, a league title, three John Player Trophies, a Premiership and two Lancashire Cups, as well as playing his part in the 1987 World Club Challenge win over Manly.

In 1988 Gill, after a guest stint in Australia with South Sydney, scored another mesmerising try, returning down under in a Great Britain jersey, during a 26-12 win over Australia. Gill's passion for music joined him on the field with his try celebration, prompting the commentator to say, 'He does a bit of a boogie.'

'I'd never had anything planned – it just came out. I think it was excitement,' said Gill when asked where the reaction came from. 'When I scored that second

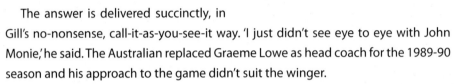

Henderson Gill races away against Hull FC at Wembley in 1985.

try against Australia it did something for me. I'd done one of the top fullbacks. I always knew if I was out on a one on one with Garry Jack I could do him, and doing him in an Australia shirt made it so much better. I got Gary Kemble in '85 too.'

So what made him leave Wigan behind in 1989?

The answer is delivered succinctly, in Gill's no-nonsense, call-it-as-you-see-it way. 'I just didn't see eye to eye with John Monie,' he said. The Australian replaced Graeme Lowe as head coach for the 1989-90 season and his approach to the game didn't suit the winger.

Gill continued: 'He disrespected me as a person. It was his attitude towards me and I didn't like it. I will not shut up and put up, I've always been like that. As far as I was concerned I had a pedigree the same as him if not better within the game and I was not going to have anyone talk to me in a certain way. It started off the first time he arrived. He had this approach in the way he spoke and some lads just had the attitude to get on with it but I always believe you need to get to know someone a little before you start bleating out at them. I've always been a temperamental player anyway and his style didn't suit me anyway. I think the incident that was the turning point was when I arrived late for training one night. I was waiting to speak to him and had me stood there for three quarters of an hour outside in the cold. He didn't say anything to me and just carried on with the training, and I thought well I'm not having this and I left the training ground, got into my car and went home. The next thing I knew I was picking up a newspaper and it was saying I'd failed to turn up for a game.'

Gill returned across the Pennines to play out the twilight of his career at Odsal, but the acrimonious nature of his departure from Wigan left an acid taste.

'I've still got the bitterness from how it was done, most fans are aware it cost me a testimonial,' said Gill. 'I'd have thought I deserved one for what I did. I missed out on that and other players have as well. People like Steve Hampson – he is another prominent player that didn't get one. You have to ask yourself why. It makes you wonder sometimes.'

Gill pauses for a moment with the memory brought to the surface and measures his words: 'I think after leaving Wigan – you leave Wigan, where do you go? It is a club I'd seen built until we got to the top of the tree. I left Wigan and that was it.'

Apparently that's Nicky Kiss being held aloft by Henderson Gill – another win to celebrate in 1988.

But fallouts with Wigan can't last as we all know. The club is bigger than an individual. We have all strayed from the touchline at times because of a gig, a love interest, even a period of despondency – but, as Gill illustrates easily, the passion is tattoo permanent whether we want it to be or not.

'If you cut me open I bleed Cherry and White,' said Gill. 'The Wigan supporters are the best in the world. You will never go anywhere and find anybody like the Wigan fans. From day one, coming from the second division to the very top I felt that. I'm in Wigan all the time – every chance I get and all my friends are there.'

MAURICE LINDSAY

Former Wigan Rugby League chairman

Triumph is synonymous with Wigan's sporting heritage. The FA Cup resides in our town courtesy of Wigan Athletic, and Wigan Warriors are once again challenging for silverware. Wiganers also regularly appear on the world stage in rugby union.

Maurice Lindsay has been involved in all three sports, beginning with reviving Wigan Rugby League's fortunes in the 1980s. Lindsay was chairman at the cathedral that was Central Park as the Cherry and Whites became the sport's most famous, successful, loved and hated institution.

Maurice Lindsay leads out Wigan Warriors for the 2002 Challenge Cup Final.

'It was in 1979 and the then chairman came to see me,' recalls Lindsay. 'I had a plant hire business in Wigan and he came to my office one morning and asked me if I would join the board. I didn't know at the time that it was because they were going bankrupt – they didn't tell me that bit. So I went to this board meeting and they asked me to take on the role of finance director on the very first day, which I felt was a bit strange.'

The stricken club were soon relegated. On 20 April 1980, Wigan played their final Division One game at Central Park in front on just 4,017 spectators, losing 20-12 to Leeds. The Championship-winning year of 1960 was a long-lost memory.

Lindsay said: 'There was a lot wrong with the club, not just from a finance perspective. There was no confidence in the club from the public. The members of the public had deserted Wigan. The crowds had gone and Central Park was like a graveyard.'

As finance director, Lindsay was faced with sleepless nights from the very first day. He said: 'I went to see the bank manager and he said there are cheques here on the desk which are not going to go through – what are you going to do about it Mr Lindsay? So that was a nice introduction.'

Wigan needed a concoction of a drastic overhaul and a good dose of patience. Lindsay said, 'The best schoolboys weren't signing for Wigan. Joe Lydon, Andy Gregory, both went to Widnes, Mike Gregory went to Warrington. It wasn't just a financial reconstruction needed, it wanted a complete top to bottom overhaul, which was what we managed to do thankfully.

'I think the most important thing I had to do to get the club back on track was to have a sit down with the people who ran the Wigan schools rugby league. They had lost confidence in the club and weren't producing juniors any more, so I had to help them understand that the club had lost its connection with the schools and to rebuild that relationship – we also had to understand how hard the schools were working.

'We began to build that and that's how we were able to sign people like Shaun Wane, Shaun Edwards and we gradually began to build up the club. It didn't happen overnight – we took the club over in 82 (Lindsay as chairman with Tom Rathbone, Jack Robinson and Jack Hilton as directors) and it wasn't until 84 we got back to Wembley.'

The last jaunt to Wembley for Wiganers had been in 1970 in a 7-2 defeat to Castleford. The Riversiders hadn't won the Challenge Cup since 1965 in what was then regarded as the most entertaining cup final – a 20-16 win over Hunslet.

'Everyone in Wigan kept telling me, Maurice, it's been that long since we've been to Wembley they've built a motorway down – all the jokes were flying,' he said. 'We weren't ready, but we learned how not to prepare for Wembley.'

Wiganers Lydon and Gregory were on fire as they tore their home town to shreds in a 19-6 Widnes win.

But in hindsight this was a test flight – and the following May Wigan were back beneath the stadium's Twin Towers. 'We went back with Brett Kenny, John Ferguson and Greame West and we won the cup. That really was the start of the revival,' said Lindsay. Wigan won a 28-24 thriller, with Kenny providing a masterclass and becoming the first Australian to lift the Lance Todd Trophy for man of the match in a cup final.

The following year wasn't exactly barren (Wigan won the John Player Special Trophy and the Lancashire Cup), but the Wembley train was derailed by eventual winners Castleford at the quarter-final stage. In the League Championship, Wigan were still improving and finished runners-up to Halifax. Finally, under Graeme Lowe, the Championship Trophy was back on the sideboard at Central Park at the end of the 1986-87 season. This led to Lindsay persuading Australian giants Manly to face-up to a challenge to discover the best league side in the world, with Wigan winning 8-2 in front of 36,895 people.

But by 1992, five straight Challenge Cups and three straight League Championships provided proof Lindsay had created a monster. 'By '92, when the rugby league came knocking on the door, Wigan had begun to win everything,' he said. 'There was a joke that Taffy and Keith, the two kit men, at Wembley used to pack up the kit bags, and the man who used to look after the dressing rooms would say next year, see you next year. That was true.'

Rugby league's health was arguably being affected by the dominance of a full-time professional club. The 1990-91 season had climaxed with Wigan facing a run of eight games in 18 days, but they dropped only one point in that run to lift another championship. A new chapter had to open in Lindsay's career.

Lindsay said, 'It was one of the Wigan school teachers who said to me, "Do you realise, Maurice, that for eight or nine years no one has been to Wembley except Wigan?" Just think about it – schoolboys who were six or seven, introduced by their fathers to rugby league, hadn't seen anybody else win the cup except Wigan. And this struck me because we played Widnes in the final as my last game before I left, and they scored the first try, were leading 6-0 and everyone in the royal box jumped up and cheered. Then Wigan scored to level and no one jumped up to cheer. It was almost as though they were desperate for someone else to win and I just thought I had to help rugby league generally.'

It wasn't so much a task of having to peg the Wigan powerhouse he helped create back – he had to help the rest catch up.

Lindsay continued, 'I couldn't do any more to help Wigan – I had given it the whole of my life and I was ready to try and help the rest of the league, and indeed Great Britain, to be more competitive, which of course they did. I became Great Britain manager and we began to beat New Zealand and Australia. It was great and a fabulous time for rugby league in the country.'

Lindsay played a heavy role in the introduction of Super League and switching the sport's season to summer. He also helped organise the 1995 World Cup. 'They had always run the World Cup on a basis of points in the test matches played, which was a stupid system really, so I persuaded Australia and New Zealand to have a 10-team World Cup.

'Australia were a bit reluctant because they didn't think anyone else was any good – they were probably right – but we had South Africa , Fiji, Tonga and Samoa and it was a great World Cup in that respect.'

The World Cup hosted in this country in 2000 was widely regarded as a disaster, putting the organisers of the 2013 tournament under pressure. Lindsay said, 'The trouble is everyone keeps comparing it to '95, but '95 was a different concept with fewer people.'

Maurice Lindsay left Wigan after his second stint as chairman in 2007.

Despite playing down the inevitable comparisons, Lindsay hoped for a successful 2013 World Cup. It was, with healthy attendances and England reaching the semi-final, before going one better to reach the decider against Australia in 2017.

After bringing the game up to speed, Lindsay returned to the Warriors in 2001 after a turbulent few years in their history. Central Park had been sold to ease mounting debts and the JJB Stadium became home, thanks to Dave Whelan's takeover. But five trophyless seasons between the Challenge Cup win of 2002 and the end of the 2007 season saw him and Whelan step down as Ian Lenagan took the reigns.

'A lot of credit must go to Ian Lenagan,' said Lindsay. 'He has worked hard with Shaun Wane to put this team together and I think they have done a great job. They have strength and depth. 'The Wigan schools are providing the juniors now in abundance. It's a wonderful tribute to the coaches, and I think Wigan will rule the range for the next six or seven years.'

Lindsay took over as chairman of Orrell rugby union in 2001 and, under Dave Whelan's ownership, a return to the heady heights of the code's premier division was the aim before Whelan ceased his investment, and the club is now in the amateur ranks, but rebuilding. He was also appointed to the board of Wigan Athletic for a short time in the 2000s and described his joy at the 2013 FA Cup triumph. Lindsay said, 'Well – let's just say what it is. It's a remarkable achievement. Anyone 10, 20 years ago suggesting Wigan would even get to an FA Cup Final – nevermind winning it – would just have been in the realm of fantasy. The main tribute must go to Dave Whelan. It's his determination and his commitment and never-say-die attitude that got Wigan Athletic to Wembley and got them to win it.'

In business and sport, Lindsay has been a prominent figure in Wigan for more than 30 years. Looking back, what Wigan means to him is very simple. 'Wigan has been my life,' he said. 'I met my first girlfriend in Wigan, I started my first business in Wigan. I bought my first house ever in Wigan. Wigan means everything to me. It took a lot out of me running the rugby club and building it but now I am able to watch it from the back benches - it's wonderful. I go to the stadium when I want to and I love watching the team. I still get stopped to talk about Wigan.'

Not every sports fan has always agreed with Lindsay's approach, but when he speaks of his first love, the Warriors, it is hard to question his intentions. He describes a familiar feeling amongst supporters, a feeling in the pit of the stomach like when someone hears the right song at the right time. 'Just to see the Cherry and Whites run out,' said Lindsay before pausing. 'When you think we rebuilt Wigan so it wasn't just known all over the world but it was the most famous and successful name. I'm very proud of Wigan and the people who live in Wigan.'

BRIAN CASE

Wigan debut: 16 January 1983, away at Workington Town (won 31-12).
Last Wigan match: 12 March 1989, at home to Bradford (won 20-13).
Appearances: 198
Tries: 14
Points: 54

Before any game, but especially a World Club Challenge, players prepare for the match with the precision expected of modern athletes. Sports science, diet, training and recovery make up just part of their routines – and one thing certainly missing is a day of manual labour just hours before kick-off.

But this was exactly how prop Brian Case spent the day leading up to Wigan's 8-2 win over Manly in the 1987 World Club Challenge. Despite holding a Challenge Cup-winner's medal and collecting caps for Great Britain, Case could be found working in his home town for St Helens Council when away from the rugby field.

'That day I was working until dinner time,' he explained. 'We were taking a floor up and I filled a skip so that was part of my pre-match preparation really. What I remember about the build up to that game was we were only part-time then. We had to break through a floor in a house and fill the skip and we were done by dinner. I then went to meet the lads for the pre-meal and pre-talk and all that.'

Case's situation was pretty normal back in 1987. Wigan were among a handful of clubs starting to lead the way with full-time professionalism, but, even so, only

Brian Case – Brian won his first John Player Trophy at the club in what was only his second appearance for Wigan as they beat

a select group of players could have rugby as their sole focus.

'I think when I played there were certain players, like Ellery Hanley and Shaun Edwards, that were fully professional. Three quarters of the team were still semi-professional – that's just what we did in those days,' he added.

It seems weird to think how a man can go to work filling a skip in the morning to running out in front of 37,000 people the same evening in one of the biggest club rugby league matches in history at the time – and the sparks in the Central Park air that October night certainly had an influence on Case and the rest of Wigan's team.

He said, 'I remember realising before kick-off how big a deal it was with people not being able to get into the ground. We also knew it was a big deal because we had stopped in a hotel beforehand. The first thing was the delayed kick-off because there were that many in the ground there were queues outside and they couldn't get everybody in. It was a fantastic atmosphere. The official figure states there were 37,000 people out there, but I wouldn't be surprised if it was more. When you came out, everywhere you looked there wasn't a spare place in the ground, thousands outside trying to get in and there were fireworks going off, smoke, it was surreal. It wasn't just Wigan speccies, they came from all over the country to watch us.'

For fans, the match was played out on top of an undercurrent of unbearable tension. Even now, knowing the final score and the jubilation afterwards, the DVD is hard to watch without sacrificing a few fingernails. David Stephenson's calm goal kicking saw Wigan home in a game with no tries scored – but many moot points.

Brian Case, Joe Lydon, Richard Russell, Steve Hampson and Andy Goodway in the bath with the trophy after beating Manly in the World Club Challenge match at Central Park on Wednesday 7 October 1987.

'The game itself was very tight,' added Case. They battered us and we battered them. It was a great team performance.'

In the game's ill-tempered moments, Manly forward Ron Gibbs was shown a red card for use of the elbow and in back play, after tackling Joe Lydon, Dale Shearer stepped on the Wigan man's head. Case didn't escape a moment in the thick of the action too – he was caught up in a dust-up with Shearer after the Aussie was lifted in the tackle.

But Wigan held their nerve, and the lead, to take the title, with Case's friend, fellow prop and current Warriors coach Shaun Wane taking the man-of-the-match award.

'We just gave everything that day and Waney deserved man of the match,' reflected Case. 'I respect Shaun and am made up he's doing so well.'

And for the Blackbrook lad who still lives and works in St Helens, Case is a Wigan fan – carrying the mantle for the Cherry and Whites on the dark side of Billinge Hill. 'Every week I watch Wigan. Wigan will always be my team even though I live in St Helens,' he said. 'I get some stick from the local people over it. They know when I go in the pub to watch a game who I support.'

Henderson Gill, Mike Ford, Ian Potter, Brian Case and Brian Dunn with physio Keith Mills celebrate Wigan's 1988 win over Halifax at Wembley.

1986-87

Liverpool had won the first all-Merseyside FA Cup Final while children were returning to school to sit GCSEs for the first time instead of O Levels. And for Graham Lowe's Wigan, a landmark season awaited the Riversiders as they were to win their first league title in 27 years and sweep-up every other honour – except for the Challenge Cup.

But this year it became official – a new era for the club had begun.

AUGUST

Henderson Gill opened his season with a hat-trick, and Ellery Hanley scored twice as Wigan opened with a comfortable 42-12 win over Salford on 31 August.

SEPTEMBER

Their winning start took Wigan through September without defeat, with Barrow (18-6) and Leigh (35-0) the first victims before Rochdale provided the opposition in the first round of the Lancashire Cup on 14 September. Dean Bell made his Central Park debut in the easy 52-0 win, but that was short-change compared to St Helens' 112-0 win over Carlisle in the same round.

Wigan travelled to Odsal on Sunday 21 September, with second-half tries from Joe Lydon and Steve Hampson helping Wigan to a 20-10 win. Ray Mort and

Hanley scored four tries each the following Wednesday in the second round of the Lancashire Cup, when Whitehaven were beaten 74-6. Back in league action on 28 September, Wigan kept up the pressure on St Helens, the only other unbeaten team in the competition, with a 34-7 win over Hull – Hanley again scored four.

OCTOBER

More than 28,000 turned up to Central Park to see Wigan beat Saints in the Lancashire Cup semi-final on 1 October, thanks to tries from Andy Goodway, Martin Dermott and Hanley. But the following Sunday, Wigan would lose ground on their rivals in the league with a first loss of the season at the hands of Warrington.

On 12 October, the touring Australia side visited Central Park for their opening match, with 30,622 watching Australia battle to a 26-18 win thanks to tries from Peter Sterling and Wally Lewis. Winning ways were to return on 19 October though, with Shaun Edwards scoring twice to help Wigan to their first trophy of the year in the 27-6 Lancashire Cup Final success over Oldham at Knowsley Road. This was followed by a 12-6 win over Castleford on 29 October.

NOVEMBER

Wigan had slipped to third in the league by the time they beat Wakefield 62-10 on 2 November, but two straight nillings, 34-0 against Salford and 31-0 against Leigh, helped them back up to second place and on the tail of leaders St Helens.

Lydon, David Stephenson, Gill and Goodway all faced Barrow on 23 November, despite playing for Great Britain against the Aussies a day before. Wigan won 16-8.

The BBC cameras were at Central Park on 29 November to show delayed highlights of the opening John Player Trophy round for Wigan, and they made light work of Leeds, winning 32-10.

DECEMBER

The John Player Trophy second round took place on 7 December, with Ian Roberts getting on the scoresheet in a 20-14 win over Swinton after Wigan had been cruising at 16-4 at half-time. Hanley scored in the 6-2 quarter-final win over Leigh a week later before Wigan travelled to Leeds to take on Hull in the semi-final on 20 December. Hanley scored twice in a tense 12-11 win over the Airlie Birds before league action returned at Knowsley Road with a Boxing Day win over Saints by 38-14.

JANUARY

Wigan started 1987 without scoring a try in a 6-4 New Year's Day loss to Warrington, putting St Helens back at the top of the table but with a game in hand. But three days later they got back to winning ways against Widnes before the John Player Trophy Final, where they would have a quick chance to gain revenge over Warrington.

At Bolton's Burnden Park, 21,144 fans saw Wigan win their second trophy of the season on 10 January. On the same day, England lost their fifth Ashes Test to Australia but won the series 2-1. A 12-try rout of Workington followed on 18 January as Wigan won their Preliminary Challenge Cup round 68-0 in a match where Andy Gregory made his Wigan debut after signing from Warrington earlier in the week. Youngsters Denis Betts and Ian Gildart also made their debuts in this game, with Betts scoring a try. On 25 January, Wigan kept up their title charge by beating Hull KR 23-6 at Craven Park.

FEBRUARY

After being postponed the weekend before due to a frozen pitch, Wigan's Challenge Cup campaign met a premature end away to Oldham on Wednesday 4 February. Dean Bell scored Wigan's only try in the 8-10 defeat. But that was it as far as losses were concerned, and Lowe's men went on to win a staggering 18 straight games.

Their quick chance to gain revenge over Oldham on 8 February was postponed due to Great Britain v France Test call-ups, but convincing wins over Castleford, Leeds and Widnes followed to put them level with St Helens, who still had a game in hand, at the top of the table.

MARCH

On 1 March, Hanley scored five as Wigan stuffed mid-table Bradford 60-6 at Central Park before beating Leeds 30-0 at Headingley on 11 March to go top of the table. A 12-8 win over Halifax followed before two more straight nillings, against Hull KR and Featherstone, put the title race firmly in their own hands.

Two hat-tricks at Belle Vue, for Hanley and Gill, saw Wigan to an easy 72-6 win over Wakefield in a record away win, which wasn't to be beaten until Shaun Wane's men won 84-6 at Hull KR in 2013.

APRIL

Wigan's charge to the title saw them go nine points clear at the top with a 42-2 win over Halifax on 1 April, with the league sealed against Featherstone on 5 April. Wigan had five games to clinch the title, but only needed the one as Hanley scored four and Gill a hat-trick in a 62-7 demolition of Featherstone. The win was significant in securing Wigan's first title since 1960 – all after Featherstone had taken a 1-0 lead through a Deryck Fox drop-goal.

Revenge over Oldham for the cup defeat was gained the following Wednesday with a 54-2 trouncing of their Lancashire rivals before Hull, St Helens, and Oldham again were beaten to close the league season, with Hanley scoring in each to stretch his try-scoring run to 11 straight games. Wigan faced Widnes on 26 April for the first round of the Premiership and survived a scare – being 14-6 down at the break, before fighting back to win 22-18.

MAY

More than 22,000 turned up to Central Park on 10 May to see the new champions beat Halifax 18-10 to book their place in the Premiership Final at Old Trafford. 'Fax, who won the Challenge Cup by beating St Helens in the final the previous weekend, took a half-time lead, but tries from Goodway, Lydon, Hampson and David Stephenson saw Wigan to the final.

On 17 May Wigan would face an arm-wrestle against Warrington in their first Premiership Trophy Final, and the first final to be played at Old Trafford as part of a double header with the Second Division Final.

Live on BBC 2, Lydon scored the only try of the game to help Wigan to a 6-0 half-time lead before they went on to win 8-0 and pick-up their fourth trophy of the season.

STEVE HAMPSON

Wigan debut: 6 November 1983 John Player Special Trophy round one at home to York (won 30-13).
Last Wigan match: 9 May 1993 Premiership Trophy semi-final at home to Castleford (won 25-8).
Appearances: 304
Tries: 55
Goals: 48
Drop goals: 3
Points: 319

All successful teams need a rock. Dependable, solid and with the ability to come up with magical moments of flair to turn a game on its head.

And great teams need a great rock. Steve Hampson fit the bill for Wigan in 10 trophy-laden seasons between 1983 and 1993.

The stats against his name speak for themselves – 296 starts in 304 appearances, 55 tries, 48 goals and three drop-goals ensured he was never far from the limelight – not to mention the countless try-saving tackles and bomb disposal feats which

Steve Hampson celebrates Wigan's 1989 Challenge Cup win over St Helens.

were better than a Hollywood thriller. Predictably, his mind is lit up by wonderful memories from a distinguished career.

'I had a great nine years and eight months at Wigan,' he said. 'There are so many memories because we won about 20-odd trophies [it was actually 30].'

Even for someone who graced Wembley five times (a feat more remarkable seeing as he missed the finals in 1984, 1985 and 1988 through injury) one game stands out. 'I think the one that sticks in my mind is the game against Manly,' he said

Steve Hampson won the League Championship and the Challenge Cup five times each with Wigan.

of the 1987 World Club Challenge, an 8-2 win over Manly at Central Park. 'It was the first World Club Challenge, no tries scored and it was probably one of the toughest games I've ever played in, even through my 10 years at Wigan.

'Playing for Wigan was more of a pleasure than anything. You had to fight for your place because we had so many decent players. We had players that could play anywhere. There were players like Joe Lydon who could take up any position on the pitch – I know he wouldn't go into the forwards but Joe would play anywhere in the backs. You had to be on your toes at all times and make sure you played well to keep your spot.'

Steve Hampson goes in for a try during Wigan's 27-0 win over St Helens at Wembley in 1989.

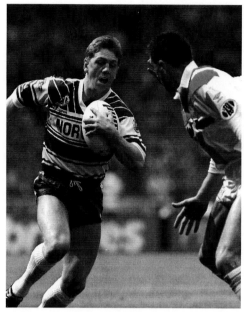

It was St Helens at Wembley again in 1991 – with Steve Hampson again ending up on the winning side.

Every kid on the terraces dreams of playing at Central Park – and players like Hampo were their heroes. The old ground has a special place in the hearts of players who played there, home and away – and Hampson is no different. 'It was brilliant because you were guaranteed every home game would be between 12 and 15,000,' he remembered. 'When it was St Helens or Warrington it was in the 20s. Even in this day and age it's great when people come up to you and remind you of some of the games you played in. It's an absolute privilege. Once you retire you live off your memories and mine were brilliant.'

Aside from his duties in Cherry and White, Hampson played 12 times for Great Britain in an era when the national side were riding high – meaning he faced tough competition from elsewhere for his place. 'I was a bit disappointed I didn't play a few more internationals than I actually did, but when you've got people like Alan Tait and Graham Steadman all fighting for one spot I wasn't too down when I didn't get picked,' he said. 'You always want to get picked but you knew either one of those would do a good job at full-back.'

1991-92

As the 90s found its feet, bomber jackets and Nirvana set trends, while Sonic the Hedgehog was capturing the minds of youngsters all over the world. And if household battles for the TV allowed for a night without the blue hedgehog, fans watched rugby league on Sky for the first time.

Some things didn't change, though, and the 1991-92 season saw Wigan again dominant on most fronts – though without quite the same drama as the 'mission impossible' of the season before, when they won the title after playing eight matches in an 18-day spell.

A 13th League Championship, 13th Challenge Cup, second World Club Challenge and victory in the Nissan World Sevens in the February were supplemented by Charity Shield and Premiership Trophy wins, ensuring fans posing with a huge collection of trophies from Central Park at the end of that season would be found stored away at the back of wardrobes decades later. Thankfully, there was no such thing as timehop back then.

AUGUST

Wigan made the trip to Gateshead on 25 August to kick off the season with a Charity Shield match against Hull. Ellery Hanley's departure to Leeds was drawing nearer, and, while still on the books at Wigan, he didn't play in the 22-8 win in which Dean Bell scored two tries.

SEPTEMBER

The season proper got underway for The Riversiders at Castleford on 1 September, and in scorching conditions of 25 celsius it was a miserable afternoon for Wigan. They never quite recovered from going 12-0 down in as many minutes and lost 38-26.

Sky's cameras rolled up to Central Park the following Sunday for a 6.15pm kick-off when Wigan faced Widnes. Hanley's departure had been confirmed the previous Thursday, and more than 15,000 turned-up to Central Park for a tight game which hung in the balance before Frano Botica scored in the final minute to seal a 26-18 win.

On 15 September, the first round of the Lancashire Cup took Wigan all the way to London as the Crusaders played in the competition. A crowd of 1,893 saw Wigan beat the second division side 28-10.

A brief return to league action on 22 September saw another win over Hull, with Denis Betts scoring a double in a 30-4 success that put Wigan second in the league behind unbeaten St Helens. The league campaign took a backseat for the second round of the Lancashire Cup, where Wigan warmed up for the World Club Challenge with a comfortable 42-12 win over Leigh.

OCTOBER

Wigan lifted the World Club Challenge for the second time with a 21-4 win over Penrith at Anfield on 2 October. Sam Panapa and David Myers scored tries in a game that never had Wigan behind on the scoreboard, though surprisingly the only television coverage was in the form of delayed highlights on BBC's Sportsnight.

They returned to the league campaign on 6 October with a straightforward 52-10 win over Featherstone at Central Park, with Gene Miles scoring a try on his debut. The following Thursday, Wigan crashed out of the Lancashire Cup at the semi-final stage when a certain Gary Connolly scored a try in a 28-16 St Helens win.

Wigan's second league loss of the season followed at Wakefield, putting them fifth in the table before wins over Swinton and Halifax settled the ship, and on 29 October Third Division leaders Dewsbury were cast aside 34-14 in a Regal Trophy preliminary-round match.

NOVEMBER

A first win for Leeds at Central Park in 11 years was made sweeter for the Loiners by the fact they were the first team to nil Wigan at home since 1979. The Yorkshire set recorded a 19-0 win on 3 November before the following week's match against Salford was moved due to GB call ups for their Test against Papua New Guinea. That was played midweek on 13 November, with Wigan losing 24-10 to fall five points off the pace in the title race with nine games gone.

They would have to wait a month before returning to league action, with Regal Trophy round one and two wins over Swinton and against Keighley on the day of Freddie Mercury's death on 24 November.

Salford managed to knock Wigan out at the quarter-final stage on 30 November, but they were knocked out by runners-up Leeds in the last four.

DECEMBER

Fans would have no idea that they had seen their side lose for the last time in the season already when Betts, Myers and Shaun Edwards scored in a 23-14 win over Widnes on 8 December. Throughout the rest of the month, wins over Hull Castleford and a 16-6 Boxing Day win over St Helens put Wigan in second place – one point behind Leeds.

JANUARY

Wigan welcomed 1992 with a New Year's Day win over Warrington at Wilderspool, and provided escape for fans dealing with the effects of a deep recession and looming general election by pulling into the outside lane for the rest of the campaign. Wakefield, Bradford Northern and Halifax were all beaten to send Wigan top before their Challenge Cup journey began away at Salford. They had to wait, though, as the match scheduled for 25 January was postponed twice because of a frozen pitch.

FEBRUARY

The re-arranged cup tie against Salford bumped the league match against Hull KR back to March, with Wigan reaching the second round with a 22-6 win. Salford's defeats of Wigan earlier in the season had encouraged the BBC to pick the tie to show live – with neutrals undoubtedly hoping they could end Wigan's four-year dominance of the competition, but it wasn't to be.

The following week the campaign was set to one side, as Wigan flew down under to show their stuff in the Nissan World Sevens in Sydney. The three-day tournament started on Friday 7 February, with Wigan beating Cronulla 20-6 before losing 16-10 to Perth the following day. In a three-team pool, each finished with one win, with Wigan going through to the following day's quarter-final on tries scored, where they beat Penrith 22-8.

Later that day Wigan beat Manly 12-8, before the final against Brisbane which still makes great viewing now on YouTube, with Martin Offiah's weaving runs sending Brisbane defenders into various puddles all over the pitch.

Back on British soil, Wigan were allowed to put back their Challenge Cup second-round tie at home to Warrington because of the World Sevens, but this did no harm to their momentum as Kelvin Skerrett and Offiah scored tries in a 14-0 win. St Helens were up next the following Saturday, with Frano Botica's drop-goal easing the pressure for Wigan in a 13-6 win to book a place in the semi-final again.

MARCH

Wins over Swinton and Hull KR opened the month before Wigan made the mouth-watering trip to Leeds on 15 March. Leeds had nilled Wigan earlier in the season and this was Hanley's first game against his old club. With nearly 21,000 packed into Headingley, the home section of the crowd were left disappointed as Phil Clarke, Myers, Bell and Edwards put Leeds out of the title race.

This was followed by a 28-7 win over Salford before Wigan returned to Challenge Cup action with a semi-final against Bradford at Burnden Park. Few would have predicted what happened that day, though, as 13-try Wigan, including five from Offiah, blitzed Bradford 71-10 to set-up a Wembley date with Castleford, who had a much tougher semi-final in their 8-4 win over Hull.

APRIL

A rearranged trip to Hull KR was won 17-2 on 1 April, thanks to tries from Panapa and Miles, before Wigan beat Featherstone 34-13 in front of the Sky cameras a week later. They were on Granada TV the following week to clinch the title with two games to spare by handing out another walloping to Bradford 50-8, and The Riversiders wrapped-up the league campaign with wins over St Helens and Warrington.

On 26 April, Wigan warmed-up for Wembley with a Premiership Trophy quarter-final win over Widnes at Central Park.

MAY

Lance Todd Trophy winner Offiah struck twice, and Edwards and Steve Hampson added a try each as Wigan won an unprecedented fifth Challenge Cup in a row. The final score against Castleford was 28-12 in what was also Andy Gregory's last game for the club. They rounded-off the season with Premiership Trophy wins over Leeds and then St Helens by 48-16 in the final at Old Trafford.

ELLERY HANLEY

Wigan debut: 22 September 1985 at home to Widnes (won 52-5).
Last Wigan match: 27 April 1991 Challenge Cup Final v St Helens (won 13-8).
Appearances: 204
Tries: 189
Goals: 9
Drop goals: 2
Points: 776

Perhaps the ultimate rugby league player, many fans regard him as the best player they have ever seen. Versatile, skilful, indestructible, it's impossible to pick a favourite highlight provided by Ellery Hanley.

Arriving in 1985 from Bradford Northern, where he had already become a household name for feats such as scoring a length-of-the-field scorcher in the 1983 Challenge Cup semi-final against Featherstone, Hanley had grabbed Wigan's attention with a trademark display against the Riversiders in a Challenge Cup match at Odsal.

During an eventful stay at Central Park, Hanley was the first man to captain a club to three successive victories at Wembley, between 1989 and 1991, and he also led Wigan to their 8-2 World Club Challenge victory over Manly in 1987.

Ellery Hanley was inducted into the Rugby League Hall of Fame in 2005.

The magic of Hanley is augmented by the fact he won the Man of Steel Award three times, in 1985, 1987 and 1989, as well as picking up the Lance Todd Trophy in 1989 for his display in Wigan's 27-0 win over St Helens in the Challenge Cup Final, which included a stunning try after 25 minutes to put Wigan two scores ahead.

Playing centre during the infancy of his Wigan career, Hanley moved to stand-off to partner Shaun Edwards until the arrival of Andy Gregory from Warrington.

Moving to loose forward, Hanley discovered a new-found freedom to stamp his signature style on the team.

During his time with the club, Hanley guested twice for Australian clubs Balmain, in 1988, where he played in a Grand Final, and Western Suburbs, in 1989, and received his MBE the following year.

His time at Wigan was not always a smooth ride, and a dispute saw him transfer listed at £225,000 in January 1988, which saw him absent from the side for more than a month. But, after a resolution, Hanley's professionalism saw him earn his place in that year's cup final and he was chosen to captain the 1988 Great Britain Tour to Australia.

His final match for Wigan was the 13-8 Challenge Cup success of 1991, again against St Helens, which produced his fourth winner's medal in the same season that he claimed a third Championship medal.

He moved to Leeds for a then record £250,000 despite having turned 30. Returning to Wembley twice more to face Wigan in 1994 and 1995, Hanley didn't

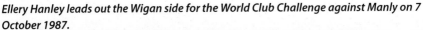

Ellery Hanley leads out the Wigan side for the World Club Challenge against Manly on 7 October 1987.

taste success in a cup final again but such was his reputation as a supreme athlete, it was reported he could play for London Monarchs in the newly formed World League of American Football, though a gridiron appearance never materialised.

Hanley coached Great Britain and England before coaching St Helens between 1998 and 2000. The legend crossed the divide to coach Bristol, Bath and England rugby union before coming back to league, first to act as a coaching consultant at Castelford in 2004 before taking over National League Two side Doncaster in 2008, where he left after seeing them win promotion.

Hanley was inducted into the Rugby League Hall of Fame in 2005 and became one of the 11 members of the Wigan Hall of Fame in 2007.

DEAN BELL

Wigan debut: 7 September 1986, away at Leigh (won 35-0).
Last Wigan match: 30 April 1994, Challenge Cup Final v Leeds (won 26-16).
Appearances: 253
Tries: 96
Points: 384

Fans packing terraces, the sun beating down on the famous pitch and some of the most memorable action unfolding before him – the youngster in front of the TV screen dreams of someday running out at Wembley. The scene sounds as if it

is straight from the front room of a house in Wigan, but this television set was revealing the magic of the Challenge Cup Final to a household in New Zealand. Dean Bell not only realised his dream, but did it in a fashion beyond what he could have ever hoped for – becoming not just a firm favourite with the Central Park faithful, but also a player coaches and parents still refer to when showing children the best ways to play the game.

'If I had to pick one I'd probably go with the first Wembley in '88 against Halifax,' Bell said, after a pause for thought, on a stand out memory while at Wigan. 'Some of the players

Dean Bell with Wigan coach John Monie in 1992.

Dean Bell returned to Wigan as head of youth development in 2000 before moving back to New Zealand in 2007, where he was appointed New Zealand Warriors' development manager.

at Wigan had been before but it was my first time. It had been a dream of mine since I was a little boy, probably since I was young kid watching from New Zealand. I watched the football FA Cup Final and obviously the Challenge Cup Final as well. It was always a goal of mine to play there. My dad used to get us up early in the mornings and our main TV channel would show it in the early hours of the morning. When I was playing for Leeds we got knocked out in the semi-final against Widnes so I got fairly close then, so to get there with Wigan in my second year at the club was certainly a great experience.'

Bell's fond memories of his first Wembley experience, the 32-12 defeat of Halifax, given his impressive medal collection, shows what the cup final means to players, and particularly Wigan. 'We didn't have any stadium anything like Wembley. Certainly, back in those days,' he explained. 'Even now we don't have a stadium that could hold close to 100,000 people, which was the crowd that particular day.'

Bell's time at Wigan couldn't really have been more successful. In 253 appearances, the uncompromising enforcer nicknamed 'Mean Dean' picked up seven Challenge Cups, six League Championships, four Lancashire Cups, four Regal Trophies, two Premierships and a World Club Challenge. Such was Wigan's dominance at the time,

the Kiwi, who also served as captain, even appeared on *This is Your Life*.

'I was very, very fortunate to join the side at a time when there were so many good players in the team,' Bell said. 'The coach at the time was Graeme Lowe. He was the New Zealand coach and Maurice Lindsay and the other directors gave him free rein basically to put a strong side together and he approached me.'

Bell had made 22 appearances for Leeds and guested in Australia for Easts before joining the revolution at Central Park. He explained, 'Ironically I'd already said yes to Leeds. Harry Jepson, a good friend of mine, was the chairman at the time and I sort of had to turn my back on Leeds even though it was a very strong club. But I wanted to follow Graeme Lowe and I was also attracted by the sort of squad Maurice said he was going to build. To me it's always been about winning and I went for Wigan and it turned out to be a good choice. It was unbelieveable.'

He also found the passion of Wigan fans unique, even if their priorities did seem a little odd to him at first. 'I was accepted really well. It was good to go to a town that

lived and breathed rugby league,' he said. 'Being brought up in Auckland, which was a big city, rugby union is our national sport so to be surrounded by fans day-in, day-out was nice. They made me feel welcome and I always remember walking up the town centre and a Wigan fan stopped me. What this guy said really surprised me. He said, "I don't care what you do this year as long as you beat Saints on Boxing Day." Obviously,

Dean Bell is still remembered as a favourite by Wigan fans for his professionalism and fearless playing style.

it took me a while to understand the rivalry. I thought, surely they want to win a trophy or win the Challenge Cup or something, but all that mattered to that fan was to beat Saints on Boxing Day.'

After his glorious time at Wigan, Bell went back to Leeds as coach for the first Super League season in 1996 – a difficult time for the Yorkshire giants, in a season where they struggled towards the bottom of the table to the point where Bell even put himself in the side for a game. But he believes the struggle sparked the development of the successful Leeds side we have seen more recently, since the arrival of Gary Hetherington as chairman.

'It was a tough time. The club sort of ran out of money so it was very difficult to bring new players in. The one good thing to come out of it was it allowed me to blood a lot of young players,' Bell said. 'Those young players went on to play a massive part in the success Leeds have had over the last 15 years or so. That was nice because I always believed in giving your local talent a go even though it was sort of forced on the club at the time. Obviously with Gary Hetherington coming in they have the reward they deserve really.'

Having such an influence across two clubs, including serving as Wigan's youth development manager from 2000 to 2007, Bell's interest in Super League is still strong, and he admits he pays special attention to the Warriors on this side of the globe. 'I watch the TV games on Thursday, the Friday and maybe a Saturday sometimes – especially if Wigan are playing. You don't have to ask – I watch them very closely,' he said. 'And Shaun Wane's a very good friend of mine to so I have vested interest. I'm a very keen supporter.'

ANDY GREGORY

Wigan debut: 18 January 1987 Challenge Cup preliminary round at home to Workington Town (won 68-0).
Last Wigan match: 2 May 1992 Challenge Cup Final against Castleford (won 28-12).
Appearances: 182
Tries: 17
Goals: 22
Drop goal: 6
Points: 118

Of Wigan's eight successive Challenge Cup victories between 1988 and 1995, there is one fans treasure the most. Challenge Cup Finals are incredible experiences for fans and players, with Wigan being blessed with more than their fair share of visits during a time when they would eventually go on a 44-match unbeaten run in the competition.

But on 29 April 1989, the final that took place on that day became the most famous of all those games – not because of a superhuman try or a classic tussle with the lead changing hands, or an audacious comeback. It was the day Wigan nilled St Helens at Wembley. Known simply as '27-0' to Wigan fans, their club's halfback on the day Andy Gregory scored a try and kicked a drop-goal on his way to a fourth cup-winner's medal.

Andy Gregory played his part in Wigan's eight-year Challenge Cup run and was also the coach to end it in 1996 when his Salford Reds knocked out the holders.

'Whenever I'm asked what was my best, I played in seven and never lost, [in 1982, Hull beat his Widnes team after a replay at Elland Road] I always say when we beat St Helens 29-0,' recalls Gregory. 'You always then get the one St Helens fan who says "It was only 27". I then say, "I'm sorry I get that one wrong, but I always get your score right – nil."'

Andy Gregory shows the cup to the fans after victory over Warrington in 1990.

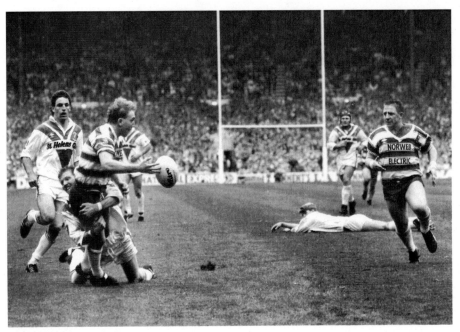

Shaun Edwards passes to Andy Gregory to score against St Helens at Wembley in 1989.

But, joking aside, Gregory, like many before and after him, took playing against St Helens seriously. Up to that point, the clubs had only ever met in the Wembley finals of 1961 and 1966, with St Helens winning both. And despite Wigan's superior record in the competition – even then – Gregory was more motivated to settle the score.

'I'd been on quite a few occasions, but you don't need any motivation when you are playing St Helens at anything,' he said. 'The Saints players were exactly the same – to me it's the best derby in any sport. You can't beat a Wigan v Saints derby.'

The Wigan line-up included names influential enough for fans to commit them to song, such as Ellery Hanley, Shaun Edwards and Kevin Iro. That's not to mention players who gave the Central Park faithful goosebump-evoking memories such as Steve Hampson and Nicky Kiss.

Wigan had lost their last two games leading up to the final, the first away to Widnes, which cost them that year's title, and the second a 4-2 loss to Wembley opponents St Helens in the first round of the Premiership Trophy, just six days before the sides met again in the capital. But such form counted for nothing according to Gregory: 'When we went there we were confident. We were the cup kings at the time, but with St Helens you never know,' he said. 'All week we trained really well and we were basically ready to play anybody that week. Unfortunately for St Helens they took a good hiding. It ranks in my memory as a great time, a great game.'

It took less than two minutes for Wigan, playing in their away strip of blue and white hoops, to open the scoring through Iro, who barged past 17-year-old and future Central Park favourite Gary Connolly.

'It would have taken a mighty good side to beat Wigan that day,' added Gregory, whose try came in the 65th minute, 20 minutes after his drop goal. 'Edwards made a break and passed the ball inside, I caught it only five, six yards away from the line. I put the ball down under the sticks and my little contribution helped us lift the cup.'

Despite losing to Saints in Wigan's last game before the final, in which they took the cup home for the 10th time, Gregory doesn't remember any worry in the camp before the game. Only fond memories come into focus.

'We'd play the last game on the Sunday and you'd just feel relieved walking off the field whether it was Central Park, Headingley or wherever,' he said. 'You wanted that hooter to go at 4.30 and then you knew your next game was Wembley. On the Monday morning you'd come down, have a bit of a workout – you were still stiff from the day before, then on the Tuesday you'd do a light weights session and some running in the afternoon and then it started building up. You get your t-shirts for training, your brand new embroidered Wigan tops, and you were as proud as punch that you were representing for me what was my home town club. On the Wednesday, you'd do your training then we'd set off on the Thursday after training from Central Park. We'd have something to eat at the old Central Park then at 12 o'clock, or one o'clock, we'd get on the coach and make our way down to Wembley.'

The day before the final, the teams visited the stadium for the traditional Wembley walkabout, but Gregory feels that part of the week didn't help too much with preparation, describing the ground as 'totally different' when empty. But the venue didn't matter to that Wigan side, according to the ex-Great Britain scrum half.

'You get up on the Saturday ready to play in a final,' he said. 'On Wembley Way you see the different colours, you see the Cherry and White of Wigan, and it's just a tremendous feeling but you've got to concentrate on the game.'

Andy Gregory puts a kick through with Kelvin Skerrett looking on.

Concentrate they did. As well as Iro and Gregory, Lance Todd Trophy winner Hanley and Steve Hampson added tries to worsen the nightmare for Saints, who had flown reinforcements Michael O'Connor and Paul Vautin over from Australia specially for the tie. And they experienced something that never happened to Gregory...

'I don't know what it's like to lose there – memories which will stick in my mind forever,' he smiled.

KELVIN SKERRETT

Wigan debut: 19 August 1990, in the Charity Shield against Widnes at Swansea (lost 24-8).

Last Wigan match: 8 September 1996, in the Premiership Final against St Helens at Old Trafford (won 44-14).

Appearances: 176

Tries: 21

Points: 84

Uncompromising, fearsome and adored by the Central Park faithful, Kelvin Skerrett was an unforgettable player. Born in Methley, West Yorkshire, the rugged prop forward arrived at Wigan from Australia's Western Suburbs, and went on to make 155 appearances in a six-year stay.

Skerrett was often a marked man for his reputation as an enforcer, such as in the 1994 Premiership Final win over Castleford, when Dean Sampson elbowed the Wigan No.8 in the face, but Skerrett insists he never took his own grudges onto the field. 'If anyone was obstructive, the plan was to sort that problem out,' said Skerrett on his role in the side. 'I never put a personal emphasis on playing – what had to be done had to be done.'

Sonny Nickle meets his nemesis in the shape of Wigan prop Kelvin Skerrett during the Greenalls Lancashire Cup Final at Knowsley Road in October 1992.

When looking back at the fixtures he most looked forward to, despite having played in every domestic final, just one opponent sticks out in Skerrett's mind: 'Saints-Wigan was always the big game,' he said. 'Everybody knew what was on for the supporters and the club – on both sides. You did what you had to do to win that game and if it meant missing a few games afterwards then it meant missing a few games afterwards!'

But one particular battle fans remember him for wasn't against Saints. As tempers got heated during Wigan's 32-4 Challenge Cup quarter-final win over Featherstone on their way to Wembley in 1994, the prop literally flew into the middle.

'It was a poor entrance,' he laughed. 'It was an aggressive game and there were things going off. I was quite a way back, saw the trouble and just wanted to get involved. I was a little bit too excited I guess – I didn't hit anybody. I wasn't aiming and I basically ended-up pushing people away.'

Even though Skerrett had his own reputation for being a hard man, there are many opponents he holds in such regard, and the players he points out may come as a surprise given his imposing frame and no-nonsense approach. There were many characters, but, as far as tough, I remember playing John Pendlebury,' he said. 'When you see a bloke at 12 stone, hard as nails and doesn't back down to anything

Kelvin Skerrett in action against Halifax in 1996.

then I see that as tough. Players like Bobbie Goulding, not as big as others but never took a backward step. It's ok being tough when you're bigger than the opposition, but when you're not then you're actually tough.'

Skerrett finished his Wigan career against Goulding as Wigan defeated St Helens 44-14 in the 1996 Premiership Final at Old Trafford. The victory saw the prop pick up his third Premiership-winner's medal to add to his collection, which included six league titles, a World Club Challenge and four Challenge Cups.

Skerrett also played for Great Britain 16 times, and represented Wales in the 1995 World Cup, an honour he describes as 'the pinnacle of any player's career'. He left Wigan to join Halifax for the 1997 season, where he stayed until the end of the 1999 season.

MIKE FORSHAW

Wigan debut: 7 January 1990, at home to Bradford (won 12-0).
Last Wigan match: 16 May 1993, Premiership Final against St Helens (lost 10-4).
Appearances: 41
Tries: 6
Points: 24

Some matches are never forgotten. And the most unforgettable carry a common theme: Wigan's win at Murrayfield to beat St Helens 21-12 in the 2002 Challenge Cup Final, their win in the last Good Friday Derby at Knowsley Road, 27-0, beating St Helens with a last-gasp try in 2011, the list goes on. Fans, players and neutrals all remember derbies, and the 2015 Good Friday win for Wigan brought back vivid memories for Mike Forshaw.

The current Sale Sharks defence coach was at the DW Stadium to witness Wigan's 12-4 triumph, and admitted it brought a smile to his face. 'I was at that game on Good Friday [2015] and it reminded me a lot of the tough, low scoring games I used

Mike Forshaw only played 41 times for Wigan,
but is remembered as a tough competitor.

to play in,' he said. 'I played in 1993, Kevin Ward broke his leg, and it reminded me a lot of that game because you don't see a lot of rugby league matches in the mud anymore. It's a different stadium but the atmosphere took me back to Central Park. It was an 8-8 draw – an epic game really.'

It was billed as the title decider, when really the result meant Wigan had to win their remaining games against Warrington and Castleford to claim the title, in Forshaw's last season at Wigan.

Having signed from St Pat's as a teenager, he played 41 games for Wigan before moving to Wakefield and then Leeds, before more successful stints at Bradford Bulls and Warrington. 'Signing for Wigan was the start of some great times,' said the forward known as 'the ultimate professional'. 'There were a lot of talented players in Wigan and early memories of playing in Wigan Colts with a host of young players I'd played with all through school. Just being part of that professional club was huge as a youngster. It was a great environment to be in. I learned a lot of lessons about how to really push myself as a player and it was great. I've always had fond memories of my time at Wigan.'

Even though Forshaw's time at Wigan brought him four League Championship medals and a World Club Challenge, in the 1991 win over Penrith, Forshaw has fond memories of his time at Warrington, and carried lessons learned at Central Park with him throughout his playing career.

'I got a call from Paul Cullen, they were going into a new stadium and I had a good 12 months there,' he explained. 'To be quite honest with you I probably could have played another year but I had played from 17 to 34 and I was a player that was more often than not playing for 80 minutes in a position where there's a lot of tidying up to do. I just thought I'd had enough – I pushed myself to the limit physically and I thought I'd had enough. What was good at Wigan was we had a lot of lads who were similar players in similar positions. I was with Phil Clarke, Ian Gildart, Denis Betts. Then you add the lads like Andy Platt and Andy Goodway and we were all very competitive.

'I remember the brutal pre-seasons at Haigh Hall and one thing we did learn together was how to push ourselves really hard – I was always looking for a cutting edge.'

Forshaw moved into rugby union, coaching in 2013 after stints as strength and conditioning coach at Warrington and then Wigan. He spent three years working with Ireland and Connacht, before coming back to England. 'The big thing about rugby union is you have to learn the game,' he said. 'You really have to learn the game and I looked at my time in Ireland as an apprenticeship as a new coach.'

But his success as a coach hasn't come without hard work – and Forshaw says his Wigan peers have helped him master his new trade. 'I really enjoyed the transition

Shaun Wane, Mark Bitcon, Mike Forshaw and Kris Radlinski.

from rugby league to rugby union and I think the change was just at the right time for me in coaching,' he said. 'I went there with an open mind and I had my own ideas – I made some mistakes, everybody does, but I spoke to Shaun Edwards and Andy Farrell and people who are still in the game – I know Mike Ford well and I put my own slant on it.'

But rugby league still holds Forshaw's attention when he has enough time away from work to catch a game, and he has seen enough of the current Wigan crop to be impressed. 'I like John Bateman,' he said of the Canberra-bound forward. 'He reminds me of a young Andy Farrell, how he runs the ball, he has that little bit of difference about him and he's a puppy who bites.'

ANDY FARRELL

Wigan debut: 24 November 1991, Regal Trophy at home to Keighley (won 32-8).
Last Wigan match: 8 October 2004, Super League play-off away to Leeds Rhinos (lost 40-12).
Appearances: 370
Tries: 111
Goals: 1,326
Drop goals: 19
Points: 3,115

As the first captain to lift the Super League trophy for Wigan, the man who led Wigan to the 2002 Challenge Cup Final and the first name on the list as Great Britain

Andy Farrell as The Phantom in June 2004.

skipper, there's a lot to remember Andy Farrell for. But one memory sticks out above all the rest.

It was a warm June evening when our hero was leading his Cherry and White army into battle against Super League's leaders at the time Leeds Rhinos. With the Rhinos looking to stretch their lead and Denis Betts taking charge of Wigan as coach, while Mike Gregory was watching from the stands as he took a backseat through illness, the Warriors were fighting to climb the table.

Half an hour into the intense battle on 19 June 2004, with the score locked at 12-12, Farrell tackled Leeds' Kevin Sinfield on his own 40-metre line, but it was clear he had paid a price for his bravery. Rising to his feet, Farrell immediately left the field with a broken nose. But, unbeknown to everyone, his important role in the match was just beginning.

Swiftly returning with the blood cleaned from his face, Farrell's next clash, when Sinfield and Matt Diskin conceded a penalty for going high on the captain, aggravated the injury. But still the towering Orrell St James product could not be forced out of the game. Farrell had led Wigan to a disappointing Challenge Cup Final defeat against St Helens at Cardiff the previous month, and success in Super League was the only way to make amends for what would have been Wigan's 18th cup victory.

In what was his 400th career appearance, Farrell emerged once more with his disjointed nose held into place with heavy strapping, and he was compared to The Phantom for his appearance. At this point, Wigan held a delicate 57th-minute, 22-20 lead.

Farrell kicked Wigan in front once more with 15 minutes to go, after Sinfield had levelled the score with a penalty of his own to create a dogfight for the 14,140 supporters at the ground to enjoy. The nail-biting intensity seeped into the dying seconds of the match, with Sinfield attempting a short drop-out as Leeds tried everything to wrestle the match in their favour. But, to cheers from the home crowd, the ball sailed out on the full, leaving Farrell – still barking orders at his players – to slot the final points between the posts and cap the win.

The Warriors finished fourth in that regular season, wedged between St Helens and Hull FC, and managed to claw within a whisker of the Old Trafford Grand Final.

Andy Farrell kicks a goal at the first match at the DW Stadium in 1999, a 14-10 defeat to Castleford.

But eventual champions Leeds were too strong on that occasion, in what would be the twice Man of Steel's last match in Wigan colours. Farrell went on to join Saracens rugby union in 2005 and earned eight caps for England to go with his 34 Great Britain caps in rugby league and 11 England appearances.

He is now on England's coaching staff at Twickenham.

MARTIN OFFIAH

Wigan debut: 5 January 1992, at home to Wakefield (won 20-2).
Last Wigan match: 21 June 1996, at home to St Helens (won 35-19).
Appearances: 159
Tries: 186
Goals: 1
Drop goals: 3
Points: 749

Ask people to think of rugby league and London and many will see Martin Offiah sprint past in the mind's eye. Not only was he one of the quickest, most flamboyant and famous players of his generation – he also ensured Wigan's foothold as the game's giants was anchored down with arguably the single most iconic moment in the game's history.

We are at Wembley in 1994. Wigan are seeking their seventh successive Challenge Cup Final victory.

The opponents are Leeds and the score is 0-0. There are 12 minutes and 37 seconds on the clock when Offiah takes the ball in his own 20-metre area. Amongst

Martin Offiah was a favourite among Wigan fans. Here he is being mobbed in 1992.

the roar of the crowd, a blur, a scattered defence and a beaten Alan Tait, Offiah touches down 13 seconds later. He drops to his knees and holds his head in his hands – history created.

'I think at the time when I sunk to my knees I realised that was probably going to be the pinnacle of my career,' Offiah admitted. 'It was my Olympic moment. It has become my legacy to the sport. I'm always going to be remembered for that try and I'm just honoured and privileged that I was in the right place at the right time to score it.'

Obviously 'that' try, which contributed to the 26-16 win, was not Offiah's only moment of greatness in a Wigan career that spanned from 1992 until his departure to London Broncos in 1996. The jet-heeled ace from Hackney returned an astonishing 186 tries from 159 appearances for The Riversiders and a less remembered yet equally significant footnote in his career also happened in the capital.

On 3 December 1995, at Charlton FC's The Valley, 'Chariots' needed a 43rd career

hat-trick to register 400 in his incredible career in front of 8,338 fans. It was a career in which he scored more than 500 tries for Widnes, Wigan, East, St George, London, Salford, England and Great Britain, and played the game with a style and swagger that frustrated opposition fans as much as it delighted those cheering him on.

Opposition fans dreaded the ball arriving in his hands, he was ready to vanish within a stride

Martin Offiah's reaction to 'that' Wembley try in 1994.

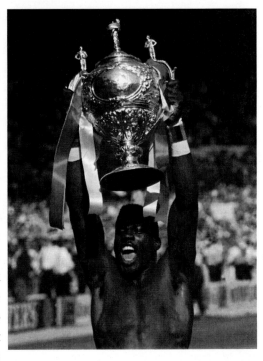

Martin Offiah with the Challenge Cup after Wigan's win over Leeds in 1994.

and be caught up by teammate Shaun Edwards for a nod, nod, high-five try celebration. And while Offiah certainly enjoyed scoring tries, he admits he had to face adversity.

'I started out in boarding school in London where I played rugby union,' he said. 'Then I went north to play a pretty tribal game called rugby league in the 1980s. I took to it like a duck to water on the pitch, but that didn't endear me to opposition fans. Because I was a bit of an exuberant player it attracted a lot negative attention. I had to deal with it, accept it, to overcome it and be successful.'

And successful he was. Winning his second World Club Challenge in 1994 (his first came with Widnes in 1989), Offiah needed space on the sideboard for seven Championship medals (two with Widnes), four Challenge Cup medals, six Premierships (three with Widnes), three Regal Trophies, two Lancashire Cups (one Widnes), and three Charity Shields (all Widnes).

It was from humble beginnings, first at Ipswich RU and then Rosslyn Park, that Offiah learned his craft, before moving to rugby league and Widnes in 1987. But he had caught the rugby league bug before then. 'I think my earliest memory of the Challenge Cup is watching the 1985 final,' he said. 'And the classic

Martin Offiah causing defenders problems at Wembley again – this time against Castleford in 1992.

Martin Offiah in action for Wigan during the 1995-96 centenary season.

between Wigan and Hull, which the Cherry and Whites won 28-24, could not have provided a better lasting memory. Obviously I'd seen rugby league earlier in the 80s being played in the mud, but my first vivid memory is that final between Wigan and Hull when Henderson Gill scored his famous try. I'll never forget his big beaming smile after he scored in the corner,' he added.

And Offiah acknowledges how special the team he was part of was – in his days at Central Park – during an era in which winning silverware was almost a given. 'It was an awesome team I played in,' he explained. 'Gene Miles, Andy Gregory, Shaun Edwards, Frano Botica, Andy Farrell, the list goes on. It was a great place to be – fantastic times.'

Humble as Offiah's words are now his playing days are over, of all the greats to choose from, he was cast in bronze along with five other legends of the sport for the rugby league statue unveiled at Wembley. Alongside fellow Wigan greats Billy Boston and Eric Ashton, as well as Alex Murphy and Gus Risman, Offiah's image represents the sport's great heritage in London – and the winger admitted he was lost for words. 'It is a great honour to even be nominated. I'm lost for words to describe the feeling,' he said. 'It's a little overwhelming and it's a fantastic honour to be up there with legends of the game – it's pretty esteemed company.'

1994-95

After Wigan's World Club Challenge defeat of Brisbane in June 1994, they could hardly have done better the following season. The 1994-95 campaign was huge for the Riversiders, running into 45 games over four competitions, with Wigan winning them all, including a record-breaking eighth Challenge Cup in a row.

More impressive was the fact Wigan only lost three times in those 45 games, and one was against the touring Kangaroos – though there was also a nerve-shredding draw in the fourth round of the Challenge Cup against St Helens at Central Park in February 1995. The record-breaking season would see Wigan score 1,735 points from all their matches and appear on the BBC eight times. It had humble beginnings though.

AUGUST - NOVEMBER

A 26-0 lead inside the first 22 minutes had Wigan's opener at Featherstone's Post Office Road wrapped-up with an hour still to go. They eased off the gas to register a 36-24 win in front of 5,504 fans, a week before 13,807 saw Wigan cruise past Sheffield 40-16 at Central Park.

Wins over Oldham, Leeds, Widnes, Castleford and Wakefield made their league campaign seven from seven, with Wigan's lowest score at that point being the 31 points they managed at Wheldon Road.

A crowd of 20,057 turned up on 8 October to see Australia take on Wigan at Central Park, and the 'Fourth Test' billing and slot on BBC Grandstand illustrated the club's status at the time. The 30-20 score in Australia's favour was a disappointment, but normal service resumed with six more league wins on the bounce.

DECEMBER - JANUARY

Wigan entered the Regal Trophy at the round-two stage, and a hat-trick from Kris Radlinski helped them to a fairly routine, if muddy, 34-12 win over Rochdale on 4 December 1994. The following Sunday brought the first league defeat of the season though – when, despite scoring six tries, Wigan came away from Headingley with a 33-28 defeat, ending their 13-match unbeaten run in the competition.

Memories of that soon faded as Graeme West's side won the traditional clash with St Helens on Boxing Day 32-25 after a fightback, and reached the Regal Trophy Final against Warrington on 28 January. To get there, though, Wigan had to squeeze past St Helens 24-22, two weeks after the Boxing Day clash, and 23,278 came to watch.

The BBC elected to show Castleford's win over Leeds instead, making this a rare derby not to be televised, and friendlies aside, every Wigan v Saints game since has made it to the small screen. The final at Huddersfield's McAlpine Stadium was a routine 40-10 win for Wigan with Va'aiga Tuigamala scoring two tries.

FEBRUARY - MARCH

St Helens were proving to be a problem for Wigan this season including in the Challenge Cup on 11 February. With Wigan's proud Challenge Cup record, undefeated since 1987, on the cards, it was nearly over as Bobbie Goulding struck the post with a drop-goal attempt in a 16-16 draw. The shake-up worked for Wigan though, and on the following Wednesday Wigan won 40-24 at Knowsley Road to set-up a round-five clash with Batley.

Routine league wins against Castleford, Wakefield, Workington, Widnes and Salford punctuated the cup campaign, with 3,800 the lowest crowd to watch Wigan that year, turning up at Mount Pleasant on 26 February to see Wigan brush Batley aside 70-4.

An away quarter-final against Widnes was won 26-12 two weeks later to set-up a semi-final against Oldham on 25 March. The passage to Wembley was smooth, though, and after leading 48-4 at the McAlpine Stadium, Oldham scored three late tries to give the scoreline a respectable look as Wigan won 48-24 to meet Leeds in the final for the second year in a row.

The month ended in a shock for the champions though. A snowy Thrum Hall saw Halifax beat Wigan 18-16, just the second league loss for the Riversiders all season.

APRIL - MAY

A quirk in the fixtures saw Halifax travel to Central Park four days later for the return fixture, and after the midweek shock, Sky Sports showed the clash live as fans across the country watched to see if 'Fax could spring a repeat performance. The reality was very different, as tries from Jason Robinson, Phil Clarke and Radlinski saw Wigan leading 30-0 by half-time in this 62-6 win.

Doncaster were taken care of the following week as the Championship became a formality. It would take a big slip for Leeds to have any hope. A press conference on 8 April at Central Park announced Super League was on its way in 1996, and the following day Wigan got the better of Bradford 60-34.

With two games to spare, Wigan wrapped their sixth title in a row up by beating St Helens 34-18, with 26,334 fans joining the party, and the formality of the league season was completed with wins over Warrington and Hull.

The Challenge Cup Final took place on 29 April, and Wigan wrote history again as Jason Robinson, Martin Hall, Henry Paul and Tuigamala scored tries in the 30-10 win over Leeds. Leeds were also the victims in the Premiership Final at Old Trafford.

Wigan had beaten Sheffield and Warrington to get there, and unleashed a 69-12 hammering on the Championship runners-up to seal a season of dominance.

JASON ROBINSON

Wigan debut: 28 August 1992 away at Sheffield Eagles (won 46-6).
Last Wigan match: 14 October 2000 Grand Final against St Helens (lost 29-16).
Appearances: 281
Tries: 171
Drop goals: 1
Points: 685

It was a common sight for the Wigan faithful. From dummy half, a loose ball out of nowhere, a cherry and white blur would come flying out of the blocks and before fans could put their pints down he'd have scored. So good was Jason Robinson at creating points from nothing, the sequence happened 171 times in his 281 Wigan appearances.

Signed as an unknown 17-year-old from Hunslet Parkside in 1991, Robinson went on to win every domestic honour in a Wigan shirt – and win his place in the affections of the club's fans.

And despite going on to become a world-famous rugby union star, lifting the World Cup with England in 2003, Robinson's years at Wigan are close to his heart. 'I'm Leeds born and bred and passionate about Yorkshire, but when it comes to rugby league – rugby league for me is Wigan,' he said. 'In certain quarters I might be known for playing rugby union for England, because of the success of the 2003 World Cup team, but I have some great memories from Wigan: The Lancashire Cup '92, beating Saints 5-4 – making my debut in 1992 against Sheffield, the win in '94 over to Brisbane, '95, scoring two tries in the Challenge Cup Final, '98, first Grand Final.'

Jason Robinson crossing the tryline for Wigan was a familiar sight, and he went on to win the Rugby Union World Cup for England.

Jason Robinson on the run against Leeds in 1996 with Shaun Edwards in support.

When fans think of a dream team, Robinson is often one of the first names on their team sheets. But ask the man himself, and the great players he made those memories with deserve the credit. Scoring tries, celebrating cup final wins, playing for England and Great Britain are all achievements most players can only dream of. And Robinson acknowledges he couldn't have done any of it without his teammates. 'You think of so many great players. I was so privileged to have played with so many great players. It's unbelievable,' he explained.

'For me, because a big part of my life has been shaped through Wigan, as soon as I think back to Wigan, I just think rugby league. I start reminiscing. I was reminiscing about some of the games we had at Central Park where we had almost 30,000 people in there. The atmosphere and how people used to turn up an hour and a half before and stand in their place every game. They'd be there without a doubt and it brings so many great memories back.'

Robinson won a World Club Challenge, a Super League title, four Rugby League Championships, two Challenge Cups, four Premierships, a Lancashire Cup, a Charity Shield and three Regal Trophies.

And he admits nowhere else would have come close during those years. 'For my development as a player it was fantastic, there was no better place for me to learn my trade than Wigan,' he explained. 'As a result of that, it's led me on to other opportunities so I'll always be thankful to Wigan Rugby League and the supporters for their support. The supporters are the best and you can never get away from that.'

Cup final homecomings, of which were winning ones all but once for Robinson, also provide fond memories. 'I can always remember coming down on the bus,' he said when asked about Wembley homecomings. 'You'd have people lining the streets everywhere, then you'd get to a certain point and there'd be a 'wave at the flats' – great memories which you never forget, no matter where you've been.'

Robinson's passion for Wigan means he is still close to the action at the DW Stadium. His son Lewis Tierney played for Wigan before moving to Catalans, and among the more recent successes for the club, one player stands out as a shining example for Robinson. 'Lockers reminds me so much of Andy Farrell, which is funny because there's the link there,' he said. (O'Loughlin is Farrell's brother in law). 'The way he has taken on that role as captain, it's a lot of pressure and over the years he's developed really well. With him you know what to expect week-in week-out, but for me you measure success for players not just by coming in and having a good season but you know what you're going to get with him, it's that consistency year after year. He's been there, galvanised the team and been a fantastic servant to Wigan.

'Wigan are known for producing fantastic players and we have some great young lads coming through. While we lose players they still bring in players and also manage to keep lots of the good players coming through so it's a conveyor belt.'

Robinson's last game for Wigan was the 2000 Grand Final loss to St Helens before he embarked on the first chapter of his rugby union career with Sale Sharks. While he has experienced a privileged life, travelling the world and being renowned for

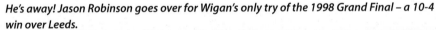

He's away! Jason Robinson goes over for Wigan's only try of the 1998 Grand Final – a 10-4 win over Leeds.

being one of the best players of either code, Robinson has never forgotten his roots. 'My job when I first left school, while it wasn't the greatest job, it paid me a wage, and I was so grateful to come home with my first wage packet,' he said. 'There's a quality in that – there's a reward, you work hard, you get a bit of money. I've never forgotten that.'

1998

You have to go right back to 1998 to find a Wigan side that made a better start than 2017s four Super League wins and a World Club Challenge success over Cronulla Sharks. After an indifferent 1997 by Wigan standards, 1998 brought a new hope with the return of John Monie as head coach, and success was delivered with victory in the inaugural Super League Grand Final in the October.

But the blistering start the side made that season, with new recruits Danny Moore, Mark Bell, Robbie McCormack, Tony Mestrov and the returning Denis Betts, could not have ended in a worse fashion – that year's first defeat came at Wembley.

FEBRUARY-MARCH

The Challenge Cup took sole priority in the early months of 1998, and it was difficult to judge Wigan's prospects for the year on a routine 76-0 fourth-round win over Keighley on 15 February and a 56-0 win over Dewsbury on 1 March.

A better test came against St Helens in the quarter-final on 15 March. In front of the BBC cameras, Moore, Betts, Simon Haughton and Jason Robinson scored tries in a 22-10 win in front of 17,179 fans to end Wigan's two-year absence from the competition's last four. And Warriors wrapped-up March with a straightforward return to Wembley thanks to a 38-8 win over London Broncos at Huddersfield – things were looking good for the start of Super League at home to Castleford on Sunday 5 April.

APRIL-MAY

Wigan's start to their title challenge couldn't have gone any better, with wins against Castleford, Halifax and London supplementing a comprehensive 38-18 dismantling of St Helens at Knowsley Road on the Good Friday on 10 April. But heartbreak was around the corner on 2 May as Wigan fans trod the familiar path to Wembley following a two-year absence.

Many saw the final against Sheffield as a sure thing and expected Central Park to be welcoming the cup home for a record-extending 17th time. Instead, the watching world, and the Wigan players, were given a shock as Sheffield recorded a 17-8 victory, which Warriors fans would never be allowed to forget.

May flung up another loss, away to Leeds, ending Wigan's five-match unbeaten opening in the league and letting the Rhinos go two points clear at the top of the table. This was a week after Wigan had demolished Sheffield 36-6 at Don Valley – eight days after the Eagles' cup final triumph. But normal service was resumed for the rest of the month, with a 46-0 win over Huddersfield being followed up by a 38-16 win at Hull Sharks, keeping Wigan within touching distance of unbeaten Leeds at the top.

JUNE-JULY

Wigan went through June unbeaten, with Lee Gilmour, Moore and Betts crossing the line in a routine 34-6 defeat of Salford on 7 June, before a 28-12 win over Bradford at Odsal the following week put Warriors top of the table. Leeds lost 22-10 at Hull the following night, putting Wigan top on points difference, a position they wouldn't relinquish for the rest of the campaign.

Paul Johnson and Jason Robinson were among the scorers as Wigan demolished Warrington at home on the longest day by 56-8, and Castleford were swept aside before St Helens' visit on 5 July marked a four-game run to be televised by Sky.

Wigan prised open a two-point gap at the top of the table thanks to their 38-14 win over their arch-rivals, while Leeds' 33-22 loss at home to Bradford saw the Rhinos drop off the pace slightly. And a quirk in the fixtures saw Warriors face St Helens back-to-back thanks to a round of 'on the road' fixtures. At Vetch Field, home of Swansea City FC, a Kris Radlinski double was the highlight of a 36-2 win in front of 8,572 spectators.

Wigan wrapped-up July by hanging onto their place at the top of the table with a tense 20-14 away win against play-off hopefuls Halifax.

AUGUST-SEPTEMBER

Mark Bell and Tony Smith scored tries in a very tense 18-15 win over London at The Stoop in front of nearly 8,000 people to kick-off the final straight in the regular season. The sting of Wembley was also still evident when Sheffield came to Central Park the following Sunday, with 10,175 watching a 44-6 win. Fans limited to home games saw Wigan lose for the first time on 21 August, when Leeds won 15-8 at Central Park, prompting fears Warriors' new bogey team could sour the play-offs – especially if Monie's men finished top and didn't claim the title. But the rest of the regular season went without a hitch – with Huddersfield, Hull, Salford, Bradford and Warrington all beaten before the play-off campaign.

Andy Farrell lifts Wigan's first Super League crown in 1998.

OCTOBER

We were into new territory on 11 October as Leeds came to Central Park for Wigan's first ever play-off match. In a qualifying clash, where the losers would get another chance to make the Grand Final and the winners going straight through, Gilmour broke the deadlock as Bell's try helped Wigan to a 10-0 half-time lead.

Despite a try from Francis Cummins after the break, Henry Paul scored a try to make sure Wigan reached Old Trafford. The win earned Wigan a week off, and Leeds were again the opponents for the first-ever Super League Grand Final.

Rhinos' Richie Blackmore scored the first try – in front of the Wigan fans – but it was to be Warriors' night, with a wonder try from Robinson before half-time playing a huge role in helping Wigan to their first title since the switch to a summer season.

MARTIN HALL

Wigan debut: 3 February 1993, at home to Wakefield (won 38-14).
Last Wigan match: 25 August 1997, away at Bradford Bulls (won 33-18).
Appearances: 141
Tries: 29
Goals: 18
Drop goals: 1
Points: 153

As underdogs, Wigan, as Super League champions and Challenge Cup holders, entered the unknown by taking on Sydney Roosters Down under in 2014. For almost 20 years, no British club side had

Martin Hall poses for a press photo in 1998.

crossed the whitewash into an Australian arena with just 80 minutes and a different breed of opposition standing between them and the right to be called the best club side on the planet.

But former Wigan hooker Martin Hall knows exactly what the players were feeling that night, even if the outcome of their 36-14 defeat was different to when Hall played in a special game. Hall was part of the last Wigan side to lift a World Club Championship in Australia in June 1994 when the Cherry and Whites defeated Brisbane Broncos 20-14 at the ANZ Stadium after a gruelling 50-game campaign (including a New Zealand tour match and a match against Featherstone called-off after 13 minutes due to fog). And Hall saw parallels with the 2014 squad and the class of '94.

'Andy Platt and Dean Bell had gone to Auckland Warriors – not too dissimilar to what Sam Tomkins has done actually and there were the injuries as well,' Hall said. 'Playing in Australia against an Australian team always adds a bit of spice and it was an exciting time.'

The bookies granted Wigan a 16-point start against a hulking Sydney Roosters squad, mixing a similar potion to the decider of 1994, with many accounts suggesting the Wigan players felt their chances were so slim they would treat the trip as a party. But Hall's version of events is different to the impressions many fans have enjoyed retelling in pubs across Wigan since the trophy came home.

'I wouldn't go that far,' Hall said when asked if the trip was a party. 'We had a long season that year. We'd won at Old Trafford [a 24-20 Premiership Final win against Castleford] – we'd had 40-odd games and had a lot of injuries. It had been a long season, players had left and we were down to the bare numbers. When we got to where we were based on the Gold Coast, we had a training session at five o'clock, it was on a Wednesday if my memory serves me right, and then basically Westy [coach Graeme West] said "right guys we're not playing for a week, go and enjoy yourselves for a few days and we'll meet for training at five on Sunday." Obviously we were a group of lads, we'd had a long season and I'm not saying we didn't have a good time in that period, but we trained well when we arrived and trained well on the Sunday and twice more before the game. It was a great experience. We trained hard but I will add we did party afterwards.'

Hall was on the substitutes' bench, coming on with Wigan 12-0 in front thanks to tries from Denis Betts and Barrie Jon Mather, replacing the injured Martin Dermott. 'Derms was carrying an injury,' Hall explained. 'We started with Derms to see how far he could go because he was playing injured – I knew I'd be coming on quite early. I don't know exactly when it was, but it was in the first half and I remember the intensity.'

Hall entered the fray after 23 minutes, with the home side cutting Wigan's lead to 12-4 three minutes later thanks to a try from Wendell Sailor. But his contribution

Martin Hall is told to take 10 minutes in the sin bin against Leeds in 1996.

throughout the match proved invaluable as Wigan never slipped behind, scoring further points through a Jason Robinson try, converted by Frano Botica, before Brisbane fought back.

With 20 minutes to go, Brisbane were only four points behind thanks to a Michael Hancock try and a try and a goal from Julian O'Neill, before Botica nudged Wigan two more points in front with a quarter of an hour to go. But Hall was confident Wigan were up to the task of defending for their lives in the final stages to take the match.

'We had trained well, even though we had some time off, we knew what we were facing,' he said. 'We were ready for it and it was a high intensity and fast game. We stuck at it and in particular our defence held strong and we did enough to win the game.'

Hall struggles to find words to describe the feeling of winning that night in front of 54,223 mostly Australian fans, and thinks the current crop of stars shouldn't see the disproportionate crowd as a disadvantage.

'The crowd was into the 50s that night, there were far more Brisbane fans there than there were Wigan fans and that was another aspect of it,' he said. 'It was actually quite inspiring. It was another factor that played as a positive as opposed to something to be subdued about – it spurred us on if anything.'

The former Wales international, who now lives in the Exeter area and works in property, explained just what that night meant to him. 'I was quite lucky to play in a lot of decent teams when I was at Wigan but that night in Brisbane was the ultimate win. The feeling was euphoric, one of the best things – other than my children being born – that I've ever had.'

GARY CONNOLLY

Wigan debut: 24 September 1993, at home to Widnes (won 32-2).
Last Wigan match: 2 September 2004, at home to Leeds (drew 12-12).
Appearances: 312
Tries: 137
Goals: 6
Points: 560

Phone calls cause people to change their plans on a daily basis. Where to meet for lunch, which day to go shopping, whether you have got the job. But imagine if a simple phone call was so significant it changed what side you were on in the most famous derby in rugby league.

For Gary Connolly, a call from across the globe did just that. The former St Helens fullback recalled, 'It wasn't I didn't want to go and play for Wigan because I'd have been stupid not to because they had such great players. But I was a St Helens lad and all I wanted to do was play for St Helens.'

Connolly was in Australia completing a summer stint at Canterbury where he played 15 games, and with his St Helens contract coming to an end, he was left to make the biggest decision of his life. 'I got a phone call saying St Helens had sold me to Wigan and that was the first I knew about Wigan's interest in me,' he said. 'I had to make a big decision – either stay in Australia or come back and play for Wigan, and obviously with the Wigan team

Gary Connolly signed for Wigan from home-town club St Helens in 1993.

at the time I chose Wigan.'

All Connolly had known was Saints before his move to Central Park. It was his home and he had lived all over the town, following his dad's business of running pubs. The Blackbrook Royals amateur appeared for St Helens at Wembley, aged just 17 in the 1989 Challenge Cup Final defeat to Wigan, and by the time he was 20 he had already been selected to tour with Great Britain. But an unprecedented run of success wasn't far away for Connolly as he put himself in the line of fire from opposing fans' chants for years to come, as well as setting his allegiance to one side.

'I can understand why St Helens let me go,' he said. 'But I was going to a team that had just won six Challenge Cup Finals and were probably the best side in the world, so I just thought it was a great opportunity to win a lot of things.'

To move to Wigan to win was probably an understatement. In his first six years at the club, Connolly had 13 medals to his name, including two Challenge Cups, three League Championship medals and a winner's ring from the inaugural Super League Grand Final in 1998.

But his most cherished medal is from the 1994 World Club Challenge, where he lined up for Wigan at full-back as they beat Brisbane at the ANZ Stadium. 'That was probably the highlight of my Wigan career,' Connolly said, before reflecting on the following season where the Riversiders swept up every honour, losing just three games of a 45-match campaign (and one of those was a tour match against Australia). 'In my second season I think we won every major honour. It was phenomenal to be part of such a great side.'

In 1995 Connolly earned an England call-up for that year's World Cup but didn't feature in the group stages, which included a 46-0 win over South Africa, the country where he had lived for some years during his childhood. But he did play in the final at Wembley, a 16-8 defeat to Australia.

The 1998 Grand Final win was Connolly's last trophy for Wigan. He stayed until 2002, moving to Leeds where he famously picked-up the Lance Todd Trophy in the

Gary Connolly in action in 1998.

2003 Challenge Cup Final, despite his side losing 22-20 to Bradford Bulls.

In 2004, the Warriors fans' favourite returned to make 11 more appearances for Wigan, including his 300th start, before his final game, a 12-12 draw against Leeds on 3 August of that year. He drew the curtain down on his league career with Widnes in 2005, before playing rugby union for Munster.

But of all the clubs he has represented, Wigan is the one that remains close to the St Helens lad's heart.

'I'm a Wigan fan now and I always will be,' Connolly admitted. 'Even though I was a Saints lad growing up, Wigan were so good to me, so I support Wigan now.' Connolly, now a care worker for children in St Helens, still keeps up with Super League, and despite being best known for his exploits as a classy centre, it is a different kind of player who catches his attention these days. 'I like Liam Farrell – I think what he brings to the side – he's constantly good,' he said. 'You need people like him for his work rate, which is second to none – for me he's my first name on the team sheet every week.'

KRIS RADLINSKI

Wigan debut: 31 October 1993, away to Castleford (lost 46-0).
Last Wigan match: 11 August 2006, away to Leeds (won 20-18).
Appearances: 323
Tries: 183
Goals: 1
Points: 734
Appointed to board of directors at Wigan Rugby League Club in 2014.

'The story of the 2002 Challenge Cup Final was really the week before. The Sunday before I was at the Trafford Centre with my girlfriend at the time, just doing some shopping, and I didn't feel right. I was walking around and I could feel my foot getting tighter in my shoe. I didn't think much of it and then I got to a point where my foot was bursting out of my shoe.

Kris Radlinski was awarded an MBE for services to rugby league in 2007.

'We decided to leave, and on the way home I phoned the doctor and the doctor met me at my house. He took me straight to hospital and said he didn't know what it was but it looked like some kind of bite or blood poisoning. I was on a drip and spent four days in hospital leading up to the game, and it was touch and go whether I played.

'I slept with my foot on top of a suitcase the night before the game and stayed in the same position all night. I looked at my foot the morning of the game and it was fine, so I started walking around and it all drained down and it just wasn't right again.

'I went down for breakfast and Dr Zaman calmly finished his breakfast and took me up to his room with a few of the lads and slit the top of my foot open. It all weeped out and I had gap in my foot. He didn't stitch it, he just strapped it because he said if he stitched it then it'd fill up, and I played the game with one boot bigger than the other.

'I did some decent things in the game, but I think the story leading up to the game was probably what earned me the man of the match. That's what's spoken about, but Adrian Lam was the best player on the field that day. I probably got a number of the votes because people weren't expecting me to play, but I've not shied away from it, I've said all the way through we wouldn't have won the game without him.

'We went in as underdogs, Saints were red hot at the time, and people weren't expecting us to win. It's a day I'll always remember, playing in that team with people who mean a lot to me. Obviously Tez was there as well so it's one for us all to remember forever.

'But there are many reasons I was privileged to play for Wigan, and playing at Central Park was one of those. I'll never forget the last match there in 1999 when we beat St Helens. Right at the end there's a chip over and I managed to get the ball, and then the hooter goes, I was the last person to have the ball at that ground.

'I took it in the changing rooms and I gave it to Keith Mills, who has been associated with the club for 50 years. His son still has it in a glass case. I was very aware of what I was doing at the time, but Keith deserved it more than I did. It's a tragedy really that people will not grow up experiencing rugby league at Central Park. It was a place like no other. I remember warming up that day against St Helens and when they were calling all the ex-players out the atmosphere was just electric. It was a sad day for the town when it went and we all still miss it.

'People also talk to me about when I came out of retirement in 2006 and we ended-up avoiding relegation. I'd watched from afar and you could see it was a team playing with no confidence, but I've too much respect for the game to think I could have so long out and just walk in, it wasn't about that.

'If you went in the changing room at that time you could see it was quiet. Lack of confidence is an inhibitor and they were going out not believing they could win. I was just a voice. I always felt no matter how fit I was or how far away from the game I've been, if I was defensively strong I could do a job.

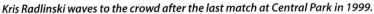

Kris Radlinski waves to the crowd after the last match at Central Park in 1999.

'I was confident no one could get around me, and if I could be an extra voice on the field, in the changing room, behind the posts and things like that then I knew we'd have a chance.

'I think I played six games, and it was hard, but we managed to survive and I don't reflect or dwell on that period much. It was just something I was asked to do and I'm glad I did it, but I don't think it was down to me to save them from relegation. I was just a voice and a bit of experience.

'I obviously still watch a lot of rugby league, but there are challenges behind the scenes in the modern game. The living room experience now is so good that getting people to a game is a challenge for us all.

'When Wigan aren't playing on Thursday night I love watching it, the last couple of hours on a Thursday pass quick because you know you're going home to watch a game. But from a hospitality point of view people don't want to go out on a Thursday night and have a few beers. It's been a difficult sell. Parents don't want to bring their kids on a Thursday night because it's school the day after and we've suffered with that from a crowd point of view. But Sky pay the wages and that's what we have to do for now.

'On the field, we recruit a certain type of player. When the going gets tough they'll put their arms up. The elusive ingredient we look for is that competitive nature, you can't quantify it. If the shit's up against the fan, this guy's going to put his hand up. We try and find that ingredient where some other clubs might want a guy who scores three tries. When I look at players I see a mistake and look for his next action. If he puts his hand up straight away you know he's tough.

'Since I've finished playing I've been general rugby manager at the club and I was made a director by Ian Lenagan in 2014. The chairman called me and I knew something was up because he Skyped me, which he never does. He was on the other end in his Wigan suit and he told me, but told me not to tell anyone over the weekend. I knew it on the Friday before the Grand Final, but, as we know, the events of that weekend took over.

'The chairman announced it at the end-of-season dinner and I literally hadn't told a soul. I remember Waney looking at me in absolute disgust because I hadn't told him! I told him I was told not to tell anybody and I'd actually forgotten about it because of everything that happened. With things like that, you think you're prepared. When Ben Flower got sent off in that final I left my seat and ran down the tunnel to see him straight away and I went and got his dad. It's Man United policy that when someone gets sent off there's a car waiting for them to take them out of the stadium. I didn't know this and the guys at Man United who I've known a while told me his car was there. I got him back to Wigan so he was in Wigan before the game had even finished.

'Looking after player welfare has always been there but anybody could be your welfare officer and it was a very much tick the box exercise until recently. Now more money is being put into that area and it's a designated person. The courses they're going on to prepare players is far greater than it's ever been.

'People forget probably only five per cent of what I do is actually rugby league related. It's other stuff people will not appreciate or not even see. We have to remember our players have lives as well, families, the issues of life to deal with. But people expect them, as soon as they cross the white line, to perform at their best.

'Dan Sarginson also experienced it recently with the death of his brother, but when he crosses that white line he'll be focused. There's no right way of dealing with it though.

'I went to pick Dan up from the airport with Shaun Wane after it happened, and Shaun asked every question he shouldn't ask. But he kept him talking. I thought, I've just heard a master at work. I was thinking 'don't ask that!' but it just worked.

'He helped Sarge. He was absolutely unbelievable. Everything they tell you to stay away from he did, but it worked. But that's Shaun, he's the best at what he does and people don't see half of it. It's been amazing while he's been in charge.

Kris Radlinski in action during the 2002 Challenge Cup Final, a 21-12 win over St Helens.

'He's probably proved a lot of people wrong. He's grown himself, he's grown as a person. He'll leave with so many friendships, so many memories and all the lessons he's learned... he'll kill his next job. It's all amicable, it's all good. He came into my office with a letter and it was emotional, but he felt the time was right.

'The last eight years have just been madness. Things we've had to deal with off the field, winning in 2010, the double in 2013, winning in 2016 was massive when everyone wrote us off and the World Club Challenge the year after was phenomenal, as was going to Australia at the start of the 2018 season. You learn a lot about yourself through experiences like that.

'I still don't have a qualification or anything and I've literally just been thrown in and been given access to how the club runs. I've worked hard, but I've come to think you can put me in any situation and I'll be alright. I'm eternally grateful to Ian for giving me that opportunity and showing me the faith, but I'm also conscious I worked hard to do it.

'I'm still a fan and I still have to pinch myself sometimes that I'm now the guy making the decisions. I go to Italy and send a brief over for the kit, have a hand in designing it. How has this happened? Every single day I appreciate it. Don't get me wrong, it's stressful and people in this town are hard to please.

'Towards the end of the 2017 season, over the off season to the beginning of the following season, not a lot of people had a lot of good things to say about the club but you have to stay strong. It's the nature of the job. It's a tough town and people will tell you what they think, but I take the responsibility very seriously, it's not a job for me. Everyone knows I don't have a day off, it's your life. But I'm incredibly lucky.'

VA'AIGA TUIGAMALA

Wigan debut: 4 February 1994, away to Widnes (won 27-12).
Last Wigan match: 8 February 1997, Challenge Cup round four away to St Helens (lost 26-12).
Appearances: 102
Tries: 62
Goals: 3
Points: 254

Off the field he was a mild-mannered giant, but the gentleman was an animal on the field and the Wigan faithful loved him for it. Va'aiga Tuigamala made 102 appearances for the Cherry and Whites between 1994 and 1997 – not a lot by the standards of most

players held in the same regard – but Inga brought something unique to the arena. The Samoan bulldozer scored on his debut in a 27-12 win over Widnes at Naughton park on 4 February 1994 and returned a very respectable 62 tries for the club, many of which involved scenes of tacklers sprawled across the pitch in his wake.

But incredibly, despite his fearsome reputation and uncanny ability to send hopeless defenders flying in the most theatrical fashions, (who can forget how he sent Leicester's Jamie Hamilton spiralling to the deck in the 1996 Middlesex 7s at Twickenham?) Tuigamala only scored one hat-trick in his Wigan career.

Warrington were the hosts on New Year's Day 1996 as just 5,123 fans paid the visit to Wilderspool for the noon kick-off and Wigan were in no mood to wish any Wire fans season's greetings as they were on course to lift their seventh successive championship by defeating Bradford 15 days later.

At Warrington, Simon Haughton opened the scoring for the away side on the quarter-hour mark to notch his 12th try that season, before Warrington threatened to force a contest a few moments later when Mark Forster, the last player in the game to have scored a three-point try, finished a smart move started by Paul Sculthorpe and former Wigan halfback Mike Ford. But Warrington's resistance wouldn't last for

long as Inga bashed through Salesi Finau to open his account in the 19th minute.

From here, the outcome was fairly straightforward for a side which stormed the season, shortened to 20 games in order to accommodate the start of Super League, by eight championship points. Tuigamala wasn't to score his second until there were

Va'aiga Tuigamala takes on the Castleford defence in 1994.

only seven minutes left to play, after taking a Rob Smyth pass to complete a simple score. And a hat-trick looked off the cards until injury time, when Shaun Edwards dinked a nifty chip over the defence to set the centre on his way to the line again, this time sliding over feet first in a concoction of muddy slutch.

Two weeks later, Tuigamala picked-up a Regal Trophy-winners' medal to go with that year's title, and played a key role in Wigan's inaugural Super League campaign, despite being unable to help his side to the trophy.

His last medal came in the 44-14 Premiership Trophy demolition of St Helens that year before he played his final game for the now Warriors almost four years to the day since his debut. The 26-12 loss to St Helens in the fourth round of the Challenge Cup was a sad way for Inga to bow out of rugby league before a high profile switch to Newcastle rugby union – but his stay at Central Park was legendary.

HENRY PAUL

Wigan debut: 28 August 1994 away to Sheffield Eagles (won 40-16).
Last Wigan match: 24 October 1998 Super League Grand Final v Leeds Rhinos (won 10-4).
Appearances: 147
Tries: 78
Goals: 119
Points: 550

Raw talent will often take a player so far, but it is never a substitute for hours spent in the gym keeping an inch ahead of rivals, as well as time on the field honing skills and gelling with teammates. But every once in a while you get to see a player with skills that can't be taught – that talent is visible through the hard work. These players provide the moments stored in fans' memories – and one who had the ability to do that more than most in a team of world class players was Henry Paul. At Sheffield's Don Valley Stadium on 28 August 1994, Wigan fans got their first glimpse of him.

Henry Paul bursts through in the 35-19 win at home to St Helens in 1996.

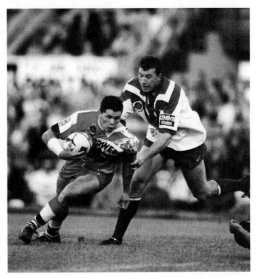

Henry Paul looks for a gap in the 31-24 World Club Championship win over Canterbury Bulldogs in 1997.

In his early days at the club Paul plied his trade at full-back, but was perhaps better remembered for his exploits at stand-off, with sharp skills that oozed class. In 35 appearances in his debut year after arriving from Wakefield, Paul returned 19 tries and 25 goals, picking up the Championship, Challenge Cup, Regal Trophy and Premiership in his first season.

On Good Friday of that season the Kiwi showed exactly the type of flamboyance only certain players can get away with when he scored an unforgettable try. Wigan were leading 22-12 after 51 minutes, Andy Farrell launched a drop-out from the Whitbread Stand end of Central Park and it bounced just before the half-way line. With three St Helens players around the ball, Paul shot from nowhere, scooped up the ball and raced clear, showing the 26,334 fans in attendance what he could do. Wigan went on to win 34-18, wrapping-up the title with two games to spare that season.

Paul never failed to pick up a trophy in any of his seasons playing for the club, winning the Championship and Regal Trophy again in the 1995-96 campaign and Premiership titles in the 1996 and 97 Super League seasons.

He also played his part in the inaugural Super League Grand Final win over Leeds in 1998, having scored his final Wigan try in the 17-4 play-off win over the Rhinos two weeks earlier. Paul left Central Park at the end of that season, having made himself a firm fans' favourite. He joined Bradford Bulls, where he stayed for three years, picking-up the Lance Todd Trophy in the 2000 Challenge Cup Final win over Leeds, and helping them beat his former club in the 2001 Grand Final.

ANDY JOHNSON

Wigan debut: 12 October 1994 away at Workington Town (won 30-6).
Last Wigan match: 20 June 1999 away at St Helens (won 24-18).
Appearances: 80
Tries: 27
Points: 108

Andy Johnson in Joining Jack colours.

When Andy Johnson broke into the Wigan first team, he is fair in describing the season as a transition for Wigan. The club were, in 1997, playing their first season as Wigan Warriors, caught-up in the Americanisation of the still new Super League, they had a new nickname (compare Warriors to Riversiders) and a terrible new kit to match. Gone were the traditional cherry and white hoops of the two seasons before and in was a design which could be described as busy, complete with warrior face in a horned-hat which looked more viking than what it was supposed to represent.

On the field Wigan weren't faltering by most side's standards but were by their own. Star player Martin Offiah had left the club midway through the previous season and Va'aiga Tuigamala's departure to rugby union was compounded by Shaun Edwards leaving for London Broncos – his last match being a disappointing Challenge Cup exit to holders St Helens in February 1997.

Wigan won nearly three times as many league games as they lost, though, and still picked-up silverware.

And for Johnson, who played 31 games, it was his big season in the first team after playing mostly a supporting role while waiting for his chance since making his debut in 1994.

'I signed as a 17-year-old. I had the choice to play for Wigan Academy, which was building block for Wigan,' he explained. 'Having done a year in the Academy, Andy Goodway was the coach and he was pleased with a couple of the amateur lads who had a decent year. He put us forward to be signed by the club. It was a choice between Wigan and St Helens at the time and I signed for my home-town club for quite a bit less money, just because it was Wigan and that was the team I'd always supported and played for, so that's where I wanted to be. I worked my way through the academy and reserves, started getting first-team games and enjoyed every single minute of it.'

He had come into the first team for the 94-95 and 95-96 title-winning campaigns, but it was when Super League kicked off in the summer of '96 that Johnson became a regular.

His 21 appearances that term produced five tries, and he came off the bench to help Wigan wallop St Helens 44-14 in the Premiership Final at Old Trafford, though it was scant consolation for missing out on that year's Super League title by a single point. But even in the '97 campaign, which was fraught with off-field debt problems at the club and the planned sale of Central Park bringing its own logistical problems and unrest from fans, Wigan still produced a trophy.

They beat St Helens again in the Premiership Final – the last one before it was replaced by the Grand Final – and Johnson weighed-in with a try. 'It was a transition period,' he admitted. 'It had gone to summer rugby. There were no kind of mega signings, on the Australian front there weren't any big names or any monster names coming in, but we still had Jason Robinson, Andy Farrell and Kris Radlinski leading the charge. The team was scattered with superstars and in '96 and '97 we won the Premiership Final. One of the first years I played was '95 and we won the Championship, so it was good to be around the place.'

Despite those Premiership Finals not being held in as high regard as a Challenge Cup or World Club Challenge, Johnson remembers the build-up to them being treated like any other final – and it would have especially been the case given these two were the last chance for the club to win silverware in each of these seasons. A trophy had come back to Central Park every year since 1985.

'It was a big event, it was the thing to close the season off with,' he remembers. 'Any final, especially with Wigan involved – they were all considered the same. I don't think they were layered as one bigger than the other. It was an opportunity to play of the big stage and lift some silverware. It was taken as every other final, the dressing rooms were all pumped up, the semi-final was a thing we needed to make the final. It was all wrapped up to be as big a thing.'

The Wigan machine was back the following year though. Super coach John Monie had returned to the club and 1998 was supposed to be Johnson's big year.

A return to Wembley was on the cards (we'll skip over the result) and they would go on to top the Super League table for the first time and win the inaugural Grand Final. But Johnson didn't play a single game.

'In '98 I ruptured my achilles so I missed all of it, and Wigan went to Wembley that year, something I'll never be able to get out of my head,' he said. 'I never made a Challenge Cup Final – it will haunt me forever – but there you go.'

The injury would ultimately cut Johnson's time with Wigan short. He made seven appearances in 1999 before finishing the season at Huddersfield, then played for London, Castleford and Salford before his career was ended by a recurring back injury in 2005. But at Wigan he made priceless memories, and despite missing Wembley, running out at Central Park is certainly a more than adequate consolation.

'Central Park is a ground a lot of people my age went to visit and see the teams on the park and never thought they'd end up there themselves,' he said. 'Central Park has a special place, as the old Wembley did for a lot of rugby league people, so it's upsetting that it's gone. I think a lot of Wiganers still have a special place in the hearts for Central Park and I think the big attendances you used to get at derbies and whatever else there. It was a pretty magical place.

Andy Johnson with Henry Paul in 1997 after Wigan had ended Bradford's unbeaten run that season.

'Wigan were going to Wembley every year and the superstars reached the top. Coming through the Wigan system, there were always players that didn't make the first team that would scatter the A team, so even if you were playing in the reserves at Wigan you'd be at an exceptional level in those times.'

Johnson's point about playing in the academy is worth pondering. In a modern era where only two Super League teams run reserves sides at the time of writing, and where players on dual-registration face the prospect on months on the sidelines once the Super 8s start and moving between clubs isn't allowed, discussion has been rife on how to give players too old for the under-19s but not quite ready for regular first team action a fighting chance.

When Johnson was coming through the ranks, things were very different, and 20 years ago player development in this bracket seemed better than it is now.

'You'd play alongside Martin Dermott, Bobbie Goulding and some quite big names that were in there,' he'd say when remembering the standard of even Wigan's second-string in those days. 'You were playing with elite players in an A Team game.'

'Those games where ferocious. I'd say those games were harder games than the first-team games – the first-team games just seemed faster. They were massively physical games. It would test you whether you were up to the mark in the physical side of the game. It's a real shame now the reserve game doesn't exist for all ages. I don't know whether the first-team players now are above dropping back – I don't know how they would feel about that. I know anyone who was pushed back into the reserves to prove their fitness or prove their worth then that's what you had to

do. Nobody enjoyed it, nobody wanted to be doing that on a Friday night but that's what you needed to do to get your first-team spot. That's how it was, it's a real shame it doesn't exist anymore.'

And it's not just in the reserve grade where Johnson has noticed cracks behind the scenes in the sport that gave him his livelihood 20 years ago. Falling attendances and criticism of the competition's structure and how the game

Andy Johnson in 1997.

is packaged and promoted by broadcasters are frequent topics of conversation among fans who feel the game has lost ground on other sports.

'I think everyone's a bit negative at the moment,' Johnson said. 'I think it's easy to say the game's in trouble but you can sit down on a Friday night and watch an absolute spectacle can't you. You can watch a real humdinger of a game and that's what it's all about. The game as a product is an incredible thing. Sky, I think, have taken their foot off the gas a little bit with the marketing. They can revamp it a little bit to give it a chance to compete with all these other sports and I think they need to get a reserve team in action across each club.

But away from the politics and debates about rugby league, Wigan, as a club and town, has stood above what sport means for Johnson's family. A dad of two, Johnson and wife Alex want what any parents want: happy and healthy children. But the reality for them is the fight of their lives to raise awareness and funds into the research for treatment and ultimately a cure for Duchenne Muscular Dystrophy.

After starting the charity Joining Jack, Johnson has seen Wiganers join people from all over the world in raising funds and awareness for his son Jack's condition, and it's another part of what makes people's relationship with not just Wigan Warriors but the town unique. 'It's been amazing,' he said. 'We've called on the Wigan club and the fans to support us. Did I think that they would support us? The answer to that is yes. To support us in the way they have supported us, it's just been mind blowing. I've said this many times, we would be nothing without them. We set the charity up to make a difference and I think we've done that. Realistically that isn't just me and Alex because if we were knocking on doors and asking for help and nobody answered then it soon becomes a lost cause. The town has reacted massively.'

One of the highlights for Johnson where the club's involvement with Jack's charity is concerned was when the club wore a special one-off kit to face St Helens in a home game in 2012.

Changing from their traditional cherry and white hoops to green, red, blue and white in a nod to the jumper Jack is wearing in a well-known photograph, and fans bought the replica in droves to raise money.

'One thing that stands in my mind is the day Wigan had the Joining Jack jersey,' Johnson remembers. 'We set up the stalls and everyone was on the phones excited saying they were selling jersey after jersey, wristband after wristband, and it was just a frenzy of activity of everyone wanting to get behind the charity. I want to say a massive thank you to everybody. It's made a real difference and the Wigan public need to know that. The amount of money we've put into various things, gene therapy is becoming reality now. This is not just a special rugby club but a special town. The

Andy Johnson and son Jack model the Joining Jack kit in 2012.

Wigan club and town is pushing research to a level that's never been there before.'

But Johnson also stresses that their battle is not just for Jack, but for the thousands of boys in the world suffering from DMD, and it's the actions of many others as well as Joining Jack supporters that is moving gene therapy in humans closer to reality.

'The condition affects so many boys throughout the world . Yes, other charities exist, yes other charities have made waves and there's no point saying that we're the leading force, we're not,' said Johnson. 'There's a hell of a lot of work that's been done by families that have been in this desperate situation. We're building on work done by others but we're certainly making big strides forward. I don't think we'd do it unless we thought a difference could be made so we push on and we're hopeful that fairly soon a treatment will be available.'

DARRELL GOULDING

Wigan debut: 14 August 2005, away at Widnes (won 48-24).
Last Wigan match: 27 July 2014, away at Bradford Bulls (lost 18-6).
Appearances: 174
Points: 288

You can't imagine. But many of us try to. Watching their heroes in cherry and white and clutching a rugby ball on the walk to school – thousands try to imagine one day crossing the touchline to go into battle for Wigan. But for Darrell Goulding, the reality was much, much more than he ever dreamed of. The feeling of progressing through the ranks, from junior to Grand Final winner, is something he admits will stay with him forever.

'To come through the academy with a lot of lads I grew up with was all a great experience,' said Goulding, reflecting on a time when the players fans have since seen conquer Super League were coming through the ranks. 'Then to get to first team and win trophies was all I ever dreamed of.'

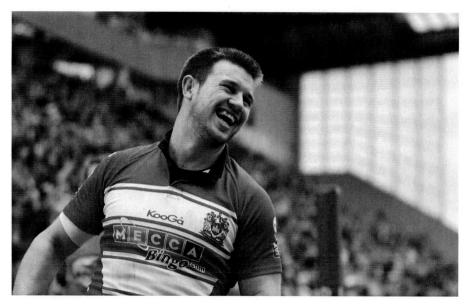

Darrell Goulding at the DW Stadium in 2010.

After a successful nine years in the first team at Wigan, Goulding's career was cruelly cut short while playing for Hull KR. At the age of just 27, he had to call it quits due to concussion. The news wasn't just upsetting for Hull KR fans but also the Wigan fans who saw him enjoy being part of the squad that brought the good times back to the town.

Goulding, a classy, underrated centre, is popular with fans across the whole sport for his genuine personality as well as his gifts as an athlete. With patience and eloquence, Goulding shows no hint of bitterness at the sudden nature of his retirement – and chooses to focus on the special games shared with the mates he progressed through the ranks with.

'I have many fond memories to be honest,' he said of his time at Wigan. 'I started playing there at such a young age. Michael Maguire came in and clearly changed the culture of the club. I think that's the one memory that sticks out more than anything – finishing that 2010 Grand Final. To go from a team that was really struggling to champions – to go and win the Grand Final and become league leaders was out of this world really.'

The 2010 Grand Final win was the first of two Grand Final and two Challenge Cup wins for Goulding – and he contributed to the win over St Helens at Old Trafford with a try. 'Some people say it's just another game but when you walk out on the pitch you know just how big a game it is,' he explained.

'To score in it – I didn't have to do much, just put the ball down, but it will be a memory that sticks for the rest of my life.'

Darrell Goulding during the 2013 Challenge Cup Final win over Hull FC at Wembley.

Following his retirement, Goulding has wasted no time in preparing for life after rugby. Joining forces with a friend, he moved back to Wigan and set up a sports compression wear company called Sports Doctor.

But rugby league still played a huge role in Goulding's life and he is now coach of the club's under-19s. 'I'm very good mates with the lads – especially the likes of Mickey McIlorum [now at Catalans] and Lockers – people I've come through with,' he said. 'This club will always be very special to me and I will imagine I will be a Wigan fan for the rest of my life.'

Darrell Goulding goes over for a try against Warrington in the 2013 Grand Final.

It's not just friends who have made Wigan special for Goulding, though. Fans have shown their support through his career and after he announced his retirement – and he has always been happy to listen to what they have to say. 'The support I've had… probably after retiring I think it was a big shock and obviously not a nice experience,' he explained. 'The support I got from fans – it was brilliant – every time I've bumped into someone it's been a pleasure speaking to them. That's the thing with Wigan having such a big fan base.'

2010

Genuine cause to celebrate for rugby reasons had been a long time coming for Wigan fans. Since the Challenge Cup success of 2002, there had been no silverware to toast and there had even been two seasons without a play-off appearance – not to mention the 'Great Escape' of 2006. And despite quiet optimism ahead of the 2010 season, with a new coach in Michael Maguire, perhaps even the most optimistic Warriors fan wouldn't have predicted what was coming.

They'd maybe settle for a strong league finish and, if they were being greedy, a Grand Final appearance.

They got a lot more, though. Two trophies, a trip to Old Trafford, a Championship. But more importantly, foundations were laid for a more successful future.

FEBRUARY

Round one of the season brought ex-Wigan coach Brian Noble back to the DW Stadium with his Crusaders outfit, who were beaten thanks to a seven-try show in front of 13,680 fans. It was enough to send fans home happy that night, and there was a feeling they could be onto a good thing the following week when the DW saw a near-identical performance in the 32-6 win over Hull KR. But the real test was around the corner, with a trip to the HJ Stadium in front of them, a ground where Wigan had never won a league game up to that point.

A jaw-dropping display by Amos Roberts, who crossed for his third double in as many games, helped Wigan go top in a 22-20 win over Warrington, then the following week Pat Richards broke the record for the club's points scored in a single game during the Super League era. His five tries and nine goals in the 58-0 win over Catalans for 38 points eclipsed Andy Farrell's 34 against Huddersfield-Sheffield in 2000.

MARCH

Observers would have been wrong to treat Warriors' first defeat of the season, to a struggling Bradford side on 5 March, as the end of their flying start. If anything, the reality check did anything but tether Wigan's new-found momentum, as it sparked a seven-game winning run.

Hull FC, Castleford and Leeds Rhinos were all swept aside by the end of the month, ensuring confidence was high for the Good Friday trip to St Helens and the last Easter derby at Knowsley Road.

APRIL

A cold and wet Good Friday saw 17,500 squeeze into Knowsley Road for what would be the last meeting between Wigan and St Helens at the old ground. Darrell Goulding and Iafeta Paleaaesina scored tries in an 18-10 Wigan win that demonstrated the full force of Warriors' new defensive powers.

Richards scored a hat-trick the following Monday, while Roberts ended a two-week break from scoring tries with a customary double. A visit to Salford produced an 18-4 win before Challenge Cup action got underway with a trip to Sheffield Eagles.

Eagles fans took the opportunity to remind their opponents of the 1998 cup final shock by wearing old shirts and waving Wembley flags at the clash played at Bramall Lane, with Wigan winning the high-scoring contest 50-34 to set-up a round-five match away at Widnes. The following week, a frustrating performance saw Harlequins become the second side to beat Wigan that season, winning 38-26 at the DW.

MAY

May began with a 28-10 defeat of Huddersfield at Magic Weekend in Edinburgh, with Goulding, Sam Tomkins, Karl Pryce, George Carmont and Thomas Leuluai scoring tries in an efficient performance, while Widnes had no answer to a 12-try display in the next round of the cup, which might have had fans dreaming of a long-awaited return to Wembley. Wigan then came through a tricky trip to Huddersfield 38-30 before completing the double at Crusaders RL, winning 46-26 with Pryce scoring four tries.

JUNE

The trip to Headingley for the Challenge Cup quarter-final threw up a tense match against Leeds in front of the BBC cameras. Wigan scored no tries in the 12-10 defeat but were leading 10-8 in the closing stages thanks to five Richards penalties. Lee Smith scored the decisive try in the final minute, leaving Wigan's wait for cup success to enter a ninth year. It was a hard defeat for Maguire to take, and he said, 'We wanted to go all the way in this competition. Now it's not to be and it's hard to take.'

In Super League, normal service was resumed with a 38-22 win over Castleford and a 48-6 success over Wakefield before St Helens visited the DW. A typically close clash between the rivals went St Helens' way by 26-24 in front of 20,498, but Wigan were soon back on track, closing the month with a win over Harlequins on 26 June.

JULY

Warriors won their next two games, against Catalans and Salford, before Warrington arrived at the DW in front of a season's best crowd of 22,701. A Lee Briers drop-goal sealed a 23-16 for the Wolves, blowing the race for the League Leaders' Shield open with five regular season games to go. Wigan headed up the race thanks to following wins over Hull FC and Leeds.

AUGUST

They blew their chance to seal the league leaders' spot for the first time since 2000 with an 18-16 defeat to Huddersfield on 15 August, but they managed to fight back against Hull KR the following week to secure the club's first silverware in eight years.

SEPTEMBER

Wigan closed the regular season with a 34-12 win over Bradford, with 17,058 fans attending to witness the presentation of the League Leaders' Shield. The first round of the play-offs didn't go so smoothly against Leeds, with a last-minute penalty attempt from Pat Richards not quite hitting the mark in a 27-26 defeat, but the visit of Hull KR the following week was more straightforward, with Wigan winning 42-18.

This set-up an elimination semi-final against Leeds, as had been the case in 2007 and 2008, with the Rhinos booking their place in the Grand Final on those occasions.

Liam Farrell leads Wigan's Grand Final celebrations in 2010.

This time round, though, Wigan were in no mood to let the chance slip, securing a 26-6 win to book their place at Old Trafford.

OCTOBER

St Helens were fittingly the opponents for Wigan's first Grand Final appearance since 2003, but right from the start this was always going to be Wigan's night. Ex-Saint Martin Gleeson scored two tries in a frantic start, with one of his tries being easily one of the best team tries scored at Old Trafford. A late Saints rally only dialled up the tension slightly, as Sam Tomkins added to Goulding's earlier score to secure Wigan's second Super League crown.

PAT RICHARDS

Wigan debut: 11 February 2006, away at Catalans Dragons (lost 38-30).
Last Wigan match: 5 October 2013, Grand Final against Warrington Wolves (won 30-16).
Appearances: 224
Tries: 168
Goals: 896
Drop goals: 4
Points: 2,468

When Pat Richards took a looping pass in the 2013 Grand Final to score a try that pretty much sealed the Super League Championship, the realisation struck that this was his last match for the club. The Aussie, known as 'Superman', was a favourite as much for his mild-mannered personality as his astonishing strike-rate and monster kicking ability. And the fact he is third on Wigan's all time points scoring list, behind Jim Sullivan and Andy Farrell, only tells part of the value of his contribution.

But it looked so very different when his Warriors career began in Perpignan in 2006. Richards scored a try but Wigan lost to Super League new boys Catalans Dragons 38-30, and no one could've predicted what was around the corner for the club.

'In 2006 it wasn't a very successful season on the field for me and also the team – we did struggle that first season,' the 2010 Man of Steel said. 'I was at the club for a long time and by my last season the surroundings were very different. I loved my time at the club and it was definitely a nice way to finish.' Wigan went from avoiding relegation by the skin of their teeth to champions in 2010, then double winners three seasons later, with Richards an integral part of the machine.

Pat Richards signs off from Wigan with a try against Warrington in the 2013 Grand Final.

During his eight-season spell at the DW Stadium, Richards amassed 2,468 points from his 224 appearances, including a 168-try haul, which puts him 16th on the club's all-time try-scorers' list. Considering the likes of Billy Boston, Martin Offiah and Jason Robinson occupy higher places, it is another stat the Ireland international can be proud of.

Impressive records aside, Richards also gave Warriors fans priceless memories. His drop-goal in the Super League play-offs against Bradford in 2007 comes to mind – when the one-pointer completed a stunning comeback from 30-6 down for Wigan to win 31-30.

His legendary boot saw drop-outs regularly clear the halfway line, and, despite the result, Warriors fans still watch clips of his drop goal against St Helens in July 2013. At a tight angle, and just in from the halfway line, he booted his side 15-14 ahead with 23 minutes to. The injustice was the mammoth effort given in a game that finished 22-16 to St Helens.

His try in the 2013 Grand Final win over Warrington was the ultimate send-off for such a legendary servant to the club – as well as an unforgettable night for fans witnessing another great comeback.

'I have a fair few great memories,' Richards reflected, admitting it's not easy for him to

Pat Richards with the Super League Trophy in 2013.

Wigan's Pat Richards grabs Les Catalans' Laurent Frayssinous on his debut in 2006. He would join the Dragons later in his career.

pick stand-outs. 'It's hard to go past the trophies – they're all special in their own different way but there's also a fair few other ones as well, so obviously I was lucky to have a fair few to choose from. 'Celebrating with the boys sticks in my mind.'

Richards returned to Wests Tigers, where he signed from after scoring a try in the NRL Grand Final in 2005, before finishing his career back in Super League with Catalans Dragons. And as well as having fond memories of seeing the club rise from a brush with relegation to winning the Super League title twice, Richards is confident the club will continue to enjoy success thanks to its reputation for developing the next generation of top players. 'You have that at Wigan – they have good juniors to pick from and we're starting to see those guys in first grade which is great,' he said.

And it is not just Richards who has fond memories of his time in Wigan. His two children, Aidan (who played for Orrell St James') and Brianna, were born in England, and Richards and wife Kim are in the company of plenty of families to have spent time in the town. 'We try to catch up with those guys as much as we can – we're always talking about our time over at Wigan and how good it was,' he said.

PART TWO

IN THE STANDS

IN CONVERSATION WITH WIGAN WARRIORS FANS.

SEAN LAWLESS

I didn't really have much choice regarding the rugby team I was to support. Being born into a family in which my grandmother worked at Ellgren making Wigan shirts, my grandfather worked at Heinz and my father played for the Wigan academy, I would say the die was cast before I was born. In fact, as soon as I was born I made my Wigan debut, entered by my parents into the matchday programme for the 1989 Lancashire Cup game against Widnes.

An overriding memory from my childhood was my visits to Central Park. Attending a Catholic school, it was important that we made an annual pilgrimage, but being a Catholic school in Wigan meant that the pilgrimage was a trip to Central Park – whether you were 4 or 11, you just did it every year without fail.

The annual school trip seemed to be very consistent year by year. There was an educational part of the day that probably involved some maths along the lines of working out how many tries Martin Offiah had scored, and some science which may involve calculating the force of Andy Farrell's handoff and the angle of certain conversions from Frano Botica. That was usually followed by a tour of the ground, including what, at that time, was a glittering trophy cabinet.

A visit to the changing rooms would follow and a fight between all the kids to sit where their heroes would be getting changed that weekend. The fight for Shaun Edwards, Martin Offiah and Tuigamala's pegs ensued, and those who weren't that into rugby and weren't too taken by the fight to get to a space were ultimately left sat by Paul Atcheson's peg!

The main part of the day, though, always came after lunch – the running out of the tunnel pretending you played for Wigan and then the training session. Wigan had a training field just behind the Kop end at Central Park on the hill. The school trips seemed to always finish with some skill and activities by the community coaches, presumably to give the teachers an afternoon off! This wasn't just a skills session or a fun session for me, every year this was a trial. This was my opportunity to get signed up for Wigan, at the age of 6. These were the days on the calendar that were more important than birthdays or Christmas. I took them very seriously.

The rest of the kids would get changed into their PE kits or favourite football shirts, but not me. I had the Wigan kit on, full kit – head to toe. Getting changed by Shaun Edwards' peg, putting on an Offiah replica jersey – I would psych myself up, gum shield in and scrum hat on, only for Mr Halliwell to say, 'Lawless, it's touch and pass this afternoon!'

The training session (sorry, trial) would continue all afternoon, with silky skills being showcased from me, even though as a youngster I was a prop – playing rugby union! Every year, I would leave blood, sweat and tears on that pitch hoping against hope that one of those days, I would be spotted. I had convinced myself that the community coaches who ran the school trips were obviously talent scouts as well.

In 1997, my time had come, I was sure of it. The session ended and the call came: 'Farrell, Farrell.' By this point, I had moved on from Offiah on the back of my jersey as Offiah had moved on himself. Andy Farrell was now my player of choice. If Farrell had his hair shaved, so did I, if he was growing it long, so was I. I answered the call of 'Farrell.'

'Yes Sir,' I said.

The time had arrived, the papers were waiting to be signed, the *Wigan Evening Post* were probably waiting back down at the ground to photograph Wigan signing their next prodigal star. I even wondered whether they had called my parents to make sure that they would be in attendance for the signing of the contracts.

'Farrell, Farrell!'

'Yes Sir?'

'Don't forget your Halifax ticket when you hand the cones in.'

Bubble burst, dream shattered.

I hadn't been singled out to be the next Wigan player, I had been singled out to collect the cones and to make sure I didn't forget to collect my free ticket for that weekend's game against Halifax Blue Sox. The joys... a free ticket to a season ticket holder. The free tickets that were given to all the school children who attended the school trip were a well-intended reward from the club.

A free ticket to a child meant, in all probability, they would be accompanied by a fee-paying adult – the chairman was a smart man! The downside for kids like me was that the more children attended the game, the less room there was on the sponsorship boards to sit. Naturally there were no reserved spaces on those sponsorship boards, so to speak, but there was a pecking order. If you didn't have a season ticket and you just turned up to a game for the first time and decided that you had a place on a board, you would be challenged. One young lad might question: 'Tha' weren't 'ere last week,' or 'That's Tommy's space tha' knows.' Heaven forbid you take a place on those boards if you hadn't earned it! Perhaps a milder version to the present day of sitting on the back row of the South Stand at the DW Stadium.

The routine of getting to Central Park, walking through the River Dougie stand to see the Academy sides coming out of their changing rooms to play the curtain raiser and no doubt my dad pointing out, 'That's Andy Farrell's brother Chris and that's his twin Phil,' was always the same.

Then onto the kop were the parents who would ultimately place their kids on an advertising board with aplomb for the duration of the game, whilst they went a little higher up the Kop. The kids placed on the boards were the first real challenge for the visiting sides that warmed up in front of the Kop. If they kicked the ball into the stand, they weren't getting it back without copping some well-intended abuse from a young kid. I remember a particularly young player for St Helens called Lee Briers warming up in front of the Kop. He was practising some long-range passing with Sean Long only to drop the ball and for it to bounce into the Kop. The ball fell into the lap of the young Wigan fans, and if Briers was to get the ball the back he was going to have to earn it.

A game of Briers in the middle followed as he walked towards the Kop, one young fan passed the ball over Briers to another fan sat in the Popular Stand and vice versa. After a minute or so of being caught in the middle, Briers gave up and headed back to his team. That was the beauty of Central Park, a small enough ground that generated an atmosphere to make the opposition players know that they were in a game before it had kicked off.

At the age of 29, those same aspirations that I had in 1997 of getting the call to play for Wigan are still alive and kicking. The dreams that an injury crisis hits Wigan and they have to call up a 29-year-old who has had two cruciate ligament injuries and hasn't played the sport for 10 years are perhaps as faint as they were back in 1997 – but I continue to dream!

Lance Todd Trophy winner Kris Radlinski with the Challenge Cup in 2002 after climbing off his sick bed to play with an infected foot.

MATT MACAULAY

It is 20 minutes to eight o'clock on the evening of 22 June 2018. The day has been blisteringly hot but it is now finally showing signs of cooling down. This is a relief.

I am wearing a three-piece dinner suit and a pink cravat. The jacket is velvet. And I'm sat in a pub, but it is not a nice pub. It is the sort of pub where men in velvet jackets and pink cravats normally fear to tread.

Strictly speaking, I should now be in a fancy hotel about three miles away, saying goodbye to our year 11 pupils on the occasion of their 'Leavers' Prom'. Instead, I'm sat in a grotty pub in a forgotten village on the raggedy edge of Gloucestershire. And the burly, sweating men at the bar are clearly keeping a watchful eye on me. Those who are more blessed in the ocular department are keeping two eyes on me.

I sup tentatively at my pint. In the morning I may well be discovered in a shallow grave with a mouthful of cravat and unspeakable injuries, but I can't worry about that right now. I have weightier concerns.

None of this is at all unusual. I have spent countless years of my life surreptitiously absenting myself from all manner of social occasions in order to sit on my own somewhere. Somewhere with a signal.

Over the years the signal has changed…. analogue, FM, 3G, 4G, 5G, wifi… but the cause has always remained the same. Wigan are playing. And it's on the radio.

There is a part of me that wishes it wasn't like this. It is probably the same part of me that doesn't like waking up with a mouthful of cravat and sore thighs. Life could be so much easier. My wife could be so much happier. But, alas, that is not the path I follow. It is the great dichotomy of fandom. Sometimes you enjoy the sweet taste of success and the sheer wondrousness of utter joy at the very core of your being. Other times all you can taste is last night's cravat and there is nothing but pain anywhere near the core of your being.

Why do we do it? Because we are in love.

Love is never easy, and heartbreak comes with the territory. As do hope, anxiety, exhilaration, frustration, elation and despair – you frequently get the whole lot crammed into eighty minutes of rugby league action. And all of them burning with an intensity that rarely troubles life in the real world. Ah yes, the real world.

The gentleman at the bar are now glowering at me with open hostility. With my earphones stuffed in, I've inadvertently been providing them with a running commentary on the action from the Mend-a-hose Jungle. They don't understand.

Down here in Gloucestershire they may talk of cherry and white, but those are hoops of a different hue. These men know nothing of…

Shoeless Mabel and Uncle Joe's Mintballs

Edwards' cheekbone and Radlinski's foot

Starving strike-breakers and pie cuisine

Mission Impossible and eight-in-a-row

Pineapple rings and prime-ministers

John Ferguson's crafty fag and slag heaps slagged off by George Orwell

It's all lost on them. But to me it provides a rich seam of culture and heritage that infuse each tackle, pass, play-the-ball and try with real meaning. Those hard yards up the middle aren't just a battle for territory on the pitch. They are testimony to the history, culture and heritage of our great town and its rugby club. They are why it matters.

Of course, Gloucester has history, culture and heritage too. But, quite frankly, Wigan is prettier. This is what the yokels at the bar can't quite grasp. And why should they even try when velvet jacketed men in cravats are so much easier to grasp?

We do, at least, have one thing in common: we'd all rather I was somewhere else. The place I'd rather be right now is Castleford. Yes, the seats in that stadium's main stand might feel like they were designed by the Witchfinder General in an attempt to elicit confessions from elderly ladies, but, given a choice, I'd always prefer to be attending a game rather than watching on TV or listening on the radio. There is nothing like actually being there.

I go with my dad. I always have done, ever since my first game way back in the season we dare not name – when Wigan were relegated. Since then my father and I have witnessed so much together. The club's meteoric rise from the depths, the glory days, the Challenge Cup loss against Salford on a suspiciously narrow and wet pitch. And all the highs and lows that ensued following the advent of Super League. Together, side by side. Me and my dad.

Being from Wigan, we are not naturally gushy types. We don't talk openly of love and bromance. But at a game we will excitedly discuss the merits and de-merits of playing a second row in the centres, and that pretty much amounts to the same thing. Each year, when Santa delivers our season tickets (and he's a man who makes no secret of his love for Wigan Warriors – check his outfit!) and I look upon our seat numbers, they mean more to me than just attendance at a game.

Prior to every kick-off, I take a 'selfie' photograph of the two of us in our seats. I treasure each occasion; every single picture in that gallery is special. And as we negotiate his narrowing world – a world being slowly but relentlessly stripped by the onset of Alzheimer's disease – the rugby matches provide very welcome respite. Every sideways glance we share reassures me that he is still there. Still my dad. And no matter what happens, he'll never forget what off-side at the play the ball looks like.

It is now a quarter to ten on the evening of 22 June 2018. Final score: Castleford 19, Wigan 18. I'm trying to explain to the gentlemen in the pub the reason for my outburst of unrepeatable obscenities, but it is hard to speak with a mouthful of cravat.

Sometimes being a Wigan fan really, really hurts. This is one of those times. I want to say that it's definitely worth it, that the euphoric highs make the lows and the pain bearable. That may be the case or it may not – it doesn't really matter, to be honest. There are no choices here. It is just the way it is. It is who I am. Wigan Warriors Rugby League Football Club – it's in my blood.

JON LYON

'Aren't you glad I wasn't born in Rochdale?' Every time Wigan win a trophy my dad turns to me and utters these words. I started watching Wigan when I was eight years old. I don't remember anything of my first three games but the fourth was the 1985 Challenge Cup Final, Wigan v Hull, and this was to have an effect on me that has not only lasted but grown in the subsequent 34 years. If my dad is to be believed, I burst into tears when Kevin James scored an early try to put Hull into the lead. That young boy would grow to learn you never write Wigan off.

The colour and excitement of that day had me hooked on the great sport of rugby league and especially Wigan, and a lifetime obsession began. That obsession has taken me and my dad the length and breadth of the country, Barrow to Hull, Cardiff to Edinburgh, Newcastle to Wembley, the latter 17 times to date. There can't be fans of many teams in any sport who have been to watch their own club or Great Britain at Wembley that often. We are the lucky few.

My impressionable, if uninformed, early days as a fan saw me ignore the stellar talents of Edwards, Hanley, Lydon and Gregory and settle on Ray Mordt as my favourite player. Mordt was a beast of a South African winger, who must have been out chasing springboks the day God was handing out side-steps, much preferring to go through players rather than round them. I spent many a night sleeping with my hair tucked backwards under my head trying to get it to curl up the way Mordt's did. The folly of youth. I spent so much time talking about Mordt on the way to matches that even now, some 32 years later, if I ever hear Simon and Garfunkel's Sound of Silence (my dad's choice of match day tunes for the car) I'm taken straight back to images of Ray Mordt flying down the Central Park wing.

I also spent most of my school years religiously wearing my Wigan Rugby flat cap, which might go some way to explaining why I was 15 before I had my first girlfriend, although that may in part be due to my also having a pair of Deirdre Barlow's specs. I got plenty stick for that cap but I didn't care one bit. Wigan were my team and I was proud to show it.

My parents, both Wiganers, had moved to Southport by the time I was born. It wasn't easy at school supporting a minority sport my uneducated friends had never heard of when everyone else was mad about Liverpool or Everton. I took plenty of abuse for my love of Wigan but enjoyed every May when I would be off to watch my team at Wembley yet again.

By the time I left secondary school most of my friends would be asking how Wigan got on every week and wanted me to bring in a rugby ball so we could play league at lunchtime instead of football. It isn't that hard to convert people when you have such a great product to deal with, and Wigan winning every week made it easy to be passionate about it to them.

Those trips down to Wembley form many of the highlights of supporting our great club. Very early morning starts, parking up at the Heinz factory to catch the supporters coach, always wondering if the car park will be open when you get back. One thing that really makes the cup final trip is the banter between fans at the service stations on the way down and back. I can recall from when we beat St Helens in 2002 at Murrayfield, my dad and I were enjoying a quiet drink at the services on the way home when a slightly, nay, severely inebriated Wigan fan rolled in and proceeded to wind up the Saints fans with his over the top singing and dancing. It was hilarious to us, no doubt infuriating to the defeated St Helens fans, but there was never a moment when it looked like it would be taken in anything less than jest. That's the spirit of our sport that I love.

I have also spent many an afternoon mixed in with the St Helens fans at Knowsley Road, indulging in a few choice words, some friendly stick and the odd wager or two. Come full-time, though, and it has always been handshakes and hugs all round, no matter the result. Can you imagine that happening at a Liverpool v Manchester United game? The fact my dad could take me to a match and I can now take my kids with nothing to worry about is just one more reason to love the Wigan club and the sport.

Another highlight of any young supporter's life is meeting your heroes. My dad regularly took me down to Central Park early before matches so I could indulge in my new favourite hobby of autograph hunting. I can remember being absolutely terrified of speaking to the fearsome granite prop forward Kelvin 'Superman' Skerrett, but as I should have expected he was a lovely man who took the time to ask me about myself. I guess it was only St Helens' Sonny Nickle that he didn't have time for!

The battles with St Helens over the years have been by far the highlight of my time watching Wigan. The games mean so much it isn't always possible to really enjoy watching them live, it's always a little calmer watching them again back home after the match, having recorded the game.

Although I'd like to think I have mellowed over the years, where Wigan v St Helens is concerned, the result still matters too much. The difference between the euphoria of victory and the devastation of loss leaves me on the edge of my seat throughout the game. Whilst losing these derby matches usually means I write off the next day due to my foul mood, and possibly half the following week, there is no feeling quite like beating 'that lot', especially with a last-minute try. Agony to ecstasy in the space of a few seconds, if I could bottle that feeling I would be a millionaire, and we have been lucky enough to have seen quite a few games with such endings.

The following are a few of my favourites…

10 March 1990. Wigan are playing St Helens at Old Trafford in the Challenge Cup semi-final. It has been an absorbing game with the lead changing hands several times, Saints determined to avenge their 27-0 defeat in the cup final the previous year. Two minutes to go, the game is poised at 14-14 and a replay is on the cards. Enter Ellery Hanley. Taking a short pass from Andy Gregory 40 metres out from the St Helens line, with energy he has no right to have at this late stage in the game, he bursts through the Saints defence, beating three players and drawing a further three before passing the ball inside to Andy Goodway 10 yards out, who dives untouched under the posts. Cue pandemonium. I still can't watch this try without getting goosebumps. A cruel way for St Helens to lose, but I don't care, it was a sensational way to win, beating our biggest rivals and off to Wembley yet again.

22 April 2011. Battle royale at the DW Stadium. A game that swung from one side to the other as Saints led 10-0 early on, but a dominant Wigan recovered to run in four unanswered tries to lead 22-10, with two apiece from Josh Charnley and Pat Richards, and with Ryan Hoffman in dominant form. Saints, to Eddie Hemmings' delight, came back again to level the match, and with just six minutes to go Jamie Foster kicked a penalty and they led 24-22. Devastated home fans were wondering what was left in the tank and how could we have thrown away such a big lead. The minutes counted down as Wigan went close. Heart in mouth as the clock ticked away into the last minute. A good run from Lee Mossop and from the resulting play of the ball, the ball was spread wide by Tommy Leuluai to Brett Finch. Finch passed further on to Paul Deacon, and with only 50 seconds remaining Deacon slipped a sublime short pass to Liam Farrell, powering onto the ball from close range, who spun past two defenders and dived over the line past a despairing Paul Wellens as the Wigan crowd erupted. I will never forget that feeling of winning so close to the end of the game when all seemed lost. I can't begin to imagine what that must have felt like for a local lad like Farrell, but to the Wigan fans it was as good as rugby gets.

26 December 1994. Probably my favourite derby match, and there are plenty to choose from. There was so much going on in this game. Wigan started well and scored two great tries through Shaun Edwards and Denis Betts. Sandwiched in between was a blatant head butt from Adam Fogerty on Neil Cowie at a scrum. Somehow instead of a red card for Fogerty, Russell Smith showed a yellow to both players, Cowie shouting at the Saints fans as he left the pitch that Fogerty was 'having it'. Five minutes before half-time, and referee Smith made the farcical decision to send off Henry Paul for barely brushing Steve Prescott's hair as he ran past him. Smith also sent Betts off the week before and both red cards were rescinded by the disciplinary committee, not that this helped Wigan in this match. Somehow, despite being down to 12 men, Wigan managed a further try from Va'aiga Tuigamala before half-time and led 20-2 at the break. Saints blew Wigan away, though, at the start of the second half with two tries in the first three minutes. Gary Connolly was then sin binned for a debatable holding down decision, and while he was off Tommy Martyn grabbed his second try for St Helens to level the game at 20-20. Tempers frayed again as Ian Pickavance and Kelvin Skerrett traded punches on 65 minutes and both received a yellow card. Now down to 11 men, things went further wrong for Wigan as Bobbie Goulding kicked a drop goal, and from the resulting kick off Anthony Sullivan scored off a pass so far forward it wouldn't have looked out of place in the NFL. 20-2 up to 25-20 down, and a man down, it certainly had the feel that it just wasn't Wigan's day. But this is Wigan, and this is the derby. Six minutes to go and a mazy cross field run from Connolly ended with him dropping the ball off to Tuigamala 20 yards out, and Inga powered through four attempted tackles to touch down under the posts to the cries of 'Tuigamala, TUIGAMALA' from Eddie Hemmings. Just when it looked a step too far, yet again one of Wigan's superstars produced a piece of magic, and Wigan's fans went home ecstatic and Saints fans had to suffer once again. The game was wrapped up with three minutes to go with another superb solo try from Martin Offiah but the damage had been done and Saints were already deflated. To overcome some appalling decisions and play 45 minutes with a player down, this ranks to me as the best win over Saints in my time.

Watching Wigan has provided many other highlights over the years, including some very freakish moments. Can anyone forget Betts' try against Brisbane in the World Club Challenge in 1994? How Denis managed to ground the ball moving past it at such pace at full stretch is beyond physics; I can't imagine we'll ever see another try like it. The same applies for Henry Paul's try in 1995, following a Wigan drop out against St Helens. The ball bounced two metres from the half-way line, and, while Steve Prescott and Sonny Nickle dithered, Henry sprinted from under his own posts and stole the ball from between the two of them and raced untouched another 50 metres to score under the Saints posts. A magic moment from a magical player.

There was also Wigan's own 'Wide to West' moment against Bradford in August 2000. 15 seconds remaining and losing 19-14, we shifted the ball left and Andy Farrell put Steve Renouf through a gap 70 metres out and he raced clear, drew the fullback and casually popped the ball up to Kris Radlinski 10 metres out to score after the 80 minutes was up. The stadium erupted as though we'd won; seemingly forgetting Faz still had to convert a difficult kick from out wide. Not a problem for our captain, who calmly slotted over the winning two points to ruin Bradford coach Matthew Elliott's night and send 17,000 Wigan fans home very happy.

Following Ray Mordt's departure in the 80s, my new favourite player was Joe Lydon. A man who has produced more magic in his career than Dynamo, his unprecedented drop goal in the 1989 Challenge Cup semi-final against Warrington was a definite 'see it to believe it' moment. I can't think of any other player in world rugby at that time who would have thought to attempt such a kick, but from 61 yards out he kicked it with ease and turned an incredibly close game in Wigan's favour and sealed another trip to Wembley.

Being part of Wigan's tremendous fan base is something else I am very proud of. Whilst it can be true on occasions that the crowd isn't always particularly vocal at the DW Stadium for some league games, the volume and numbers of our away support, or at home in a game that really matters, the support is vociferous and passionate to the point of deafening and has visibly lifted the players on the pitch when defending their own line or chasing the game. One of the greatest features of our fans is how our attendances increased considerably during our struggles against relegation in 2006, playing a big part in keeping the club in Super League. Ancient and loyal indeed. Having had the same seats in the East Stand since we moved to the DW Stadium in 1999, my dad and I have formed some close friendships with the people seated around us, and also with the Golden Gamble ticket sellers and stewards. Wigan really is a family club.

Never too popular with other fans, the green-eyed monster changes how people look at a club. Wigan's effect on rugby league should be applauded rather than derided. Throughout our domination of the sport in the late 80s and early 90s, we faced criticism for being full-time professionals in a hitherto mostly amateur sport. Our directors of the time should be praised for their foresight and ambition to bring the club and the sport to such a level. No-one prevented any other club attempting such a thing, it took a lot of hard work and bravery to make such a move, and all these years later the sport is in a much healthier financial position and has a much stronger brand.

Other clubs also benefit from the production line of local youngsters amateur rugby in Wigan continues to develop. Not every local lad will end up in the Wigan first team, there is just too many, but looking around the league at other Super League squads, there are more than a dozen players produced in Wigan, as well as the 17 in our own first-team squad, and countless more in the lower leagues. For all the thrills seeing the likes of Brett Kenny, Gene Miles, Steve Renouf and Henry Paul in a Wigan shirt, there is nothing better than seeing a local lad make the grade, and thanks to the coaching staff at our local clubs and at the Wigan Academy, we are luckier than most to see so many of our youngsters pull on the cherry and white shirt.

A great advocate of promoting youth has been Shaun Wane, another legendary local figure who has done so much for the club as a player, scout and coach in almost 30 years at Wigan. Shaun has at times worked miracles with the players, instilling a never-say-die attitude that has seen us challenge for trophies consistently, despite, the last two years especially, having an horrendous injury list to deal with.

So yes, dad, I most definitely am glad you weren't born in Rochdale!

DARREN WRUDD

As a supporter of any sporting club, one would always assume that your own team was special in one way or another, but the Wigan Rugby League Football Club stands head and shoulders above them all in my book, I will try to explain why it means so much to me.

My first memories go back to sneaking over the back fence at Central Park just after kick-off, as that's when the stewards disappeared from 'guard duty'. We would wander down to the corner of the field and slot in, or if it was packed we got ushered onto the grass to sit right next to the action. Bill Ashurst played second row and I often hid my face if he was near as he had lived next door and might have told my mum if he had seen me there.

I managed to get to a couple of the Challenge Cup Finals on the mighty run of eight, which were the most fantastic experience and atmosphere. But by the time the run had come to an end I had been lucky enough to find my wife Glenda and settle down to married life. For a while I followed from afar as we did not attend games until the year 2000, when I persuaded Glenda to join me at a match. And this is where rugby league played its ace card. Not being a great sporting fan, I was quite surprised when Glenda enjoyed the game and quickly became a supporter, although I should not have worried as her father before her cheered from the terraces at Central Park.

In 2003, I began to write for the *Wigan Evening Post*, in a section that was then called Fans Forum, now more recently renamed 18th Man. A voluntary exercise which has brought me much pleasure over the 15 years (so far) and, to a certain extent, caused me to look a little closer at the club and the way that people think of things here at Wigan.

I began to notice the families attending games. Not just lads 'n' dads, but mothers, grandmothers, girls and boys too. In fact, several generations of the same family is not an unusual sight at home games or away. My mother comes with us too and can get more heated at the referee than I do. The appeal seems universal, but the foundations of that appeal lies I believe in the grounded attitude of everyone at the club from the groundsman to the chairman.

Everyone has access to their club and the players have such a commitment to the community and fans that it really makes us feel welcome and a part of what is going on. When a fan can sit down for a chat with some of the all-time greats of our wonderful game, it is both fantastic and endearing in showing that each and every one of the supporters are both valid and important to the club. All squad players spend time for photos and autographs after a game has finished, walking around the pitch to the applause of the Wigan faithful.

Much of this has, of course, originated from the grass roots of the sport, and in Wigan we are spoiled with such high-quality clubs for our youngsters to join and play the game. I live next to Rose Bridge and yet am only a stone's throw from St Pat's, two clubs who have produced some of the best players in the world. These clubs and many more like them are run by volunteers and family members, keen to help provide access for our youngsters to this great game in a safe and stable environment. Edna's sandwiches and refreshments at Rose Bridge for the youngsters are legendary, as is her voice as she cheers from the West Stand sat behind me. I am sure you have heard her, wherever you sit. I regularly get updates on her children and grandchildren, which makes me feel a real part of the family.

This sense of family within the club forms the bedrock of our game, on which we build everything else, so no wonder everything is so down to earth and accessible. Players and staff spend much of their down time helping charities and visiting schools, care homes, hospitals and all manner of local organisations. Willie Isa even spent his own money buying shirts to take with him and give away at Wigan Infirmary children's ward; now what does that say about the man? The whole squad is committed to improving this town and helping bring opportunities to young and old to get more from life, and I applaud them and the club for this fabulous community attitude.

Since Ian Lenagan took over at the club, things have improved so much. Our young players come off the production line and slot right into games like they were born to it. The structures in place now behind the scenes are so complete and steadfast that it really does feel like we are in good hands. In fact, the safest pair of hands that I have seen on the field of play now controls much of what happens here, and as director of rugby Kris Radlinski has played a huge part in putting pride back in the shirt at Wigan, both on and off the field. One of the most respected figures in the game, Kris is also one of the hardest working chaps I have ever met. Not willing to let things jog along, he constantly challenges himself to do better, an inspirational man to have at the head of any organisation. Mr Lenagan said when he took over the reins that he wanted to put pride back into the shirt for the fans – I would say, mission accomplished.

Within the minor sponsors' set-up, my wife and I have been lucky enough to offer sponsorships for a couple of players in recent years, Amos Roberts first and then a lovely young lad Liam Carberry, who ended up moving on to Widnes, and now we are proud to currently sponsor Kris Radlinski, one of the finest full backs this game has ever seen. My memory of seeing him at the Challenge Cup Final in 2002 at Murrayfield is possibly the highlight of all my memories following this great club. A photograph was published of Kris sat with the cup in the changing rooms after the game. That photograph, to me, sums up how I feel about this club.

So, to me, I suppose Wigan Warriors rugby league club is often like an extended family. Full of friends from all over the country who share in this need for a good and decent standard to which they can pin their flag and cheer their sporting heroes. I feel it is in good hands and will develop further in the match-day experiences we can expect as our game grows and improves as a whole over the next few years. It is about memories, new and old, and the values that our society needs to prosper, and let's not forget it's about the rivalry and local bragging rights every time we take points from the other side of Billinge Hill. This is what it means to me to be a Wigan Warriors supporter and I love it.

ROBERT KENYON

It means being proud of supporting a sports team with a dynasty that's known all over the world. There aren't many of those and I think we are the most famous and successful rugby club of either code in the world. It's also about being envied due to our rich and successful history.

Wigan means demanding the highest standards from everybody involved with the club. It's about turning up in all weather in all locations after a hard week at work, spending our hard-earned money in these austere times and wanting to be entertained by the sport and team we love as a way of escapism from all the negativity and bad things happening in the world.

It's about getting excited about new signings, promising academy products and new kit designs. It's about the nostalgia and what stands out for you. For me, its Central Park, Norweb sponsored kits and winning the Challenge Cup year on year.

It's about beating Saints on Good Friday and winding up every Saints fan you know, and then putting a brave face on if we lose.

It's about the great players of yesteryear like Ken Gee, Ernie Ashcroft, Joe Egan, Brian McTigue, Brian Nordgren, Jim Sullivan, Billy Boston, Johnny Ring, Colin Tyrer, Eric Ashton and Jimmy Leytham. Recent players like Andy Farrell, Kris Radlinski, Pat Richards, Terry Newton, Sean O'Loughlin, Ellery Hanley, Jason Robinson, Andy Gregory, Dean Bell, Martin Offiah and Shaun Edwards.

Our history and list of fine players who've played for this club goes on. It's also about having the best academy system in the country, which produces world-class rugby players in abundance, and having the faith that there's another one just around the corner.

My first memories of supporting Wigan would be trying to emulate Mark Preston in my mate's back garden in the early 1990s. He seems like an obscure player and his heroics were overshadowed with the arrival of Martin Offiah, but Mark Preston was rapid and scored tries for fun back in the day. My dad had a few VHS videos and I'd watch them often. One of them was the treble or Grand Slam, one was the 89-90 season review from Micron and I think one of them had a pink box.

The kids these days who have access to unlimited videos on YouTube won't get the same feeling as watching the same VHS over and over. Most notably for me, *101 Top Rugby League Tries* and finding out about past players like Billy Boston, Green Vigo and Henderson Gill.

Growing up and going to games at Central Park, we used to park on the car park near to the old police station and walk down to the ground. Most of the time we would stand on the popular side, with me sat on a crush barrier as we never got there early enough to get on the wall. I could have been the world's best trapeze artist with the balance skills I learnt sat on the crush barrier, with every man and his dog ducking under me to get through for a pint or a pie.

We were blessed with some cracking players, but I wasn't really old enough to appreciate how good they actually were; it's only in recent years with YouTube and, more importantly, 'Wigan TV' where I have watched past matches and realised how good players actually were, especially the likes of Ellery Hanley, Andy Gregory and Joe Lydon.

Growing up when Wigan were winning everything, you take it for granted that you'll win a trophy that year – I certainly did. So, in the later part of the 90s, probably from 1996 onwards with the arrival of Super League, everything changed. We seemed to go out and sign a load of unknown players who weren't Wigan standard, and Saints and Bradford started winning more trophies.

Central Park is special to us, but that being said the DW is a very good stadium and we have had some great games there; the 2000 play-off against Bradford, 2003

Good Friday and 2006 against Catalans where we turned a corner. And recently the World Club Challenge against Cronulla all go towards making it a home. I suppose in 20 or 30 years we will have a lot more memorable games and we will feel nostalgic like memories of Central Park do.

Come the early 2000s, growing up in St Helens with a lot of my mates being Saints fans, they won everything and I grew a very thick skin – I had to. I had to have a thick skin, especially after the 75-0 game, that still hurts now and it was the lowest point. The only way I could get over that is if we bettered that score and one day, when I'm old and grey (or greyer) when I'm at the game with my kids or grandkids, I'd love us to beat Saints 76-0, just to put that to bed.

I remember walking down the road after that game at Knowlsey Road and walking past a monumental masons, where there were gravestones being made and some smart alec Saints fans behind us shouted, 'Hey look at that gravestone, rest in peace – Wigan Rugby League'. Talk about a dagger to the heart, that comment cut me in half.

A major turning point was the 2005 season when we lost our core of players who'd been there for the last 10 seasons. Players like Andy Farrell, Kris Radlinski, Mick Cassidy, Terry O'Connor, Terry Newton, Adrian Lam all retired or left. It was left up to the young lads, who were thrown in at the deep end, and we struggled, 2006 being a really turbulent year, but if I'm honest 2006 is one of my favourite seasons.

I loved the way the fans got behind the team, I spent countless hours on the internet fishing for rumours of new players, it was a very exciting time.

In 2007 we signed Trent Barrett, a real class act, and the game away at Bradford is one of my top three games ever. Me, my now wife, my sister and brother-in-law went up to Bradford on a cold dark night and after 50 minutes the game was as good as dead and buried, then Trent Barrett stepped up along with Mark Calderwood and snatched the victory. I remember jumping up and down hugging everyone in sight when Pat slotted the drop goal. For some reason the next two games against Hull and Leeds I've got photos of me wearing a stick-on moustache for good luck.

The next few years I'd say were the steady years, with Brian Noble coaching us we were a five drives and a kick team with a lot of old heads. Nobby did a good job in settling us down as a club, but I was glad when it was time for him to move on. I thought he put too much trust in the old heads and not enough in the young lads. An injury to Tim Smith being the reason for Sam Tomkins' league debut.

Another one of my favourite seasons was the 2010 one. Michael Maguire came in and revolutionised us and Super League with 'the move', which by now I'm sick of seeing. Every time we tried it we scored, teams couldn't defend against us. The switch from stand-off to fullback improved Sam Tomkins tenfold.

More recently, with Shaun Wane in charge, we have had a team willing to put their bodies on the line for the coach, their team mates, the club and the fans. I'd say these last few years Shaun Wane has got the most effort out of his players, more than any coach I've ever seen. He will succeed in rugby union.

It has been great to have had a Wiganer coaching the team and bringing Wigan lads through, but not for the sake of it, bringing through some world class players and Waney will go down as one of the best coaches in Wigan's history.

Looking towards the future, we have a fantastic chairman in Ian Lenagan, who has got the club back into great shape both on and off the field. We have a chairman who cares passionately about the club and is here to stay. We have a good squad of players with a lot of Wiganers in the squad, a large stadium with great training facilities and staff, with a new coach taking over next season, Adrian Lam, and Shaun Edwards coming home for the 2020 season. It's a good time to be a Wigan fan, the future looks bright, but so does the past.

BEN REID

My first memory of watching Wigan Warriors came when I was seven years old. It was not only my 'first' memory, but it has forever been my most cherished. It was late August in 2000, and I remember it being a cold Sunday afternoon. It was the first time I really felt the excitement before, during and after a game. I had been going to games for years, even had two season tickets at Central Park – not that I can remember any of my time there, no matter how hard I try. I was there for the final ever game at Central Park and can't remember a damn thing about it. I see pictures of me there, as a young kid, in my shirt that was three sizes too big – so I could wear it for a few years and get some serious use out of it. Kills me that I can't remember that wonderful stadium, and my time there. If only I was born a few years earlier I could have seen some of the best times Wigan have had in their illustrious history.

So, even though I had been to my fair share of games prior to this one, I've always felt like this was the first time that I sensed it was a big game, and I felt like I wanted my team to win, and that it mattered. It's a strange thing to say, but I guess it was the first day I really became a Wigan Warrior. From that day on, I have lived every game as a fan in the stands. It helped me a lot in my younger days as a player, as I used to play rugby league for my local club. Being a 'big lad' throughout my life, I have always been a forward, and always wanted to be like my Wigan Warriors heroes – Mick Cassidy, Neil Cowie, Terry O'Connor... the list goes on.

I actually have a great story about Mick Cassidy, a player I looked up to more than most as a kid. I was in the under-8s team at my local club, and he was my hero at the time. I've always preferred the forwards than the backs. Anyway, we were undefeated in our season and got invited down to a tour of the Wigan Stadium, and it was to be run by Kris Radlinski, and we'd get chance to meet some of the other players. I could not miss the opportunity to meet my hero Cassidy. The night before, me and two other lads bleached our hair blond in homage to our main guy. We went down and got a picture with Mick and a few others, and even made the papers. It's an image and memory that will forever be in my mind. I mean, what was I thinking, bleaching my hair blond. It's safe to say I never touched my hair again – but I still got to meet my favourite player, no regrets.

I've been supporting Wigan for 25 years now, and there's been a fair few ups and downs over those years, and I've experienced and been there for the majority. From the highest of highs by winning Challenge Cups, Grand Finals and, most recently, becoming World Club Champions – to the lowest of lows, by being beaten in those finals and, of course, the infamous season of 2006. Safe to say, it's more than eventful being a Wigan Warriors fan. However, no matter what I've seen throughout the years, the one game and moment that always sticks in my mind more than others, is the 20-19 win over Bradford in 2000. That game turned out to be the catalyst of everything that was to come, and everything that is still to come.

Another time I remember arriving at the game like any other before it. I was with my dad and a few other family members. I have always sat in the South Stand – I find it to be the best stand for atmosphere. I got my ritual face-paint underneath the stands – going for good old 'Billy Whizz'. He was great. After games, we used to always go down to the South Stand Bar and meet all the players and get photos and autographs. Jason Robinson was the nicest rugby player I have ever met. He had time for everyone. I used to play rugby with his son (not Lewis Tierney who went on to play for Wigan), and we'd be running around the floor, having a laugh, it was a great time for me as a Wigan fan, some great memories and made some even better friendships.

Anyway, I remember the atmosphere feeling a little different than usual, which I always find strange looking back, as before this game I'd been to some huge ones against Saints. But this one just struck a nerve I guess, and I got that 'fan feeling' for the first time. The crowd was building up, players were on the pitch, and everyone was talking you through the game, of who was going to do what, who we'd have to keep our eye on. And, of course, how this referee will ruin the bloody game! Speaking of referees, I will never forget one of the first games my little sister came to. She must have been about six or seven years old. During this game, some of the South Stand got a bit 'hostile', should we say, and a few expletives were being aimed at the referee. One of those being, 'the referees a...' well, you probably know the rest. Anyway, after a few minutes, my sweet, innocent, baby-faced sister leaps up and shouts on top note, 'the referees a...' Oh, you should have seen the shock and awe on my dad's face. I couldn't tell if it was pride or embarrassment!

I knew this game was crucial to our season, and as the players came out, and the paper confetti was thrown, I was hooked. I could feel the adrenaline going through my veins – I was bloody pumped. It wasn't the best of starts, and that adrenaline soon turned to nervousness as we trailed from the first minute. As the game went on, we got worse, and we trailed 19-2 at one stage. The feeling around the JJB Stadium (as it was then) was unbearable. No one could have predicted what was to come. As we went into the final 20 minutes of the game, we got ourselves back into it when my fellow skullcap wearing hero Steve Renouf set up the great Terry Newton to get one back. As the game went on, Wigan got better, and Bradford started to get rattled – something that Wigan could do to a lot of teams when behind. Wigan would score again, and, all of a sudden, it seemed possible.

The fans started to roar, and the Bulls fans seemed to dip, as did the performance of their players. You could sense that 18th man for us, and it was working. Bradford's discipline steered off course as they had two players sin-binned. Something I always remember as I stood and waved them off the field, like they knew what I was doing. It was always fun mocking opposition players as a kid – I don't know why. The game went on and chances came and went. We were heading into the final minute, and we had 80-metres to go, it just wasn't going to happen. I actually remember some folk about to leave as Bradford kicked the ball deep, and Robinson retrieved to get us going for one last set. People shouting to chip over the top, pass it out wide, move the ball... just do something. It was a mixture of hope and setting yourself up for the worst. As the ball got shifted out wide, Andy Farrell played a beautiful ball to Renouf, and you just expected something from him when he had some space to manoeuvre in. He threw that little dummy and was gone. I had my eye on Renouf the whole way, and never saw Radlinski busting a gut to be there on hand to score what turned out to be the winning try.

I've honestly never heard a noise like it. I've been in Wembley, Old Trafford and even attended WrestleMania in New Orleans in packed-out Stadiums – it was deafening. As a seven-year-old, I guess it must have just sounded that bit extra loud that evening. The funny thing was, I thought we'd won at that point, and being the stupid kid that I was, hadn't noticed we needed to kick the goal. Suddenly, the whole place went from complete euphoria to absolute silence – it was so odd. I was sat on the right of the posts, so wasn't behind the sticks to see the ball go over. I remember Farrell taking that walk back, and I had my eyes on the people at the left of us to see their reactions, as I knew they'd know first. Once they started to jump and cheer, that was it, we'd won the game.

Watching it back now, I love hearing the noise of the crowd, it takes me right back. It was such an amazing game and moment for me as a Wigan fan. It's always been the one that's stayed with me throughout the years. I get goosebumps every time I watch or think about it, it's like I'm re-living the whole moment again. For me, that game was everything about being a Wigan Warriors fan.

DAVID BAILEY

Whenever I look back at my time supporting Wigan Warriors, or Wigan Rugby League as they were simply known back then, I can't help but feel lucky to have been born when I was, and privileged to be introduced to watching them when I did.

My first memory of the rugby was wanting to watch Wigan play at Wembley against Widnes in 1984. I'd have been six, about to turn seven, at the time and it seemed such a big deal. Shops were decked in cherry and white, people were buying rosettes (whatever happened to them?) and scarves and it was the talk of the town.

Wigan had come through a dark spell, which included relegation. My mum, Monica, and my two sisters, Karen and Mandy, made the trip south and I was disappointed to be told that I was too small to go. In hindsight it was probably a good thing, I don't remember much of that final, I don't even think I watched it on television (but I could be wrong).

The only things that spring to mind now when I think of it are Wigan losing to a Joe Lydon inspired Widnes and it being a miserable wet day. Fast forward 12 months to Wembley 1985, The 'Sterling-Kenny' final and a seven-year-old boy being overjoyed at being allowed to go. Back in those days, getting to Wembley was a big deal for Wigan, prior to the Widnes game they hadn't been to Wembley for 15 years, and hadn't won the Challenge Cup for 20.

I remember standing on the platform of Wigan North Western station, excited at the unknown and getting on the train. I'll be honest, I had to ask my Mum about the latter part of the journey as I don't remember how or where we got off the train but assumed we got the tube from Euston, but apparently, back in those days it was a special train that stopped at Wembley.

I remember being in awe of the twin towers and walking up Wembley way, I remember a carnival atmosphere and the contrast between the irregular cherry and white hoops and the irregular black and white hoops. The game itself was a bit of a blur. I remember being sat on the wall so that I could see, but every time Wigan scored the crowd would surge forward and I would have to be passed back to my mum over strangers' heads. It really was a different world.

That game produced so many memorable moments as a Wigan fan and really was the catalyst for the success for years to come. From Shaun Edwards's try and his awkward celebration (who knew we were witnessing the first medal of the most successful player in rugby league history), to John 'Chicka' Ferguson's shimmy in the corner, to Brett Kenny's scything try from the half-way line, and Henderson Gill's length of the field effort, and his 'smile as wide as Christmas Day'. I suppose that day was what captured my imagination, and what was to come over the next few years cemented my love for the sport and Wigan in particular.

I remember in primary school all of the camps during school holidays, and Graeme West in particular running them to get kids interested from an early age. I suppose Central Park was a huge part of that, a stadium almost in the town centre, the floodlights dominating the skyline.

There was something magical about games at night then too. Most games were played on Sunday afternoons at 3pm, except for televised games for the Challenge Cup, which would be on a Saturday. Midweek games were reserved for rearranged fixtures, which happened occasionally, but also for cup replays or the visit of the touring teams, so it was generally a special occasion. I can still remember finishing school and getting ready for the game. Going to 'Kay's Korner' and getting some sweets, usually a quarter of Uncle Joe's Mint Balls, and making our way into town. With the game being played in winter back then, the sun would have already set and the floodlights would beam brilliant white lights.

As we walked to the ground you'd see the crowds building and usually a bloke with a sandwich board telling us the end is nigh or something equally controversial (again, whatever happened to them). I was lucky enough that my mum used to help out in the office at Central Park, so rather than the turnstiles we used to go to the main entrance, which was also the players' tunnel. We'd call into the office and I'd be in awe at my heroes not only being within a few feet but also speaking to my mum and asking her if she had any sweets (or if they were Aussies or Kiwis – 'lollies').

I'd be at the club in school holidays when my mum helped out and ended up selling programmes. We'd go to the A-team games home and away, travelling to places like Hull and Workington on a Friday night following the team coach, and I even ended up being a ball boy for the A team with Graeme West's son Dwayne (of Wide to West fame). Even though it wasn't for the first team, it was still a highlight. I remember when the ball went over the Douglas Stand, a ball boy had to sprint down the pitch, down the tunnel and out of the main entrance, grabbing a huge fishing net, and retrieve the ball before it floated off past the town centre.

Each time we did it we got 50p, which wasn't a lot but compared to the cost of a replacement ball it was peanuts. I remember earning a small fortune when a certain Andy Farrell was captain of the A team.

Then in high school, I remember PE lessons for a term being run by first-team players. My first high school Cardinal Newman had a great record and there were always hard-fought battles between us and the Deanery and St John Fisher. I remember our PE teacher Mr Griffin being delighted at our year, getting to both the North West Counties and English Schools Finals. I honestly believe it's the hard work of people like Mr Griffin in the schools and amateur clubs around Wigan that lays the foundations for the Warriors to have such a brilliant youth set up and a seemingly never ending-conveyor belt of players, not only coming through but making a name for themselves in the sport.

Throughout the years, I have been lucky enough to see Wigan win everything possible. It's hard not to take success for granted when you watch your team win at Wembley eight years running, become the champions too many times to mention, when you see them win four World Club Challenges (three in the flesh), when you see them take on Bath in a cross-code challenge, and go to Twickenham, the home of rugby union, and win the Middlesex sevens, when they travel across the world and win the World Sevens Trophy in Australia.

Wigan is a unique club that combines the best overseas talent with the very best home-grown talent, whilst setting the pace off the field with ground-breaking initiatives. As the song goes, 'Cherry and white, it's in our blood.'

BILKO

I got into rugby league in the early 90s as I moved into primary school at a time when Wigan's dominance in that era was at its peak. Strangely, though, it wasn't necessarily that dominant success that drew me in. That era had also seen the launch of Cable TV in the Wigan area and it must have been cheap because my mum not only got the service herself but also afforded young me the luxury of my own box in my bedroom. I recall the first night we had cable the joy of Ipswich Town v Norwich City was on Sky Sports Monday Night Football, but it was the twice-weekly rugby league that caught the eye.

Sky's coverage today often gets hammered, but back then the coverage was fresh and exciting. Eddie and Stevo's jocular double act went on to become a poor parody of itself, but in the early days it was totally different to not only what we had from the BBC in terms of rugby league but also all other sports presentation.

Everything seemed spot on from exciting title music to an on-field product that might have been dominated by Wigan but never seemed dull to watch, even though it was played then in winter.

My best memories though came in the early 2000s. The late teens, early 20s are a great time in anyone's life when you get to socialise in the pubs and clubs for the first time and the rugby played a huge part in that.

That's why my favourite seasons are all from around that time. Wigan's trophy success may have dried up in those days, but the rugby was still great to watch. 2003 remains my most favourite season of all. We might have won nothing but it had many joys along the way. Four derby wins over Saints, three epic battles with Leeds at Headingley, two good wins over Bradford and a win on our last visit to Warrington's old Wilderspool ground.

The mental memories will forever remain, whether it's that Good Friday win over Saints with the kids or Brian Carney scoring some scorching tries including the one at Leeds in the play-off semi-final, which cost me a mobile phone in celebration. Whether I got mugged or it danced out my pocket leaping about doesn't really matter in a moment like that. Though I do miss the snake game on those old Nokias! Not long after came the sobering period of 2005-06 which included consecutive record defeats and the worst start to a season for Wigan in recent memory.

Wigan should have been relegated in 2006. Seems amazing still to write that but they should have been.

I remember the gut realisation of that prospect when Colum Halpenny denied Pat Richards a try in a crucial Saturday Night loss away at Wakefield. It was only May but it left Wigan five points adrift of safety, which didn't seem much but when you'd collected only four points out of 28 it was an absolute mountain.

A month later Wigan were playing Catalan on a Sunday night 7pm fixture, and I remember listening to the radio in the Red Robin Pub pre-match as, before we played, rivals Castleford beat Huddersfield whilst Lee Briers missed a penalty goal that left Wakefield 17-16 winners at Warrington.

As we kicked off that night, Wigan had still only won two games and found themselves EIGHT points adrift of safety. They had just 12 matches to make up the equivalent of four wins on their rivals.

The fact they managed that was remarkable in itself, but it didn't compare to how the support base rallied in those few weeks. It was like an air raid siren went off and support came out in droves, some who hadn't been for years after the Central Park departure fallout.

Wigan went on to win 10 of those final 12 matches and personally nothing trophy-wise has ever lived up to the joy of that run. I don't know why but I think the fact we'd all given up hope just led to a feeling of enjoyment and it helped that it was matched of the field. Michael Dobson only played 14 matches for Wigan but his contribution to our history is huge because without him scoring five tries and kicking 61 goals, I doubt we'd have survived the embarrassment of going down.

Further great days followed, like the remarkable play-off comeback at Bradford and the following moustache trip to Hull, but it was often mixed with dark days like Magic Weekend 2008 when I recall the zombified shock of fans as Wigan found themselves 35-0 down at half-time to Saints in Cardiff.

One thing remained consistent in that first decade of this century and that was the lack of trophies, but it made the 2010 season all the more special for a certain generation of Wigan fan. The blunt truth was that Wigan absolutely annihilated all comers that season under Michael Maguire. Only Warrington came close to halting our march and the only real worry we had was how embarrassing it would have been had we blown it.

That was a worry right up until the final hooter but to absolutely dominate our rivals St Helens in the Grand Final was a perfect ending to that campaign, and you just wonder what might have been had Lee Smith not scored in the last minute to knock us out the cup in a rain-ruined match.

GARETH DAVIES

You always remember your first time. Or at least that's how the saying goes anyway. But for me, I actually can remember my first time vividly and with a great amount of fondness as Sunday 24 October 1993 saw my love affair with rugby league really begin. Some would say that Halifax's quaint but ultimately crumbling old Thrum Hall ground is hardly the most glamorous of locations to tie this particular ceremonial knot, but that's the hand I was dealt and I wouldn't change it for the world.

You see I, unlike many, if not all of the other contributors in this book, was born and bred in the South of England. Subsequently, I was raised, sadly by virtue of my geographical location, on an unhealthy diet of the 15-man code and my only glimpses of league initially were on *Grandstand* as Bradford took on Oldham on a mud bath at Odsal, or something like that anyway.

However, the instantly recognisable tones of Ray French wouldn't be my zenith as my dad's best mate, through a chance meeting at a wedding in the 1970s, came from Halifax and introduced Mr Davies Snr to the greatest game of all.

As my love of sport rubbed off from my father, it was only natural that this interest extended to league and, despite being from a working-class family, we were lucky and had Sky television. I then started watching rugby on a Friday night, and even now, whilst sat in my front room typing, I'm humming along to that 'Seize the Day' song that Sky used in their opening credits.

By 1992, I must have shown more than just an interest in rugby league as I can vividly recall being a very happy nine-year-old when Great Britain thumped the Aussies in Melbourne and this prompted me to beg my Mum for some more pocket money so I could buy an actual rugby ball to practice kicking like Paul Eastwood. Sadly, though, Malcolm Reilly's team, like many before and those after too, lost the test series and I was so upset that I didn't want to watch the final leg of the last proper Lions tour.

It was a touch ironic that Reilly as manager of Halifax would be involved in my next league milestone: actually watching a game and experiencing all those moments that make our game so special and like no other.

Dad's mate, whose name is Phil Walsh by the way – a tough prop forward who played for the now defunct Park Amateurs club in Halifax – knew Ned, who I am led to believe was kit-man at Thrum Hall and managed to get us three tickets.

We stood on 'Fax's rickety old terraces as a packed house and a fervent atmosphere greeted a Wigan side packed with superstars and a home team that was going well, with the likes of former Wigan players Steve Hampson and Mark Preston in their side. Despite being in with the home supporters, I only really had eyes for one team and that was Wigan. Martin Offiah looked every bit the superstar he undoubtedly was, whilst Shaun Edwards organised his troops round the pitch like a conductor leading an orchestra.

There was even the rare occurrence of Nigel Wright in a cherry and white jersey as Wigan dominated the opening 40 minutes and led 14-2 at the break. 'Fax rallied in the second half, but the visiting side, who were coached by John Dorahy at the time, ran out 31-22 winners, with the final scoreline flattering the hosts who were never really in the game as a contest.

Phil Clarke, in his final season before a move to Australia which sadly cut his career short, crossed twice, as did Offiah with a young winger called Jason Robinson also registering a four-point haul. Sadly, though, Robinson, in the act of scoring his try, dislocated his elbow and my last glimpse of him on a cold October afternoon was sat in the back of an ambulance on the outfield of the neighbouring cricket ground as we left Thrum Hall.

Edwards was not only Wigan's talisman that day, he also played the role of pantomime villain too. So much so that one elderly lady supporting 'Fax barged her way to the front of the terracing to tell our Shaun that she would rearrange his head with her umbrella if he didn't pack his nonsense up. I couldn't actually believe what I saw or heard, but in a funny kind of way, it cemented the viewpoint in my mind that everything about rugby league was just magnificent.

After the game, everyone ran on the pitch trying to get an autograph, nowadays it would be a selfie or something to hashtag on Instagram, but the best I got was to pat Karl Harrison, Halifax's giant prop, on the back. Phil managed to get me a signed programme after the game and my mum even bumped into Frano Botica whilst out in Halifax that evening. Despite getting a 'Fax shirt for my birthday five days later, I really wanted a Wigan one.

Some would call me a glory supporter for jumping on the Wigan bandwagon that rolled along at break-neck speed during this golden era at the much-missed Central Park, but I just loved the game, and given Wigan's standing within it how could I fall in love with anyone else?

My next glimpse of the side was at Wembley in 1995 when Wigan lifted the final Challenge Cup pre-Super League, and that match, despite victory, was possibly the final act of their ultimate dominance.

Things unravelled pretty dramatically in those early summer rugby days, as a once mega-rich club suddenly became impoverished, and, although Dave Whelan ultimately saved Wigan from oblivion, the club selling Central Park is one that still sits uncomfortably with me as it meant I never saw a match there.

My early Wigan years had seen nothing but success, but by the millenium years, the club were going through a barren spell in which the noisy neighbours from up the road and Bradford were the dominant forces. We did have our moments and being there for the Radlinski final and Terry's tears at Old Trafford a year later were special, but Cardiff in 2004 was less so. Dad and I actually met Whelan walking around the grounds of Cardiff castle before the final that year, and he was astounded at dad remembering that he broke his leg in the FA Cup Final, but he walked off before I mentioned Central Park.

The years after were nothing short of dreadful as remembering Iain Millward's time at the club still makes me shudder! But things changed under Michael Maguire and laterally Shaun Wane. Not only did Wigan start winning things again, but they did so playing a brand of rugby that was a throwback to those early years. From Offiah in 1994, we had Joel Tomkins' stunner some 17 years later. The team was, and still is, littered with superstars and Wigan are the team to beat whilst St Helens had fallen on hard times before improving last season.

Getting to games is still a problem, especially now I have re-located from Dorset to Cornwall, but I'm still there, cheering and swearing in equal measures at my TV screen every time Wigan are on the box. My passion and desire for the game is still as strong as ever, and, although I thought rugby league would have evolved at a far greater pace than it has, our wonderful sport still gives me the same satisfaction that it did all those years ago and will continue to do so for many years to come also.

MARK ILLINGWORTH

I grew up as a skinny bespectacled kid in a football loving household in Lytham St Annes, about 40 miles north-west of Wigan. Growing up, rugby league was never at the front of my mind. This is my story on how I went from there to having a cherry and white colour scheme for my wedding.

My uncle and grandad started going to watch Wigan in the late 80s, but it was just something I knew of rather than followed religiously. It started to change for me in the late 90s. My first final was the 1998 Challenge Cup Final. I'm surprised I was allowed back after that one! But the drive down, the walk to the stadium and the atmosphere before kick-off all really got to me. Standing on Wembley Way and seeing all the red and white flags was something I'd never experienced before. And the roar of 'WIIIGAN WIIIGAN WIIIGAN' inside the ground was incredible.

Going to Old Trafford for the inaugural Grand Final and seeing Wigan lift the trophy pulled me in even more. Jason Robinson's try that night was my first 'I was there when' moment as a Wigan supporter. It is the kind of try that each time I remember it, Robinson starts from five yards further away from the line and he beats another Leeds defender on his way to score.

When we moved to the new stadium I started to share a season ticket with my brother. The big games had a real sense of atmosphere and intensity in the stands, and this was always matched on the field. Something was always happening. There were still enough of the names and faces I had seen lift cups on the TV for me to feel a sense of history – Farrell, Betts, Radlinski, Connolly. There were new fast and exciting players from overseas – Dallas, Renouf. When my brother got a job collecting glasses in a pub on a Friday night, the season ticket became all mine.

By the 2000 World Cup, I was a fully fledged rugby league fan. The M6 and the M62 had become my favourite roads to travel on. They meant I was going to see something special. Nothing that year was more special than Farrell wide to Renouf, Renouf up the touchline, then the pass inside to Radlinski against Bradford. We were sat right behind the Farrell conversion as it went over to snatch victory from Bradford.

Probably my favourite ever day as a Wigan fan came at Murrayfield in 2002. To get one over on the old enemy, playing as underdogs, was awesome. Kris Radlinski's try savers still live strong in the mind. Gary Connolly scored his try right in front of us. But driving away from the ground will always be my lasting memory of that day. U2's *Beautiful Day* came on the radio as we were driving past some Saints fans. My uncle leaned out of the window, Wigan scarf stretched out, singing the chorus at full voice.

Obviously the next few years weren't quite as successful for Wigan. And that speccy kid had become an awkward inbetweener, who hadn't quite found his place yet. Going to Wigan became a personal experience. It was a chance to release a lot of life's frustrations through chanting and cheering, clapping and shouting. There was a lot of shouting during those years! But it all meant I had found my place, I had found my identity. People who knew me now knew first and foremost that I was a Wigan Rugby League fan.

The next truly special night I vividly remember as a Wigan fan was the great play-off comeback at Bradford. Nights like that have the classic hug-a-stranger celebrations that only a special away victory brings. The game was gone after 50 minutes. Even when Mark Calderwood began the fight back, we weren't really convinced. But when Harrison Hansen took it to within one score, and all we were seeing was Wigan players streaming away from us to the far end try line, the noise and the atmosphere were incredible. I definitely felt like us fans played a part in upsetting the Bradford players into the error that Calderwood scooped up to complete his hat-trick. Then Pat Richards landed the drop goal. What a night!

2010 to 2013 was the greatest stretch in my time as a Wigan fan. Watching a team that was fitter than everyone else, more accurate and polished than everyone else, and capable of delivering on the big occasions was something I had not seen in my previous decade of being a season ticket holder.

The 2010 Grand Final will always be second only to that 2002 Cup Final for me. It was a game that never felt in doubt from the start. I have no idea why Martin Gleeson's second try that night isn't widely regarded as one of the greatest tries seen in a Super League Grand Final. I think it's right up there with Robinson's in 1998.

Wigan's 2011 Challenge Cup run had so many great tries in it that there was always going to be one more at Wembley. It was the first time watching Wigan at the new national stadium. The team had to mark the occasion in a special way, and nothing could be more special than Joel Tomkins' try that day. For me, the new Wembley gives the best all-round viewing experience of any big stadium I've been in. Everywhere you sit gives a great sense of sporting occasion. We were up in the top tier for this game, but all that meant was we had a great view of things unfold and open up, as Sam picked up the ball and skirted across the line, before finding his brother Joel, who did the rest. It was one of the purest moments of rugby league beauty I've ever seen first-hand.

When I met my future wife in early 2011, everything was great again in the Wigan world. She didn't care about rugby, but she got used to seeing me go off on a Friday night, come back happy after a solid Wigan win and then have a happy weekend as a result. We got engaged in September 2013, mid-way between Wigan winning in the rain at Wembley and clinching the double at Old Trafford. She still didn't care about rugby.

Over the next couple of years, as we planned for our big day, she started to warm up to a red and white colour scheme that she had been determined to never have. By the time the big day came, my grooms party were wearing Wigan club ties and the bridesmaids were in red. The white table cloths were complemented with a red runner through the middle of every table, with the venue getting specific instructions that it needed to look like cherry and white hoops as we looked out from the top table. The colour scheme was most definitely cherry and white, and I am ancient and loyal until I die.

MIKE GRUNDY

Mike Grundy is a professional mixed-martial arts fighter and a member of the Team Kaobon set up, from which UFC fighters such as Darren Till train. Grundy started in wrestling and won a bronze medal in the men's freestyle 74 kg event at the 2014 Commonwealth Games.

MMA fighter Mike Grundy became a Wigan Warriors fan in his childhood.

I've always supported Wigan since being a young kid. My family are rugby mad, a few of my uncles played rugby and my grandad was a coach so there are a lot of us in the family who played rugby, so I was brought up with it. Living in Wigan you're going to support them. I played a little bit when I was a kid, I quit wrestling when I was about 11 or 12 and I played rugby for a year at St Williams in Ince. I only did a year and did a few games – I didn't do much but I always enjoyed it. Coming from a wrestling background it helped in the rugby side of things.

Growing-up I remember Martin Offiah, and Kris Radlinski was one of my favourites when he came onto the scene. You always knew you'd be able to depend on him at fullback. I loved Offiah because he was so fast and Radlinski – I like the fact he came out of retirement to help Wigan out when they were facing relegation in 2006, and it was something I think all the fans who remember it will appreciate. They weren't performing, winning matches or doing too well. Radlinski came back and seemed to change them a little bit. For him to come out of retirement was amazing so he was a favourite for that too. They had a lot to do at the end of that season to stay in Super League and I think having his presence in the squad helped lift the others.

A few years after that Michael Maguire changed a lot behind the scenes as well. I went down to the club at that time as I was starting up coaching wrestling. I was only young and I've always been passionate about coaching the next generation of athletes.

I met Mike Forshaw and he was the strength and conditioning coach at the time. He took me to see how things were running and Maguire had something good going on. There was a lot I could take back to my wrestling coaching and I was amazed at the professionalism at the club.

Maguire brought the best out of his players and he liked his wrestling. It was good to see. When he came he changed Wigan and it's easy to see why they won the Grand Final in 2010. He changed the way a lot of teams play rugby league and I think we've seen more teams try to copy that. As for rugby league, I appreciate all the different aspects of the game, not just the wrestling side. It's a tough sport. There are a lot of collisions and it's hard work. You've got to be fast, you have to be able to grapple a little bit and in some sense wrestle a little bit. While being a big guy and trying to be fast as well, it's tough. The guys that play it have my every respect.

I appreciate the whole sport. I've always liked and enjoyed rugby. Looking at it from a wrestling point of view you have to appreciate those 10-second contacts. They're tough and there are a lot of technicalities in them which I don't think you always get to appreciate. If I ever get chance I watch the game at the weekend, but I'm busy a lot coaching and taking kids to competitions these days, and my passion is seeing youngsters take up sport and get the best out of it.

And it's obvious Wigan Warriors feel the same – they get on to anything that's doing well in something and help make people better through enjoying sport. It doesn't matter that not all of them are going to be the next Sam Tomkins, what matters is they are enjoying sport and getting the most out of life. They have a good system within the schools to get kids into rugby, so they're doing a good job in the community. We've had a lot of kids who play rugby come to wrestling and a lot of the skills are transferable. A lot of teams book in for six weeks blocks to help with that side of the rugby.

The wrestling helps and a lot of coaches are noticing it now right from amateur to professional – they are all realising there are areas of other sports they can borrow from, much like other sports borrow a lot from rugby league. It's not just the playing side, but also supporting the club that's good for the community. It's a great chance to come together, support a team and have something to believe in.

They're giving the town something or someone to believe in – and inspiring people. They're inspiring kids. Some kids don't have much and they need teams and people like that to inspire them to do something special. To make them get up and say I want to be the next George Williams. They want to be that person so they can make a good living and become someone special. It's massively important in our town.

BRADLEY WIGGINS

Five-time Olympic Gold medalist, 2012 Tour de France winner.

Riding in the Tour de France is hard. Spending more than 2,000 miles on a bike, in any conditions, wouldn't be a lot of people's idea of fun – this is a test for the super-fit. Winning it in 2012 was a career highlight for Bradley Wiggins, arguably the career

Steve Hampson, Bradley Wiggins and Andy Johnson.

highlight. Add eight Olympic medals to his sideboard – five of them gold – and you get some idea of the athlete on your hands.

There are countless other meals in his collection, from the Commonwealth Games to the World Championships, and in 2015 he broke the hour record at London's Lee Valley VeloPark – certainly enough there to put him among the greats. All this before you add a knighthood in 2013 into the equation.

You'd think then that for Wiggins nothing would beat the efforts of those on two wheels, lactic acid unbearably building in the calves while flying past the crowd at speeds expected of small motorbikes.

But Wiggins's love of rugby league, in particular Wigan Warriors, is well documented.

Made a life member of the club after his Tour win in 2012, he presented Sam Tomkins with the Man of Steel award that year, and he has joined the team's Grand Final celebrations.

'What they do as athletes… That's where my love for the sport comes from, because it's hard,' he said. 'Seeing the hits, they're big collisions – someone summed it up well when they said "footballers spend 90 minutes pretending they're injured, rugby players spend 80 minutes pretending they're not." Players smash each other to bits for 80 minutes and then shake hands afterwards and that's something to be admired. It's how sport should be.'

No stranger to intense preparation, to the point it takes over your life, Wiggins has an appreciation for some of the club's recent achievements, which many supporters perhaps do not. A Grand Final on the surface is just another game – physically it should require the same preparation as Hull KR away on a Thursday night. But it doesn't, just like an Olympic final is nothing like a club meet, though the motions the body does are the same, 'Mentally – no matter how hard you train – you're looking forward to those big occasions,' he says when asked for comparisons between cycling for medals and playing rugby for a trophy.

Rugby league might seem an odd choice for someone who was brought up in north-west London after moving from Ghent, Belgium, at the age of two. And football was actually his first passion, before he discovered cycling and emulated his father Gary by becoming a professional. But rugby league was always in his peripheral before becoming a fan in the early 2000s, after Wigan's all-conquering success of the 80s and 90s but when they still boasted some of the most famous names in the sport in Jason Robinson, Kris Radlinski and Andy Farrell.

'I was aware of it through the 90s,' he explained. 'Living in the south, it was the one time you'd see rugby league on the telly. Once a year, the Challenge Cup Final. To be honest, Martin Offiah was the only rugby league player anyone ever knew. He became a household name. He was from the south and transcended the sport, he brought it to the masses. I've known people within the sport who have different thoughts about Martin, but from the outside and not living here then, he was the one you were aware of, the one on the posters, the one you'd see interviewed on Sports Personality of the Year.'

It's easy to see why Offiah was the one everyone knew outside rugby league circles. It wasn't just his speed and knack for scoring tries – it's the fact he did it when others were watching, and not just people on the terraces at Lancashire and Yorkshire's rugby league grounds. He appeared in four Challenge Cup Finals, scoring four tries (two in 1992 and two in 1994) and his first in the '94 is still watched and talked about – so much so the pose he adopted after scoring it was used on the rugby statue at Wembley.

It was feats like those, in front of nearly 80,000 fans at Wembley and huge TV audiences, that made the Wigan brand almost as big as the sport at that time.

Granted, Wigan has been soaked in history for generations, but to people outside Wigan like Wiggins, this was the era when they became aware, and why you see Londoners in Warriors jerseys at the home of London Broncos whenever the sides meet in the capital.

'The players realise what it means to pull the shirt on. That is a famous shirt to put on,' explained Wiggins of the current Warriors team, which might not have an individual as famous as Offiah, but most have won accolades as important such as the Challenge Cup and World Club Challenge. For me, it's like representing your country at the Olympics, you've been chosen for a reason and that's because you've got something special.'

Having married a Wiganer in Catherine and seeing his son Ben and daughter Isabella share in his support of the Warriors, Wiggins certainly falls into that bracket of people where the town is as special as the club. His success has taken him around the world, but Wigan has followed him to more than one destination, most notably Australia, a hotbed of rugby league where the club is perhaps the most famous English side, thanks in part to an epic World Club Challenge victory over Brisbane in June 1994.

'It's funny when you go to Australia and see people walking around with old Wigan tops with Norweb across the front,' laughed Wiggins. 'It [the town] definitely got something about it. For a tiny north-west town, it's so well known around the world. It's famous because of some of the greats who've represented the club and what they've achieved.'

Bradley Wiggins was speaking to the Wigan Observer.

GREG FARRIMOND

Everyone thinks their home town is special and like no other. And, of course, that is true because if you grow up with that emotion of belonging and community, it stays with you for life. But with Wigan I genuinely believe that the attachment is somewhat stronger than most. Whether it's a northern thing or a Wigan thing, I'm not sure but the sense of community that exists within the town – its districts, its estates and its streets – is, in many ways, still the same as it was decades ago.

And it's those constants that make the town what it is; the sport, the music, the Pier, those wonderful pies, the people. It's also that warped sense of humour that allows Wiganers to not just accept but embrace the town's flaws. God help anyone else who points them out, though.

I've always grown up as someone who just wants his home town to do well, no matter what. A semi-pro boxer, a singer on the X Factor, a professional chess player, some bloke on karaoke in Benidorm... you get the picture. For me I love being able to point at someone or something and say 'they come from where I'm from'. I was on a train the other week and saw some bloke eating a packet of Uncle Joe's Mintballs and something in me just wanted to tell him they come from Wigan.

I live down south these days and it's got to a point where if I start talking about Wigan, eyes start rolling as the general expectancy is that I will end up rambling on for hours. My identity here is pretty much my home town. I think when people call me 'Wigan Greg' it's meant as a bit of a sneer but I absolutely love it. So, when we excel and sit proudly at the top, I absolutely beam with pride. True, when I watched the 2016 Grand Final in a pub in Camden no-one gave a toss about me celebrating or even the game for that matter, but Wigan was the best that day and that's all that mattered.

The town has had it rough over the years, but I love the way that sport can bring us together. Yes, we'll probably always have that Warriors/Latics divide, which I have learnt to accept and kind of understand, but one I will never, ever embrace. But behind it all, the two fan bases are incredible and share all the same values. Lifelong friendships are made out of supporting the same club, matchday traditions and following your home town the length and breadth of the country.

The year 2013 will be etched in my memory forever. For the two clubs to bring back those three trophies was something incredible. It even – albeit temporarily – united the sporting divide! Again, though, we come back to that word 'community'. The Wigan Warriors fanbase is one of the strongest I know. One of the proudest moments my family had was when my uncle, Mike Gregory, was appointed as head coach in 2003. The support he had from fellow Wiganers who loved seeing one of their own leading their club was incredible.

But it wasn't the support they showed him during his highs as he led them to the Grand Final and the Challenge Cup Final, it's what they did after that which will live with me forever. Mike's time with Wigan was struck short when he was diagnosed with Motor Neurone Disease and over the three years he battled his illness before his passing in 2007, I'm not quite sure my family would have coped were it not for the support of the Wigan community. And that doesn't just stop at Wigan Warriors fans.

When one of our own needs help and support we're there for them. Those who don't necessarily have a lot themselves give all they can, be it time or money, to help those in need. That to me is what makes Wigan great. Not the pies, not the Pier, not the music or the sweets. The people.

ANDREW HEAP

Watching Steve Hampson doing backflips after winning the Challenge Cup in 1989 is my favourite memory of Wigan Rugby League. We'd just beaten St Helens 27-0 at Wembley so it's not a bad one. I was eight. I did the 1985 final and I remember sitting right on the back row and it was just benches, watching it with my grandad. I don't remember anything about the game apart from Henderson Gill, when he scored the try, spun round, massive grin… amazing.

From that era, it tends to be Challenge Cup memories because there's so many of them. The fact 1989 was against Saints adds to it definitely, and they were nilled as well which was always good.

Do you remember those big inflatables? There were light bulbs, Newcastle Brown Ale bottles and stuff. They had bits of cardboard in the bottom and my cousin was waving one around and smashed my dad on the top of the head with one. It cut his head open on the coach on the way down. I also remember getting on the coach, we were getting on at Central Park to set off. It was a double decker coach and I'd never been on one – I wanted to sit at the front of the upper deck as we went down. We were the first ones on the coach so I legged it up, sat down, got in the seat right at the front ready to go. The driver says 'the coach has broken down, you'll have to get another one.' We had to get off and I sulked all the way down to London. We got on to another coach and were sat in the middle – someone else got to ride at the front.

The rugby meant a lot in terms of togetherness with the family. We always used to go to Central Park – there might have been 20-odd of us and we'd all stand together at the same spot at Central Park. That's what makes it more emotive when you look back – it's not just the rugby taking place but you're watching it with your family – my brother, dad, mum, cousins, aunties and uncles. It's that I think about most when I look back – using Wigan rugby to bring our family together.

My dad moved to Wigan in his late teens, early 20s. He lived with my grandad when they moved here before he went to college to be a teacher, but he's always liked rugby league and moving to Wigan made him involved in watching Wigan. My dad met my mum, whose family were fans, and that compounded the fact my dad liked rugby. He could get involved watching it with the family. We spent a lot of time at Central Park and it was a bit of a focal point in that part of our family history.

I have very early memories of being at Central Park and not even being as tall as the crush barriers. I just used to walk under those, which was how young I was when we went there. We stood in the corner between the Kop end and the Popular Stand, away fans to our left looking over the pitch from behind the corner flag. We'd stand probably about two thirds of the way up. But one year me and my mum spent a season sat in the Popular Stand because I didn't want to stand up. We got tickets in the posh seats, which were those wooden fold down seats. They made a bang when you stood up out of them and they weren't really that posh, but much posher than most other parts of Central Park.

I remember the rugby cards too, you'd go to the policeman asking for them. We thought we were asking a policeman once for some cards but he worked for St John's Ambulance. They had a picture of a player on them and a safety message on the back. It never leaves you. Someone just saying 'Wigan's won' sparks some kind of memory, then you end up going on a YouTube journey watching all the cup finals and stuff. It still comes up in conversation, talking about the outings more than anything. Big family days out to Wembley. Most of the pictures we've got are of cup finals, things like that, and those YouTube journeys bring it all back, especially when I watch the '89 cup final again.

DAVE WOODS

Voice of rugby league on the BBC.

I was two years old when my dad first took me to Central Park. So I can't remember a time when rugby league wasn't an important part of my life. But coming from Bolton it felt like a long distance love affair. It's that odd geography of rugby league that makes a game that is a religion in one town, a rare and strange entity in the town 12 miles down the road.

So, as a kid, my mate Kev became my mate because we were the only two kids at our school who watched, adored, were fanatical about rugby league in general and Wigan in particular. We made up songs about Dennis Boyd, idolised Billy Melling. We wrote letters to Maurice Bamford, worshipped Terry Hollingsworth and later jinked like Henderson Gill in the playground.

Other kids were kicking footballs, we were picking them up. So, when at 17 I decided I was going to be a journalist, I also decided that rugby league could be a specialist subject. In an incredible stroke of luck, when I rang the sports editor of the *Bolton Evening News* and offered to write about the game for his paper – the way you do when you're 17 and think nothing is impossible – he gave me a chance.

I was still at school, studying for A levels, yet found myself at Headingley on Saturday 1 December 1984 to cover a Regal Trophy tie between Leeds and Wigan. The match report was published – Leeds won 10-4 by the way – and that was it. I was back at school on Monday, but a course was set for my professional life.

By the time I'd finished my studies and exams the following June, I'd talked myself into a job with the Wigan press agency, Barnes News Service, on Bridgeman Terrace, just up from Mesnes Park. The changing nature of newspapers and news coverage means that agencies like Barnes News don't really exist anymore. But back then every town and city had an agency like ours, reporting on local news and sport and selling stories to regional and national newspapers, radio and TV outlets.

A major part of Barnes News output was based around the rugby league club, so those were heady days for a young rugby fanatic like me. One week I was in school, the next I was in a job that involved ringing the likes of Maurice Lindsay and Graham Lowe on a regular basis, then letting the leading national newspaper reporters, like Brian Batty at *The Daily Mail*, Paul Harrison at *The Sun*, Keith Macklin at *The Times*, know what the stories were from Wigan that day. It was like signing for the star team, because Wigan were the coming force.

They'd just appeared in the greatest cup final of all time – the 28-24 classic against Hull featuring Kenny, Ferguson, Gill, an 18-year-old Edwards *et al.* And with the recent appointment of the Kiwi Lowe as head coach, they were beginning to revolutionise the game.

Lowe was a fantastic personality to deal with – laid back, laconic and full of quotes. 'When you're cruising, you're losing,' was one of his favourites. Maurice was a box of tricks – colourful, charismatic and unpredictable. He banned me from Central Park once for reporting that centre David Stephenson was in dispute.

'It's far more subtle than that, David. He wants more money, we're not willing to give it to him,' he firmly told me. 'But Maurice, isn't that a dispute? You're banned from Central Park,' he shouted at me. 'For ever. Don't want to see you again. Ever.' Phone slammed down. I was a kid. The bottom had fallen out my world on the strength of that one phone call. The very next day he rang me, no mention of our last conversation just 24 hours later. 'David, I've a story I'd like you to do.'

I've no recollection of what that story was, but that was Maurice in a nutshell, as I learned many times down the years. You could annoy him, frustrate him, anger him, justifiably or not, but he never held a grudge. Life always went on. Five years at Barnes News coincided with covering some great times and great characters. The best of them were the Wembley finals – anyone remember 1989?

The players – with one exception, and you can guess who – were always a delight to deal with, and understanding when you might not get it right. So, when I wrote the story about how Wigan's ferocious forward Andy Goodway had opened a rest home and was helping to look after customers himself, it was with a laugh that he rang me the following day to say I'd misheard. It was a restaurant, not a rest home he'd opened.

Two days after the 1990 Challenge Cup Final win against Warrington, I left Barnes News and joined the BBC – Radio Leeds, to be exact. And that was the point that the passion for Wigan began to wane. Working in Yorkshire and covering the likes of Leeds, Bradford, Wakefield, Halifax etc, you begin to see other clubs' points of view. You empathise with their key characters on the coaching and playing staff. And with Wigan dominating everything, you began to realise that wasn't good for the general health of the sport.

So, I can genuinely say that since being at the Beeb, I've never sat down to commentate on any match – Radio or TV – as a Wigan fan. It's been the quality of the game that's mattered most, not who wins.

Well, with one exception… the 2002 Challenge Cup Final at Edinburgh. I have to admit that secretly throughout that game, commentating for BBC Radio 5 Live, I was desperate for Wigan to win for all sorts of different reasons. It became perhaps the most famous of non-Wembley finals, the Radlinski final.

I've had tremendous fun and good fortune through my career, travelling all over the world to cover rugby league. So far, I've commentated on six World Cup Finals,

I've covered every Challenge Cup Final as a journalist since 1986, I've had the terrific honour of being the BBC's lead commentator since 2009. And was appointed the Corporation's first ever rugby league correspondent in 2017.

But for all of that, nothing compares to the sheer innocent thrill and daily joy of being a young cub reporter in Wigan in the 80s. In those heady days when the Cherry and Whites were breaking new ground, signing superstars and breaking records, the memories of being on the fringes of that, notebook in hand, still sends a shiver up my spine. I can close my eyes and imagine every nook and cranny, every broken step and squeaky flip-up seat in Central Park. The noise, the smells, the quips, the cheers. the occasional boos are all still there in the back of my mind.

Life moves on, it's inevitable. But wouldn't it be lovely to spend a day back in a time when Wigan were undisputed kings of rugby league and the Douglas Stand felt like the centre of the world?

JENNY MEADOWS

Rugby league memories are your first memories of life almost. My dad was a huge fan so I was brought up supporting Wigan Rugby League. I remember my brother and my dad always going on a coach and travelling down to Wembley; I was always either too young or involved in athletics so couldn't go. I remember being at my nan's house watching the game and at that age it feels like a long time, it feels like three hours or something when you're young.

There was never a question every year whether Wigan would be at Wembley in the Challenge Cup Final or not, it was just kind of a given that it would happen and a given they would win really. I was just always so excited to see my dad when he got home really late at night or even the next morning because I'd gone to bed when he'd get home, just to see my dad really happy that his team had won always had the same effect on me. It's something I grew up with.

St Helens were the enemy and Wigan were the team you had to support! There was never any question.

I used to keep a scrapbook, and I've

Jenny Meadows made her name in athletics but has a lifelong connection with Wigan Rugby League.

kept it all my life, of my athletics career – in athletics there wasn't any kit other than your club vest so I've got a picture of me and my dad when Wigan Harriers won a primary school sports athletics competition and behind us we have the Wigan Rugby League scarf. My dad has one of his Wembley caps on. We're just big Wiganers really.

We're really passionate about the town and Wigan Rugby League has played its part in putting it on the map, so it's never been a question of whether I'd be a supporter or not. It was kind of a given as I grew-up. When I was younger people would always ask where I was from and I'd always think do I say Wigan or Manchester, there was always that conflict. If I said Manchester people would ask, 'is it Manchester United or Manchester City?' and I'd tell them I'm from this place called Wigan, and it was amazing how many people knew it.

Rugby league would be the connection and I would be really proud if someone had heard of Wigan rugby; it happened especially when I met Australians. I remember going to the World Junior Championships way back in 2000 and it was in Santiago in Chile. Most of the time you break down barriers through talking about what football team you support. All the Australians thought it was cool I was from Wigan. A lot of the other people would be talking about their football teams but it was nice at that time to see some recognise Wigan Warriors. I've always been proud of that connection.

I remember being at Central Park, I only went a few times, and I remember having a pick 'n' mix, sat on my dad's knee. My dad had a season ticket and I have this memory of some wrought iron steps to get to the ticket office. I always remember walking past the players' cars and seeing names on the cars. We'd be queueing up the steps for the little ticket office to get my dad's season ticket. My dad knew the people next to him so when someone in their family wasn't going my brother could go and I just sat on my dad's lap – but I do remember more of the pick 'n' mix than watching the game!

I don't really get to as many games as I like now but I try to get to one every season at least. If Wigan have had a good game it really boosts me and it still frustrates me if the match hasn't gone their way. It's just sport isn't it? But that's the thing, passion and emotion makes it what it is.

In 2012 I got a really good insight into what training they do. Unfortunately, in 2012 I missed the Olympics and I couldn't compete that season. Trevor, my husband and coach, was out in South Africa because they were getting ready for the season and I was at home with a boot on because I had an injury, but Mark Bitcon helped for that three to four weeks Trevor was away, just making sure I could see a coach twice a week.

I went into Orrell and a lot of the boys were there, it was Good Friday week and the players who weren't playing the game were there. Some had injuries and others had missed selection and that's a game nobody wants to miss. It was a really nice day and we did some work in the gym. Mark opened the doors so we could do some work outside and we all worked so hard. I remember then just getting such a respect for how hard those guys actually work. It's a bit like athletics. You see them out on the track and you see the finished product and you don't actually see what goes into it.

I'd say I'm one of the fittest athletes on the circuit, I've been competing in the sport since the age of seven, so I've always been used to being the one still going at the end of a session and the one who doesn't complain. That was the attitude from all of the boys. I was nice to be around world-class athletes and it's when I discovered these guys are athletes. It's quite easy to see a big guy on the field tackling and running, but to see what goes into it, I got much more respect when I saw them killing themselves, having two minutes' recovery and going again and being around really like-minded people.

Athletics is an individual sport and you don't have that team to go and meet every day. I realised it's not just me in Wigan trying to be world-class every day, this is happening literally a few miles down the road from me. It was really good to see. I have cast fresh eyes over it ever since I saw what goes into what happens on the field.

I'll go into a school to do a talk and you see so many children involved in sport and doing well.

I don't know, but I think we punch way above our weight in this town and it's something I'm really, really proud of. People associate Wigan with sport, especially with Wigan Athletic being in the Premier League for eight years and winning the FA Cup. It's phenomenal. I'm so proud of my town, Wigan Athletic, Wigan Harriers and Wigan Warriors.

When people think of Wigan, what they might have heard about cobbles and the industrial landscape is overshadowed by sport. I don't know what the magic formula is, I think they don't have over-inflated egos. They just work hard. In sport that is just what it takes. I had a certain amount of talent but that doesn't necessarily come into fruition for people. It's attitude and mindset and I just think people are prepared to dig deep.

That's what the boys are doing each and every day and it's not just me. I've had that connection with the club since doing my strength and conditioning programme with Mark in 2011 and Shaun Wane has allowed me to use the gym there which has been great.

Trevor and Mark share training tips and there's a great connection between the sports. We'll see the boys doing hills at Haigh Hall, and there are also Wiganers who play for other teams doing the same thing, and amateur teams.

We also all use Rivington and Formby and you see the Warriors boys do things I've done. A lot of Trevor's training comes from Chris Butler, who was Wigan's fitness

Jenny Meadows is put through her paces in the Wigan Warriors gym with Mark Bitcon,

coach in the 1990s, and what he used to do with the team. Trevor tells me a tale about David Grindley, a Wiganer who won bronze in the 4x400m relay in the 1992 Olympics. At Rivington there's a flight of steps everyone trains on and they call it the Olympic steps because of David, for a 19-year-old to do that in the Olympics is pretty phenomenal. Michael Johnson was the world record holder in the 200 and the 400, this an era before Usain Bolt, and he gave a speech at the end of his career. Someone asked Michael if he'd ever been afraid of anybody, and he said I've never been afraid of any athlete other than David Grindley. He said he thought he was going to be the one to beat him. It's amazing David used a part of Rivington where Chris Butler would take the rugby league players.

There's a story of Tuigamala doing this session up Rivington. He was a massive guy and he absolutely emptied himself up these steps and it took three or four of the boys to carry him down these steps.

David did it, some of the real legends of Wigan Warriors have done it, I've done it in my career, and the new stars of the Warriors are still going up there to fulfil their dreams. It's mindset. You don't need the best facilities to have all the plaudits. It's working hard and I think Wiganers are prepared to do that.

PART THREE

HERE AND NOW

IN CONVERSATION WITH WIGAN WARRIORS STARS AND THOSE BEHIND THE SCENES

TOMMY LEULUAI

Wigan debut: 8 February 2007, at home to Warrington (lost 16-10).

He might not agree, but Tommy Leuluai's status as a Warriors favourite was sealed on 21 March 2008. In truth the team were further away from getting back to the top than the one try from a Grand Final appearance the history books read, and out of four clashes with St Helens that year, the best they managed was a draw. Saints racked-up 40-plus points on the other three occasions. But there's one moment from the otherwise unremarkable season Warriors fans still look up on YouTube.

Tommy Leuluai in action against Warrington in 2017.

The wait goes on. Tommy Leuluai's Challenge Cup dreams are crushed in 2008.

The result was a poor one – a 46-10 defeat to St Helens is never easy to stomach, especially on Good Friday – but Leuluai's hit on Maurie Fa'asavalu might nearly have made up for the result had the opponents been different. It was the first half, and with Wigan 18-0 down the game was already gone – but the way 5ft 9in Leuluai dumped his 6ft 2in opponent felt as good to watch as any try.

Despite a win against St Helens proving elusive, Wigan finished fourth that year and were painfully close to actually reaching the Grand Final – 18-14 losers to Leeds in the semi-final, as they had been in 2007 by a score of 36-6 when they reached the play-offs by finishing sixth.

It was a familiar theme for Leuluai since arriving from London for the 2007 season. In 2009, the Kiwi's third year at Wigan, they were Super League semi-finalists again – and again lost it by four points when St Helens reached the Grand Final with a 14-10 win. Then something changed.

'The year before I arrived they nearly got relegated but as soon as I got here we were always there or thereabouts but never really kicked on,' he said. 'Until Madge got here.'

Madge, otherwise known as Michael Maguire, arrived at Wigan as head coach to replace Brian Noble, who had been at the helm since midway through their relegation-threatened 2006 campaign. An assistant coach at Melbourne Storm, Maguire's first gig leading a side was at the DW Stadium in 2010 with Shaun Wane as his assistant. And Maguire wasted no time in weaving his magic, with Wigan finishing top of the pile that season to claim a first minor premiership since the year 2000, which by then came with a prize – the League Leaders' Shield.

'It was methods, tougher mentality, we trained a lot harder,' Leuluai said on that landmark season. 'We just trained way harder. I'm not trying to discredit the stuff before that, but he came in with new standards, everything was harder. Training was harder, we were fitter, we were stronger, faster, there was a lot more detail in our attack and it changed everyone's standards. If you ask anyone who was there in and around that period and I'm quite confident they'd agree. One pre-season and it was a different club.

'What we were doing was just way more intense than a lot of other clubs. Everyone goes on army camps and stuff now and that was started pretty much from him. He changed our club and when you get a bit of success everyone copies what you're doing. Attacking-wise, defensively, we were a lot better, we were wrestling, it was a completely different club.'

Although they ended a 12-year wait to win the Grand Final that year, beating Saints 22-10 in the decider with Leuluai winning the Harry Sunderland Trophy as man of the match, they had to wait until the following August to win the Challenge Cup, beating Leeds, the side who knocked them out in 2010, at Wembley.

'They're both great,' Leuluai smiled on recalling trophy celebrations, but being so close for so long made that first Grand Final win more special. 'The first one in 2010, because we hadn't had success and been close, we'd always been knocked out in semi-finals, that was more of a relief really to get that. We always knew we had a decent team that year and it would have been hard to go through the whole year that year and not win something.'

Having missed out on the Challenge Cup, Leuluai revealed success in that competition was made a priority the following year, and he scored a try in the 28-18 win over the Rhinos at Wembley. 'Then the next year with the Challenge Cup we sort of made it our focus at the start of the year because we'd missed out the year before,' he explained, having missed out on a place in the cup final – the first at the new Wembley – in his first Wigan season when Catalans shocked the Warriors in the semi-final.

'We put a lot of energy into that. Even the rounds in the Challenge Cup before the final, they were like a Grand Final each week. We were lucky to go there, experience that and win that with a really good squad and some really good players.'

That win marked Maguire's last trophy for Wigan, leaving him just a World Club Challenge short of a full collection following that year's 21-15 defeat to St George Illawarra Dragons, and the coach left Shaun Wane to take over in 2012 after a play-off defeat to St Helens. 'We had a great year that year but we just ran out of steam,' Leuluai acknowledged. 'Things evolved under Shaun Wane.

'He definitely changed a few things but he kept a few things - you'd be silly not to. I enjoyed it. Madge was very intense to the point where it was a bit too much sometimes and you don't know how much you can keep going like that, and Waney came in and it was like a breath of fresh air for us. I think 2012, playing-wise, we played our best that year. Waney tweaked it and allowed us to play. Madge was always defence focused but Waney let us put more into attack.

'It was the same type of play but we just practised it and got really good at it. We were really unlucky not to win any trophies – we won the League Leaders' but we had crucial injuries at the wrong time of year.'

Wigan clinched the League Leaders' Shield that season by a point from Warrington Wolves, missing out on a Grand Final spot with a 13-12 defeat to semi-final bogey team Leeds. And that marked Leuluai's last season before heading home to New Zealand to play for the Warriors until returning in 2017. 'My wife wanted to come back – and I was happy to come back – I like it here,' he said on choosing to return to Wigan, where he has a coaching deal lined up for when he finishes playing. 'I was pretty close to signing at Saints,' he admitted. 'I knew everyone here and was at a stage in my career where I wanted to come where I was comfortable and I had something sorted for when I finish. That's the plan and I have a path here so if things work out… I'll give it a try.'

Leuluai met his wife shortly after signing for the club the first time, ex-Warriors player and current under-19s coach Darrell Goulding is his brother-in-law, and even though he has special memories made with the club, he still sees Auckland as home. 'I wouldn't say I'm a Wiganer, I'm still very much a Kiwi and I still call New Zealand home,' he said. 'This is not home for me, it's a place where I'm at at the moment and where my wife's from.'

Still, that's not to say Wigan isn't a significant part of his life. Leuluai's dad James played against Wigan for Hull in the 1985 Challenge Cup Final, and the youngster

who would go on to lift a World Cup with New Zealand in 2008 kept an eye on the Super League giants when watching the competition at home. 'I saw them play when Kris Radlinski and Jason Robinson were playing – those types of players – it would have been early morning back home,' he said. 'My dad didn't really talk about it so I didn't know too much about it. As soon as I got here I knew how big the club was and that it was well respected. It had all the big names and I was at London and we were one of the smaller teams. The

The wait is over. Tommy Leuluai with the Harry Sunderland Trophy after Wigan's Grand Final win over St Helens in 2010.

atmosphere was awesome when we played them and they were a well-supported club so you understood that straight away. I just wanted to play in bigger games. My first year at London we made the play-offs but it was coming to a bigger club and pushing in those bigger games that drew me here.'

It's probably why that first Grand Final win is so special to the hooker, the three-year wait and being so close for so long was a frustrating itch that was hard to reach. But even that doesn't quite match lifting a World Cup – especially when the side his Kiwis beat in the final was an Australia team tipped to saunter to the title. 'A World Cup is once every four years and it was the first big trophy I won – and the team they had… it's hard to beat that,' he said. 'The 2010 Grand Final – relief. Winning the Challenge Cup was cool but when you haven't had something for so long and you finally get it…'

2011

Long waits happen a lot in sport, and rugby league is no exception. Warrington fans waiting to win a league title. England fans waiting to see a win over the Kangaroos. St Helens fans waiting to see their heroes win a Good Friday derby for eight years.

The 2011 season saw one of those waits come to an end for Warriors fans when Sean O'Loughlin lifted the Challenge Cup – a trophy so much a part of the club's history it was referred to as 'the Wigan Cup' in the 90s by fans of other clubs. But even that image, a first for the scrapbook since 2002, is not the one that springs to mind first for many Wiganers when 2011 is mentioned. Liam Farrell is. With a face the same shade of pink as Warriors kit that season, a break from tradition of cherry and white hoops, under a pile of teammates in front of a packed DW Stadium. The celebrations for a dramatic, last second 28-24 win that Good Friday were being etched into the memories of many of the 24,057 people in the stadium. The reaction from supporters, players and coaches were what makes a derby.

FEBRUARY

Tries from Ryan Hoffman, Harrison Hansen and George Carmont got Wigan off to a flying start in the season opener against St Helens as they raced into a 16-0 lead at Millennium Magic on 12 February. For most of the game it looked as if the champions had a tight grip on their opponents until Saints fought back to claim a 16-16 draw.

The following week's trip to Bradford goes much more to plan, with an Amos Roberts double among the tries in a 44-10 win to prepare for the World Club Challenge against St George Illawarra. The clash with the NRL champions on 27 February saw 24,268 in attendance, with an impressive two-try performance from Carmont seeing Wigan leading at half-time. But despite Wigan's best efforts, they were beaten 21-15, and one particular sporting wait would go on a little longer.

MARCH

Straight wins over Salford, Hull FC and Huddersfield lifted Wigan to fourth in the table before Brett Finch made his long-awaited debut in a home clash against Warrington on 25 March. Finch, an off-season recruit from Melbourne Storm, underwent neck surgery in the off-season, and marked his Wigan debut with a try. It was all Warriors fans had to cheer though in a 24-6 loss.

APRIL

A trip to Headingley on 1 April seemed to be over with time to spare as Wigan were kept at arm's length by Leeds until the dying moments. Joel Tomkins had put Wigan in front before Leeds stormed into a 22-4 lead. With the scores at 22-20 in the last moments, Sam Tomkins landed a penalty kick to snatch a draw.

That high was undone by a poor home performance in a 47-24 loss to Catalan Dragons the following week, before Wigan were back on track with a 28-16 win at Hull KR, though they remained fifth in the table. After the game, coach Michael Maguire announced he would leave at the end of the season.

That tee'd-up the Good Friday masterpiece on 22 April, where Farrell's winner on a scorching afternoon (was it scorching? The memory thinks so) was helped along by doubles from Josh Charnley and Pat Richards. On Easter Monday, Wakefield were beaten 26-0.

MAY

Crusaders are beaten 48-16 on 1 May before Wigan defeated Barrow 52-0 in the fourth round of the Challenge Cup. Their scoring run was continued on 13 May in a 54-6 rout of Harlequins at home before a trip to Bradford in round five of the cup proved tricky, with a Richards double helping Wigan to a 26-22 win. Gareth Raynor had been sent off for knocking out Sam Tomkins as the Wigan star went over for a try, but the depleted Bulls fought back to ensure a nervy finish. Not that Sam was overly affected – he scored a hat-trick in the following week's 40-6 win at home to Hull KR.

JUNE

Wigan lost in France on 4 June as Catalans took their clash with the Warriors to Montpellier, with the follow week's trip to Castleford ending in a 22-22 draw. It was Wigan's third stalemate of the season and the second by the same score. Things picked-up on 17 June, though, as Wigan won their trip to St Helens in their season at Widnes by 32-10. They then took care of Huddersfield 46-12 to climb to second in the table.

JULY

A feisty home clash with Leeds on 1 July saw Wigan win 26-24, and Andy Coley banned for one match, while a week later Charnley was at the double in a 26-16 win over Castleford that lifted Wigan to the top of the table. A trip to Harlequins resulted in a 38-6 success, in a week that saw released Leeds prop Ben Cross join the club and Carmont delay plans to retire. On 14 July, though, Hoffman confirmed he would be going back to the NRL to join Melbourne for 2012.

Gareth Hock scored three tries in a 48-6 home win over Wakefield before the Challenge Cup quarter-final with holders Warrington. Wigan were on fire at the HJ Stadium, with Richards and Charnley scoring two tries each in a 44-24 win to set up a semi-final tie at the same venue against St Helens. Before then, Wigan kept their position at the top of the table with a 30-16 win over Hull FC.

AUGUST

Carmont, Charnley and Sam Tomkins scored tries as Wigan beat St Helens 18-12 in the cup to secure their first place in the final since 2004. This was followed by big wins of 52-18 over Salford and 60-12 over Bradford before the big day at Wembley. On 27 August prop Jeff Lima proved an unlikely hero, scoring two tries and winning the Lance Todd Trophy in a game that saw Joel Tomkins rival Martin Offiah for one of the greatest tries scored at Wembley in the 28-18 win over Leeds, ending a wait for the trophy since the Murrayfield triumph of 2002.

SEPTEMBER

The month started on a bad note for Wigan as at the HJ, scene of two triumphs in the cup, Warrington ran riot to go top in a 39-12 win over Wigan. The following week's 42-10 win over Crusaders wasn't enough to snatch the League Leaders' Shield, and Wigan went into the play-offs from second spot.

A 26-18 defeat to Saints in round one set up a home tie with Catalan Dragons, which Wigan comfortably won 44-0.

OCTOBER

Wigan met St Helens again on 1 October for the right to join Leeds in the Grand Final. Eamon O'Carroll, Charnley and Sam Tomkins scored tries at Widnes, but it wasn't enough to keep Michael Maguire's tenure as coach running for at least another week as Wigan again lost 26-18 to their arch rivals. Shaun Wane was announced as head coach on 11 October.

LIAM FARRELL

Wigan debut: 5 April 2010, at home to Wakefield (won 54-4).

It's not always about the trophies you win and reputation you create. It can also be about moments.

Liam Farrell is a Challenge Cup, Grand Final and World Club Challenge winner. He's an England international and has a reputation for a relentless work ethic. He's a favourite, not because of flashy plays, but because he's dependable. But there is also a split-second moment he will forever be associated with – a winning try against St Helens on Good Friday in front of a packed stadium. Wigan had recovered from being 10-4 down at the break on 22 April 2011 to lead Saints 22-10 with a hour gone.

Liam Farrell, Wigan's second row forward, was selected in the 2015 Super League Dream Team.

But converted tries from Jamie Foster and Tommy Makinson put the away side in front, and with moments to spare it looked like a lost cause for Wigan, until Farrell popped-up with a try in the final moments to seal one of the most memorable derby wins. Seven years on, people are still talking about it. 'I thought it would die off after three or four years but it never does,' Farrell said. 'I'm really pleased it happened to me because it's a once in a lifetime opportunity and it will be with me for a long time. That one will be remembered when I do retire.'

Ask any supporter or player of either club and Wigan/Saints games are the one. It doesn't matter if it's a cup final or a dead rubber, lose a derby match and the following week is ruined. 'The derby games are always massive fixtures and the crowds are always really into it,' Farrell said. 'The players get on really well but they know between themselves there's that rivalry between the clubs, passion and fire. On those days players get fired up and get into each other. There's respect there, but they know they have to give their all for that 80 minutes. I've been involved in some really good ones. I look forward to them every year but so do all the other players.'

It's a rivalry that quickly makes its impression on people not raised in either town, so for Farrell, a Wigan fan since being little, being part of those moments are a realisation of a lifelong dream – and he admits he didn't exactly hedge his

Liam Farrell goes over for one of the most memorable tries in Wigan's recent history, on Good Friday 2011.

bets when it came to a career choice. 'When you're playing amateur you hear about kids getting signed up and that's what you want to do,' he said. 'You play for your amateur club week in, week out and you hear about scouts being there and if they thought you could provide something they'd sign you up to the scholarship. I was 12 when someone approached my parents and asked. It's all you ever want as a kid. School isn't the most important thing, all you want to do is play rugby. I know that's not great but that's what you want to do and I was fortunate to be part of that scholarship from being 12.'

Farrell comes from two of Wigan's most renowned rugby league player factories in St John FIsher School and the Wigan St Patrick's amateur club, and he was in a busy year group of hopefuls. 'There were a few lads in my year who were signed up to the scholarship, but it becomes more important when you get to 16/17 and the club decide whether to sign you on the academy system or not,' he explained. 'I played all my amateur rugby for St Pat's and I signed for Wigan when I was 16, I'd been in the scholarship since I was about 12. As a kid I always looked up to Rads, Andy Farrell, Terry O'Connor, Terry Newton, all those kinds of players. Adrian Lam, that kind of era was really my time and I enjoyed watching them winning the Challenge Cup in 2002. I watched 2002 in Edinburgh and that sticks out more to me, and I was a ball boy for about three or four years. I did some Grand Finals, some which Wigan weren't even involved in.

'Bradford/Leeds games, Saints/Leeds, so I saw a few. The one that sticks out is 2002 because there wasn't that much success at the time and that was a memorable one for me.'

By the time Farrell was working his way up the Warriors ranks, the first team had slipped from reaching finals to missing out on play-off places in the 2005 and 2006 seasons. But the fact playing for his childhood team might not mean success didn't put Farrell off, and his gamble eventually paid off with a debut in 2010 – by which time Wigan had recovered and were showing signs of challenging for honours again, and they did by winning that year's title.

'It wouldn't have been the brightest time for the club, 2006,7,8,9. I was a teenager at the time,' Farrell recalled. 'Even though the club wasn't doing that well I wanted to be involved but it was a dream I thought probably wouldn't happen, it was always in the back of my mind. Luckily enough a few years later I got to make my debut. My first thought was to put all my eggs in one basket, I wanted to play rugby. I'm glad it paid off because I didn't have a lot behind me if it didn't, but I've been fortunate up to now.'

Looking back to the side Farrell supported as a youngster, he admits that next season he will find it strange being coached by one of his heroes when Adrian Lam takes over for the 2019 campaign. Lam was one of the stars of the 2002 Challenge Cup win Farrell watched from the stands, though he explained next coach in line Shaun Edwards's time as a player came before his dreams of being a Warriors star came into view.

'I had to sort of do the same with Rads [Kris Radlinski] when he started off as welfare manager and now he's the rugby manager, so it's going to be strange,' Farrell said when asked what being coached by Lam will be like. 'Adrian Lam coached the academy the year before I started and I wasn't fortunate enough to work with him then, but I will be next year so it's going to be a good experience. 'I'd seen a few games at Central Park when I was about seven or eight.'

Liam Farrell with the Super League Trophy in 2013.

But Farrell's gratitude for being where he is now lies with former coaches Michael Maguire and Shaun Wane. It was under Maguire, with Wane as assistant, that Farrell burst onto the Wigan scene, and he went on to become a foundation of the Warriors' pack under Wane, with too many highlights to count. 'I've had some good ones,' Farrell said. 'I made my debut under Madge and I owe a lot to him because he gave me my debut but Waney has played a big part in it as well. The 2016 Grand Final where I got man of the match was really pleasing for me. All the Grand Finals have different reasons for being special.'

And for someone whose life has been rugby, Farrell says his connection with the club will stay with him long after his playing days are over, though he hasn't thought about what he might do when he has to contemplate life after rugby. He said, 'I'll always be a Wigan fan no matter what. I'd like to try to still be involved, but if I'm not then I'll have a massive following for the club and I'll always want to be a supporter.'

2013

Looking back through history, before 2010 most of the highlights tapes Wigan fans kept were on grainy VHS tapes rather than DVDs. But as they started to take annual leave to book hotels in London for Wembley, and days off to nurse two-day Grand Final hangovers again in place of trips abroad and days to do DIY, the YouTube searches were of clearer recollections.

The 2013 season will be remembered as fondly by Wigan fans as years in the 90s when the story is told to fans who never saw Sean O'Loughlin lift a trophy as they watch a future captain's bid for glory. A Super League and Challenge Cup double were big parts of an unforgettable sporting year for Wigan as a whole, and there were many other milestones along the way.

FEBRUARY

Sam Tomkins opened his season with a hat-trick as Wigan fired an early warning shot with a 42-0 win over Salford on 1 February. Warrington visited the DW Stadium a week later for what was an early Grand Final rehearsal, with a Matty Smith drop-goal putting Wigan 17-16 in front until the Wolves secured a draw with their own one-pointer from who other than Lee Briers. This was followed by a disappointing 22-10 loss at Huddersfield before Wigan finished the month in third place on the table with a 42-10 win at home to London.

MARCH

Warriors climbed to second in the table on 3 March with a 28-22 win at Castleford but were made to work for it through a Chris Tuson try after Wigan had surrendered a 22-4 lead. The following Friday, Pat Richards scored his 150th Wigan try in his 200th appearance in a 38-0 thumping of Catalans Dragons.

The Sky Sports cameras were present for Wigan's 18-14 loss at Leeds on 15 March, where Warriors managed tries from Liam Farrell and Iain Thornley. But they soon got back on track, opening up a 13-match winning run that put them clear at the top of the table, and looking like running away with the League Leaders' Shield. The run started with a 62-4 win over Widnes on 23 March, with Josh Charnley scoring four tries – and continued with a fourth Good Friday win in a row – 28-16 in front of 23,861 fans.

APRIL

Warriors' ruthlessness showed signs of picking-up, rather than slowing down, on Easter Monday, as Hull KR had no answer to a 15-try display at Craven Park. Blake Green scored a hat-trick in the 84-6 demolition of Hull KR, which set a new record league win for Wigan, new record away win in all competitions and new record defeat for Rovers.

A home match against Wakefield was no problem on 7 April, before Liam Farrell scored a hat-trick at Odsal in a 36-6 win over Bradford the following week, and Wigan's Challenge Cup campaign began at home to Leigh. Sam Tomkins scored four tries and Pat Richards and Charnley a hat-trick each – and a certain George Williams scored a try on his debut as Leigh were brushed aside 60-10 to set up a clash at Hull KR in the next round. Before then, on 26 April, Wigan negotiated a tricky tie at Hull FC 28-20 to keep a point ahead of Huddersfield at the top of the table.

MAY

Epalahame Lauaki made his first appearance of the season in a straightforward 46-6 win at home to Salford on 3 May, which featured nine different try-scorers in a game that Salford coach Brian Noble described as a 'reality check for his side.'

And that set Wigan up for another onslaught at Craven Park in the cup on 12 May – though the 46-14 scoreline was not quite as impressive as the last time out. Sam Tomkins scored four tries in a game that saw Wigan go from 12-4 to 34-4 up in the opening 14 minutes of the second half.

Charnley, Richards and Tomkins each claimed a hat-trick in a 64-4 rout of London Broncos on 18 May, keeping the Broncos locked with Salford and Castleford at the bottom of the table – with a first appearance in a televised game in eight weeks next up at Magic Weekend. And the clash with Leeds on 26 May didn't disappoint.

A tense encounter saw Wigan edge their fourth-placed rivals 20-16 in an entertaining tie for traditionalists. Shaun Wane summed up the feeling when he said, 'It was enjoyable to grind out a win. We've not been in many arm wrestles recently.'

JUNE

Wigan clawed back from 17-10 down at the break against Wakefield on 2 June to win 36-23 and keep the gap between them at Huddersfield at the top at three points. But a more nerve-jangling clash was next up when a Sam Powell drop-goal nine minutes from full-time proved the difference as a depleted Warriors side won 33-32 at Widnes. Lewis Tierney scored a try on his debut in the 13th minute.

But Wigan's run had to end at some point, and that happened on 26 June at Warrington in a 22-12 loss, in which Wigan had fought back from 10-0 down at half-time to lead 12-10 going into the final quarter.

Warriors' lead at the top was cut to just a point on 29 June as Castleford sprung a shock 18-4 win at the DW Stadium, in which a late Charnley try was no consolation for Wane, who described the performance as 'poor.'

JULY

Two tries each for Tuson and Charnley helped Wigan stay top in a cagey 26-20 win over Bradford. The Bulls led 18-4 before Wigan fought back, frustrating their boss Francis Cummins. Wigan turned their attention back to their journey to Wembley and were much more slick than they had been, with a 48-4 win over Widnes on 17 July.

Back to Super League action at St Helens on 22 July, Wigan led with five minutes to go thanks to a drop goal from Matty Smith, but the night was remembered for an amazing 45-metre one-pointer from Richards. But a Joe Greenwood try secured a 22-16 win for Saints, and they would have enjoyed the result, knocking Wigan off the top of the table.

Worrying about the table would have to wait though. A Challenge Cup semi-final against London at Leigh Sports Village was next on the calendar on 27 July. Memories of the 2012 semi-final loss to Leeds were still raw, and Wigan were efficient and ruthless in making sure it didn't happen again by beating London 70-0.

AUGUST

Wigan kept within touching distance of Huddersfield at the top, and ahead of Warrington on points difference, with another cagey win at the DW on 3 August. Hull KR were the opponents and were level 10-10 with Wigan at half-time, before Charnley and Anthony Gelling tries helped them to a 21-16 win. But two losses before Wembley snatched the League Leaders' Shield away from Wigan's grasp. Huddersfield put one hand on the prize with a 30-12 win at the DW on 9 August before a loss at Catalans on 17 August saw Wigan drop to third.

But Wembley was on the horizon, and Wane's men weren't letting that one slip. Thornley and Tomkins scored tries in an arm wrestle of a final to see Wigan win 16-0 and take the cup home for a 19th time. Hull were again the opponents at the DW on 30 August, and a young Wigan side rallied with ex-Wales rugby union international Andy Powell scoring a try for the Warriors in a 33-32 loss.

SEPTEMBER

Leeds visited the DW on the last day of the regular season on 6 September, with both sides in special one-off Superman kits. But a super performance evaded Wigan in a 20-6 defeat, setting-up a play-off qualifier against league leaders Huddersfield. Danny Brough scored first at the John Smiths Stadium before Charnley's try helped Wigan to 8-8 at the break. And a strong second-half saw Wigan win 22-8 to book their place in the play-off eliminator on 27 September.

Leeds were the opponents at the DW, while Warrington battled Huddersfield in the other eliminator for a place in the Grand Final. Warriors prevailed 22-12 over Leeds while the Wolves booked their place in the decider. And Wane demanded improvement for the final. He said, 'There is still a lot of work to be done. Warrington are a great team but there are areas where we can improve.'

OCTOBER

After the Grand Final on 5 October, Wane's words summed up the season that had everything. A rocket-fuelled start gave way to doubt in mid-summer, then silverware followed to make highlights packages easy to compile. 'I was expecting a few apologies [from the press] after how we have been doubted this year. I can't tell you how proud I am,' he said after the 30-16 Grand Final win. 'I knew this was a good day and I can't tell you how happy I am. I have seen these players come of age but I want them to be good players and good men, and what satisfies me is to see them having good family lives as well.'

The final, like the season, saw Wigan fight back against the odds. They were 16-2 down after half an hour. Blake Green was man of the match after playing on with a nasty eye injury, and Pat Richards signed off with the try that sealed Wigan's third Super League title.

TONY CLUBB

Wigan debut: 7 February 2014, at home to Huddersfield (lost 24-8).

A lot of people wouldn't hesitate in choosing Tony Clubb as a favourite player, which could be seen as unusual when you hear him speak. His London accent reveals when growing up Clubb wasn't flying through the streets in a replica Wigan jersey, running towards a tryline marked with jumpers while rehearsing a dream

Tony Clubb arrived at Wigan from London Broncos for the 2014 season.

that only comes true for a few. Clubb was playing rugby, but it was down in Gravesend – and it was the 15-man code he knew.

But fans watching him in Super League see a man who is undeniably a Wigan player. The fact he has only one kidney and carries memories and scars from a serious neck injury that saw him miss nine months' worth of rugby in 2016 don't influence the way he carries the ball into collisions, an attitude which will make him fondly remembered when his playing days come to an end.

But when Clubb started to make a name for himself at London Broncos, making his debut in 2006, the Wigan he first encountered was far removed from the glory days most from the capital associate with the club. 'I got into rugby league when I was about 14, it was a bit late,' he said. 'Where I'm from is a massive football and rugby union area and I played rugby union from when I was five up until I was 16 and had to make a decision whether it was league or union. Once I started getting into rugby league and watching it on the telly, that's when I started hearing about Wigan. It was quite late when I got into it and when I started recognising it. When I started getting into it Wigan weren't going so well at the time.'

Not going so well is one way of putting it.

Clubb's London, or Harlequins as they were then known, were pushing for a play-off spot in Super League, while Wigan were battling relegation at the foot of the table, and, while the Warriors ended up finishing only one point behind them, Wigan were the ones enduring a nervy season and supporters would have swapped places with the side from the capital.

'When I started playing for London, Wigan were on the verge of getting relegated, so it was quite a tough time,' Clubb remembers, 'but when you look into the history of the club and what it's achieved over many years, it's fantastic.'

By the time Wigan came calling they had recovered from that lean spell that almost had dire consequences. The side Clubb joined in 2014 were Super League and Challenge Cup double winners the year before and would reach the next three Grand Finals in a row. But they weren't the reasons he was swayed to make the move north with his family. 'When it came about for me to come to Wigan, I was having a bit of a tough time at London. I spoke to Kris Radlinski at first and we only had a brief chat over the phone, but what made my mind up was when I met Waney,' he said. 'I had a meeting with him and Kris and I knew from that point on I wanted to join Wigan – how passionate he was about the club and how he sold it to me. I went away and looked at the history of the club and it's a massive, massive club. It was a no-brainer for me to join. They were double champions when I joined and London were on the verge of getting relegated so I went from the bottom to the top. It was just a no-brainer to join.'

When you think of people relocating, the expected path would be from the northern industrial town to a big city, and it's not hard to wonder what the look on his wife's face might have been when he told her his next career move, and their physical one. 'I remember ringing my Mrs and saying, "Look, we're coming to Wigan,"' he smiled. 'I had interest from a few other clubs in St Helens and a few others but once I met Shaun it was Wigan I wanted to go to.'

But those in the area, including the Clubb family now, know the Wigan that isn't the flat caps and dirty back streets often portrayed to the outside world. The borough has its proud industrial heritage, granted, but is actually mostly countryside – just take a drive five minutes out of town and look around. 'We live in Up Holland, which is really nice, we live in a cul-de-sac and my children go out the front and play and I love seeing my kids happy. That's what makes me happy and on top of that I've got a dream job,' Clubb said. 'It's a better pace of life up here too. I lived in Kingston for a few years and I lived two miles from the train. It took me 40 minutes to get there and things like that, and now I can stick the car in neutral and roll in and I'd be in in two minutes. It's quite rural up there.'

Clubb is referring to Wigan's training base in Orrell, the former home of the village's once top-flight rugby union side before it disappeared and re-emerged as an amateur outfit. But it isn't just him and his children who benefit from a quieter life at home in the north. 'I have two dogs and a young family. I've got a Staff and a teacup Yorkshire terrier,' Clubb said, describing the type of dog you'd expect a rugby league forward to have and another which is the exact opposite. 'We rescued her. We used to live near Battersea and we just used to go in and have a look and she travelled up with us. It's a horrible place but a nice place, and I've had my Staffie 11 years now and we didn't know the age of the Yorkshire but we think she's about four now.'

But dogs, children and home life aside, Clubb also feels like he's hit the jackpot on the pitch. Despite having been at the club for five seasons, he had only won one winner's medal before the 2018 Grand Final - the 2017 World Club Challenge after Wigan's 22-6 win over Cronulla Sharks. In his first season he appeared in the Grand Final loss to St Helens, and the defeat to Leeds in 2015. The following season, when Wigan beat Warrington to claim the title, Clubb sat out through the neck injury that required surgery when he was victim of a 'crusher' tackle against Hull FC.

That was followed in 2017 by the need for him to have surgery to have a dead kidney removed – a non-rugby related problem which he had tried to play on with – though he did make his return in the July, just 58 days after having the surgery.

'What had happened, the kidney was dead. It had gone,' he explained at the time. 'They said, "You can carry on playing with it in you, the only thing is you can't take on a lot of fluid." I couldn't drink what I wanted to. And me being a bit naive and a bit stupid, I said I'll have a crack at it because I'd been out for a long time with my neck, I didn't want to miss another big chunk and, to be honest with you, I wanted to play in the Cronulla game. I was probably just a bit stupid, thinking I could carry on. After the Cas game [in the April] I got rushed to hospital, the pain was too much, and I saw the surgeon and we had it out – he told me it'd be eight weeks.'

And yet the towering forward still counts himself lucky to have been successful in this brutal career path. 'It's a pleasure to play,' he smiled, as if his catalogue of injuries are just a scratch. 'To be able to play for Wigan, it's a dream job. It's a pleasure to roll

Tony Clubb celebrates a try in 2015.

in every day and do what I do. We have everything given to us, fantastic facilities, fantastic stadium. Everything and anything is top drawer. It's hard not to roll in with a smile. If we're beaten the week before it's hard not to do it because it's your dream job. For someone who's not from Wigan, when you come to Wigan the first thing you hear about is Wigan/St Helens and things like that, it's once you go into the town and see how people feel about Wigan – it blew me away.

'Coming from London and walking down the street with no one knowing who I was, you leave your house and people know who you are. It shocked me at first because it was something I wasn't used to. But then you see how passionate the people of Wigan are and there's been games I've played in and it's hard to explain if you've not done it, but it lifts you. When you're in a tough spot and someone gets a good carry or a good play and you feel the crowd pick up, it's massive for us. It's an absolute pleasure to play for Wigan and I've got a year left and I'd love to see my career out at Wigan – that's how passionate I am about it.'

Clubb's handful of years in Wigan have left him feeling like he belongs, and most supporters will agree his place in the club's history is as important as any home-grown star. So much is his affinity with the area, unless told otherwise by his wife, Clubb feels his move is a permanent one. 'It's got to the point where I won't leave Wigan now,' he said. 'My family's settled here, my wife's opened a business here, my kids – my youngest started school in September. My youngest was born here which is quite special to me and my eldest was brought up here. She was one when we came here so it's a special place for me really. People ask would I return down south and I don't want to, I see Wigan as home now. Even my wife – if she said, "Tony I want to go home", when I retire I'll do that to make her happy – but I want to stay here. It's more for our kids because our kids are happy.'

DAN SARGINSON

Wigan debut: 7 February 2014, at home to Huddersfield (lost 24-8).

When Dan Sarginson was born, Wigan's rugby league team were absolutely flying. Earlier that month, May 1993, they had beaten Widnes 20-14 at Wembley to win the Challenge Cup for a record-extending sixth time in a row and they were champions yet again, albeit pipping St Helens to the title on points difference. Not that Sarginson would grow-up aware of the exploits of the club he would go on to play for.

Born in Perth, Western Australia, he moved to London early in his life, and would go on to join Hemel Stags after an upbringing in rugby union. 'I joined rugby league really late,' he said when explaining his path to rugby league. 'I'll be

Dan Sarginson found himself playing against Sydney Roosters in the 2014 World Club Challenge.

honest, I used to watch union up until I was around 13 or 14. Even when I broke onto the London Broncos scene I didn't know many of the players, but as soon as I started to come through the academy stuff there, there was a year I started to watch rugby league.'

When breaking into Super League, the Broncos were known as Harlequins RL – the name they carried from 2006 to 2011 before reverting to their London tag. Sarginson debuted in a Challenge Cup match in 2011 – their last year under the same name as the famous rugby union outfit, and by then Wigan were back to their best and at the top of Super League. 'I'm not just saying this, I used to watch Wigan and loved watching them,' he said on his time in the capital. 'I genuinely supported them. Although London Broncos were in the Super League with them I just loved the way they played and they were such a good team you never thought they were going to get beaten. I did three years at London Broncos first team and then when the option came to come here I snapped their hand off. I wanted to come to this club.'

The Wigan side that made such an impression on Sarginson was coached by Michael Maguire – the former Melbourne Storm assistant coach who has brought a new brand of rugby to the Warriors and a league title in his first season. In 2011, they would also win the Challenge Cup for the first time since 2002, before Shaun Wane took over 2012, two years before Sarginson joined. 'It was under Madge and then won the double the year before I came. They were just such a good team to watch and the way they played,' he said. 'They mastered that block before anyone else – that block shape – and no one could defend it. You'd see the back rowers pouring through every week and just plenty of tries. It was good to watch.'

As much as rugby league gripped Sarginson, though, on his journey to playing for one of the most famous clubs in the world, it took those around him more time. 'It took my family a while to adapt to me playing league. They didn't follow it growing up and my family and all my brothers were more into union,' he explained. 'No one really knew the rules and it took them a while to understand. I was at London for a bit and they supported me but not the team because we were pretty poor to be fair. We were always bottom half of the table and losing and it's hard to support a team that's losing.'

But that changed when Sarginson signed for Wigan in 2014 and he suddenly found himself facing Sydney Roosters at Australia's Allianz Stadium for the World Club Challenge. 'Considering they'd just won the double for me to play against Sydney in the World Club Challenge just because of the pre-season I had was massive, and I can only put that down to the staff here and what they turned me into physically,' explained Sarginson on the intensity placed on training at his new club. 'In my last year at London I knew if I ever wanted to play for England or win trophies and become a much better player I had to play for Wigan. Within my first pre-season I had become stronger and fitter than I'd ever been in my life and that was massive for me.'

That World Club Challenge would end in disappointment – Wigan lost 36-14 – but they reached the Grand Final in each of the first three seasons he spent at the club, winning it in 2016 before he left to join Gold Coast Titans and fulfil an ambition to play in the NRL. 'I made sure I had a Wigan TV subscription and would stay up to three, four in the morning to watch that Challenge Cup Final,' Sarginson said on the 18-14 loss to Hull FC at Wembley in 2017. 'I felt like I was with the boys and I was gutted when they lost that one.'

But after struggling in the NRL with a shoulder injury, which limited Sarginson to just six appearances, he knew his first-choice club for a return to Super League. 'When the option for me to come back was there again after struggling for a bit at Gold Coast with injuries, I knew it was the right place to come and get back on track,' he said. 'They've made me the player I am today. I knew I needed to get into some physical shape after struggling with my shoulder injury, so there wasn't a better place to come back to.'

And the love for rugby league is finally trickling down to members of his family. 'My nan and grandad are so proud and even when I went to Gold Coast they watched Wigan every week,' he said. 'They've kind of become fans and love watching the team, and they know all the rugby league players probably better than me. Every time I ring them there's a half-hour conversation on the boys. All my family support me to the end of the earth, but they are massive Wigan fans now and love watching the team play as well. Even my friends, genuinely, they see it on Sky Sports News and see rugby league and see a few scores and before they'd never click on it. I'd never heard of it when I came through, it was eight or nine years ago. It's progressed more now but I hadn't heard of it at all.

'The friends I used to go to school with know what my last game was and how I got on. It's massive, even for a little town like Hemel where I'm from just to get the brand out there. It's amazing how many people have heard of rugby league now and know what I'm doing up here.'

But even with more people being aware of rugby league than ever, Sarginson is concerned with the challenges the sport faces with attendances falling due to various reasons and the competition it faces from other sports and technology. Most people with an interest in the sport have access to Sky Sports and social media platforms, which offer near instant updates on every game from a Wigan v Saints derby to the amateur leagues, and that coupled with scheduling on weekday nights gives supporters more reasons to stay at home.

'I always think attendances will go down because of technology,' Sarginson said, though he thinks the issue is not unique to rugby league. 'Even in the future you'll be able to watch it at home and feel like you're there. We're going to struggle with that in the sports industry, but that's a long time away, it will be after I'm finished. I still think we get good crowds to the games that matter. We're always going to struggle with smaller games, and on Thursdays it's tough for the kids and parents probably don't want to go on school nights, but the big games… we don't struggle filling those. I think we'll always fill those, which is important.'

Sarginson holds a firm belief rugby league offers sports enthusiasts enough to survive but stressed more needs to be done to bring it to a level playing field with events like international rugby union matches. 'Even with Toronto coming along and maybe this New York team, I think more and more big cities will try and get involved with that,' he said when outlining his hopes for the sport's future. 'Hopefully London can get on board with that. I think the more major cities you can get playing the game the more money into the game and the more you can do with it. You look at rugby union, it's not as exciting to watch but the corporate stuff at international level in unbelievable and the amount of money that generates is phenomenal. It keeps it above us financially.

'Magic Weekends, you speak to people who are stewards for the football, they watch it and they can't believe how exciting it is. People who haven't seen the game love it – it's not a biased view, it's genuinely exciting. We just need to get it out to as many people as possible.'

What shape rugby league will be in when Sarginson leaves is unknown, but one thing he is sure of when his playing days are over is that he doesn't want to be involved in the sport. A path into coaching or the media doesn't appeal to him and, having arrived at Wigan as a 20-year-old, by the end of his career he thinks he will be after a 'normal' life away from the spotlight.

'I don't really want to stay in rugby post playing because people do it every day and it becomes life,' he explained. 'I probably want to get away when I'm mid-30s and maybe get a normal job and be able to do some normal things with my family and friends without the restrictions like not drinking and the sacrifice we make.'

But at just 25 years old, he hopes this normal life is still quite a way away and, having come back to Wigan knowing he needed to prove himself after his NRL disappointment, his immediate plans are to stay in the matchday squad for as long as possible. 'If I'm in favour here and I get the right options to stay then I will,' he said. 'It's an amazing club for me and I get along with the boys so well so there's no reason for me ever to leave unless form or something like that makes me have to.'

RYAN SUTTON

Wigan debut: 21 April 2014, at home to Bradford Bulls (won 84-6)

Of the hundreds of youngsters to play rugby league each week, a handful stand out as definite ones to watch, and a few more on top of that show potential to become professionals. Most, if not all, harbour those dreams, but it's not always the ones with the obvious talent that go on to play for Wigan.

Ryan Sutton was one of the not so obvious future stars, by his own admission. He isn't from a long line of rugby league enthusiasts and he wasn't a whizz with a ball. But fast forward a couple of decades and in his time in the Warriors first team he has become one of the foundation blocks – a robust piece of artillery in what is known in the modern game as 'the middle.'

'When I was a kid I didn't know what I wanted to do,' he reflects. 'When I was five or six, my mate at the time played for St Pat's. He asked me to go down and give it a try because I was a big kid, a bit too big.'

It happens to many of us, and from here, Sutton's story is similar to the others – the ones with the former player for a grandparent or the ones from a long line of dedicated supporters. 'I went down, loved it,' he said. 'You make a lot of mates when you're that age and a lot of mates away from school so I started at Pat's – loved the game. I wanted to do it all the time. Get home, play rugby.' But before rugby could become Sutton's sole focus, he moved from St Pat's to Rose Bridge, and he had to be patient before others started to see there might be something about him.

Ryan Sutton will play for Canberra Raiders next season.

'Obviously as you get older you get more and more serious,' he said. 'I was about 10 – I'm not too sure of the age – I wasn't really liking it at Pat's and I moved from there to Bridge and that's when my rugby took a high. I have to credit two of my coaches, Anthony Gallagher and Chris Prescott, at Rose Bridge who took me on. I didn't have a lot of belief in myself and I think rugby's about belief. You play with your mates and sometimes you don't think you're good enough and those two just helped me on.'

Sutton revealed he always had to work a little bit harder than his peers to progress in the game he has grown to love so much, and it was after his move to Rose Bridge things became serious. 'I think through my teens I wanted to get better and I got to 13-14, I never really got selected for any town teams or anything like that, and then all of a sudden I was taking it more seriously at school and stuff and got selected for town,' he said. 'From there it just escalated. I just think I've never had it easy. I've always had to work at things because I've never been mega talented. Nobody in my family has ever played rugby. We've had to look back and there's not many.'

Dinner table chat isn't all about rugby but that doesn't mean his family haven't supported him, a common theme among top players in any sport. And it's the early weekend mornings, the money spent on petrol, the time spend getting soaked on touchlines, which are the base ingredients for a player now on his way to the NRL to play for Canberra Raiders.

'My mum's side is all football, so at Christmas you can see the conflict there,' he joked. 'Just to be a first generation rugby player... it's a credit to my mum and dad. I think without your parents you can't do it. They sacrificed a lot of time, going up and down the country, going here there and everywhere, and it had a big influence not just on me but on my brother when he started. It started from there and when I was about 15 I got signed up at Wigan. I was lucky enough to get scouted there and then it's just escalated from there.

'I think rugby's been a big part of my life and I've loved every minute of it. It sounds stupid but even the side of my family who like football, because I'm playing they watch bits. My cousin comes and watches me a lot – he's football mad and he won't admit it but he likes it.'

Sutton has played in a Grand Final, a Challenge Cup Final and a World Club Challenge, but it was a forgettable Easter Monday in 2014 that sticks in his memory the most. The record books show that the 84-6 hammering of Bradford was Warriors' best-ever home league win and it was also Bradford's worst defeat. As a match, it wasn't a contest. But win, lose, classic or not, that's not what a debut for your home-town club is about.

'It's good to be a part of something at a club like Wigan,' Sutton said. 'It's your home town. I think my debut was on a fan day and for someone 18 years old running onto a pitch playing against men – you're like 'wow what is this?''

'Honestly that debut for me, I'll tell my kids about it because it's something that means so much to you. Just from there you've progressed to where I am now. I can't credit Waney and the coaching staff here enough for giving me the chance to do it.

'I've loved every minute of playing at Wigan. I think the heritage is second to none and to be a part of it and have the heritage number is great.'

Even then, Sutton wasn't convinced he'd make it. It's true a lot of players who break into the first team don't manage to hang on to their places, and Sutton had a back-up with a job away from sport. He revealed, 'When I signed full-time I was working. I didn't know if I'd make it. I was 16, an apprentice electrician. As soon as I signed pro I carried it on because I wanted to finish it and I think that's what made me a better player, and a better person.'

Seeing his qualifications through is part of the hard-working and down-to-earth player coach Shaun Wane has developed. Wane wanted to see him stay at Wigan. After the forward's move to the NRL was announced, Wane said, 'They've got a quality player, I don't watch Canberra that often, but I will do now he's there.'

And even though reaching the NRL is a dream come true for Sutton, he insists the decision was a difficult one given how hard he had to work to get to where he is. 'It's not an easy decision because it's not easy but it's comfortable being at a club where you've grown up, you've trained, you know the people and it's like an extended family,' he explained. 'I've loved every minute here, but in my heart I've always wanted to try in arguably the best competition. I've done things over here I've never expected to do – why stop there? See how far I can go – why not? I wouldn't go there if I didn't think I could do it.

'A lot of players over there might not have made it in the past and been unlucky – I don't want to be on that list. I want to be one of the players who goes over there and makes a name for himself. Not only for myself, but, being a Wigan lad, I want to do it for where I'm from. Everything I've learned here will definitely help me over there.'

Sutton is joining a pack at Canberra with a very English feel, with fellow Wigan Warrior John Bateman also going over for the 2019 season to link-up with a pack boasting Englishmen Elliot Whitehead and Josh Hodgson, but he will be checking-up on Wigan while he's away. 'Wigan is my home-town club and I love it – it will always be a part of me,' he said. 'I'm going over there and they will think "who is this? I can't understand a word he's saying" so I'm going to be looking at what they'll be doing. They have new coaches for next year and the year after that so I'm definitely going to be intrigued to see what happens, and they're my family so I'll be in contact with them all the time.'

He'll also miss the Wigan fans: 'I want to thank them. When I did sign [for Canberra] I thought I was going to get a lot of abuse, but there's been nothing but positivity and that's a credit to the town,' he explained. 'It was a tough decision and it was something that I thought in the back of my head I was going to get a lot of abuse, but nothing but positivity. They've been great with me, ever since my debut I've had a lot of positivity, a lot of people speaking to me. I'm proud to be a Wiganer and that's a credit to them.'

But if Sutton's debut is the Wigan memory he is going to tell his kids about – what about those finals? A Grand Final winner in 2016, and being in the Wigan side that beat Cronulla Sharks in the 2017 World Club Challenge must also rank highly in his best moments.

'Walking out at the Grand Final at Old Trafford before the match. I'm a United fan and to see all the people,' he smiled when remembering the pre-match routine in front of 70,202 fans. 'I honestly can't remember a lot of the game. I can just remember walking out and seeing the crowd – that's definitely a stand-out moment. And winning the World Club Challenge. The club is renowned for winning World Club Challenges. You have to look at that and to think "we've done it". Hopefully I can come back here one day.'

OLIVER GILDART

Wigan debut: 21 August 2015, away at Warrington Wolves (won 28-0).

Dreams of playing for Wigan are rarely mixed with expectation. So many of us went to bed to have dreams of being one of the chosen few, there just isn't room for all of us to realise it. Oliver Gildart's rise to the Warriors first team was different. Though no pressure came from home, his surname carried a weight of expectation where supporters were concerned.

His dad, Ian, made 139 appearances for Wigan between 1986 and 1994, and lifted the Challenge Cup in 1990 after coming off the bench to have a hand in the club's 36-14 win over Warrington at Wembley.

Oliver Gildart followed his dad Ian into rugby league.

And Warrington are significant opponents to Oliver too. The centre made his debut in August 2015 in the 28-0 Super 8s win over the now-named Wolves, adding gloss to the occasion with every Wigan schoolboy's dream – a try.

It was a particularly sweet win for Warriors fans. Warrington had beaten Wigan 17-6 at the Halliwell Jones Stadium the month before, and Wolves halfback Chris Sandow had arrived at the Wolves before Gildart's debut from Parramatta to be immediately thrust into some cringeworthy marketing. His 'smash the pies' video was originally just strange but became funny following the Super 8s result. And since then the memories that have remained vibrant are those of Gildart racing in for his first Wigan try.

'It was a bit crazy really,' he said. 'Everything you've worked towards all your life and it was in the deep end in the Super 8s against Warrington. I didn't get eased in really, but I wouldn't have had it any other way. I've learned fast and I'm enjoying it. I managed to score so I was made up.'

Oliver was only born in 1996 – by which time Ian was in the twilight of his career at Oldham, and he admits rugby league wasn't his first love before going to St Pat's with his brother to try the sport for the first time. 'When I was really young I played a bit of football and then I went down to St Pat's, aged 11 or 12, and fell in love with the game,' he said, revealing his dad didn't nudge his children to follow his own path into the professional ranks. 'Growing up he didn't push me and then when my brother played at St Pat's I gave it a try on a Sunday morning and ended up realising I was okay at it,' he explained. 'My dad taught me everything I know growing up and he sits back now and enjoys watching me play.'

It was when at St Patrick's, a club renowned for its knack of producing star players, Gildart realised his dream was to follow his dad into the professional ranks. 'When it got more serious I adapted my life to becoming a professional rugby player,' he said. 'The success and the number of lads who want to play for Wigan. It's probably as

Oliver Gildart celebrates a try against Warrington in the 2016 Grand Final.

big as football and there's a lot of competition from a young age. When I first joined, my age group wasn't really that strong but as I got through the years we had Nick Gregson, Jake Shorrocks, Liam Marshall – we all played in the same team and ended up winning two national cups, which is the biggest thing you can do in amateur rugby. We played all through the scholarship together and now we're doing it on the big stage so it's a bit surreal really.'

Talking of big stages, Gildart has already performed on the biggest despite his years. His Super League debut came in a Salford shirt, on loan from Wigan, before he lit up the Halliwell Jones Stadium in that Super 8s match. In just his 10th career match, six weeks after that brilliant debut against Warrington, he found himself playing against Leeds at Old Trafford in the Grand Final, following that up in 2016 by going one better, scoring a try and ending up on the winning team as Wigan returned to Old Trafford to beat Warrington to win a fourth Super League title.

He then spent 2017 emulating his dad, first lifting the World Club Challenge when Wigan beat Cronulla Sharks 22-6. Ian was a substitute in the 1987 win over Manly and 1992 success against Penrith at Anfield. Then in the August he appeared at Wembley for the Challenge Cup Final but ended up on the losing side as Hull FC beat Wigan 18-14.

It makes for a treasure trove of medals and old shirts between the father and son.

'I've got pictures in the house and clips,' Gildart said of being in a rare household

Oliver Gildart leaves St Helens fullback Ben Barba tackling thin air as he goes over for a try in a 2017 derby.

boasting two Wigan stars from different generations. 'There's a lot of memorabilia there.'

Gildart's early career success has certainly caught the attention of not just Warriors fans, but eyes throughout the game. After speculation over his future at the start of the 2018 season, he signed a three-year extension with his home-town club, saying at the time he felt he still had improvement in him and wanted to reach more finals. Whatever happens in Gildart's future, though, he has already achieved more than those thousands dream of.

Where just five minutes on the pitch would do for most, Gildart already has medals, stories of triumph and heartbreak, and the prospect of more to come. And he admits it means a lot given the impact rugby league had on his upbringing. 'It was massive,' he said. 'I'm a local lad and there's a lot of history here of them coming and playing for Wigan. It's a bit more pressure for me because my dad did it as well. From a young age I was hoping one day I'd play and I've managed to do alright so far.'

WILLIE ISA

Wigan debut: 5 February 2016, at home to Catalans Dragons (won 12-6)

Growing-up more than 10,000 miles away from Wigan in Penrith, Australia, Willie Isa was still in tune with the rugby league club in north-west England. The young rugby league player had the sport in his blood, and a hugely influential figure made

Willie Isa says playing for Wigan is a privilege.

sure he was exposed to what was happening in the northern hemisphere through early morning alarms to watch Super League. 'I heard about them from my father,' Isa explained on when he first saw Wigan. 'He watched Super League early in the morning in Australia and it was the time when Andy Farrell was playing, and Jason Robinson. My dad would tell me to watch a few games when I was younger and managed to get up early and Jason Robinson and Andy Farrell... I couldn't believe Farrell was playing like a number six, for a big guy it wasn't the same. I couldn't get my head around around it.'

Farrell, Wigan's leader and loose forward, was many fans' favourite player – and not just those who adored Wigan, but those who also loved the way Farrell directed teams and used his skill as well as size. 'It was different from my perspective. Halves are usually small, but he was like a forward but real skilful,' Isa recalled. 'The closest I've seen to it in real life is probably Sean O'Loughlin. I was quite intrigued in how he was doing that and when he played for Great Britain I watched it a bit closer.'

His early morning study sessions certainly paid off, as Isa arrived in the UK to join Castleford in 2011, having played for Penrith Panthers and Melbourne Storm after playing for the Australian Schoolboys and under-15s and New South Wales under-17s, as well as playing a Test match for Samoa.

'I was born in New Zealand but I grew-up in Penrith and game through the system there. I played one game but didn't really consider that a debut,' he said. 'I played all my senior games at Melbourne. They had development squads in Penrith so you start at 12s and then when I was 15 I played in the 16s, which is the same as the scholarships here. I went from Melbourne to Cas' for one year in 2011 then I went to Widnes.'

It was after his four years at Widnes that Wigan came for Isa, putting him on the path to Grand Final glory after 30 appearances in 2016, not that his dad believed the news at first. 'He's really happy, because he's watched it for a long time. He's a big rugby league fan and he loves it,' said Isa. 'He couldn't believe it when I told him I'd

Willie Isa takes on the defence in the 2016 Magic Weekend win over Leeds Rhinos.

signed for Wigan. He's a proud man and he's happy I'm at this club – a very historic club as well.'

Isa's chance to write another chapter to the club's history came in the 2016 Grand Final, after a season that saw Wigan climb to second in the Super 8s after finishing the regular season in third place. He started the game at loose forward, with captain Sean O'Loughlin starting from the bench as he was rushed back from injury.

Warriors went into the game against Warrington as underdogs owing to an injury list that included Sam and Joel Tomkins, Dom Manfredi, Michael McIlorum and Lee Mossop, and had been written off at the back end of the season even before reaching the play-offs where they booked their place at Old Trafford with a 28-18 win over Hull FC. 'It was a big year for you, for me, for the club,' Isa said on how the players faced adversity to lift their fourth Super League title.

'We had a lot of injuries to our senior players and were pretty much at the bottom end of our squad, trying to get guys fit every week. But I always had belief in myself. It wasn't going to be easy but 2016 was a unique year. Guys like Sam Powell made a name for himself. He was very consistent for us. We had to make the best of our squad because the older boys couldn't be out on the field for us. We had Sean O'Loughlin come back for the Grand Final, which was massive for us. Matty Smith was really good for us that year. He was very durable at halfback and got us through a lot of the games. It was a big year and looking back now it's one of the best things I've done as an individual.'

Even in the final, Wigan had to battle back with their backs against the wall. Like in 2013, they were down at half-time, but only by 6-2 instead of the 16-6 deficit they were dealing with three years previously. Second-half tries from Oliver Gildart and Josh Charnley, in his last match for Wigan before a stint with Sale RU, proved the difference in the Warriors' 12-6 win. 'As a team, what we were up against, no one really took us on. Even though we're Wigan – everyone wrote us off because we had a lot of players out,' Isa said.

Isa is especially proud to have been part of that squad because of the history associated with Wigan and of getting the chance to be part of the side which were the subject of some of his rugby league lessons as a child. 'It was a big thing for me [coming to Wigan],' he said. 'The older I got, I got to know who Wigan are. I knew who Wigan were and St Helens were. Just because the first English team my dad mentioned to me were Wigan. He told me it's a big, big club and when the opportunity to sign here came up I was like a little kid, I couldn't believe it. At the same time, I thought it was like a dream but it wasn't a dream because I never thought it was within my reach because of the calibre of the club. It's weird saying that because I played for Melbourne Storm. And they are still in their early years, but it's a big club for me. Historically, no other place can come close to Wigan.'

That's not to say Isa's days at work are a breeze. He isn't afraid to admit there are dark times – like the ones leading up to the 2016 Grand Final triumph, which he and the players have to pull themselves through. And when the task seems too hard, Isa has his own way of dealing with the challenge. He explained: 'There are hard times and hard training but you put yourself in the place of that little kid who thinks "I can't believe I'm here". The local 'authentic' guys know what it is to be here and I try and put myself in their shoes because I want to feel how they feel. It means a lot to me and every time I go on their field I am reminded of who I am playing for, why I am playing and what it means to the people. I just want to do my best for the town.'

He mentions 'authentic' players, but when Isa says he wants to feel how they feel, most would agree he isn't far off when he describes what pulling a Wigan shirt on means to him. 'Privilege,' he says, without hesitation. But the word is carefully chosen. 'Simple. I said it when I first came here in one of my first interviews. I was asked how I feel and I said 'privileged'. I learned the word when I was young.

'I went to a school called St Dominic's college and we sat in the big assembly every week. The first day we got there and the deputy principal had a talk. He said, "Remember kids, it's not a right to be here, it's a privilege to be at this school." I learned the word early but I don't use it for a lot of things. This is the type of club that doesn't knock on people's doors for fun. I take this club seriously and it's not a right, it's a privilege to be here.'

MARK BITCON

Mark Bitcon has worked at Wigan Warriors as director of performance since 2009. He left to join Manchester City at the end of last season.

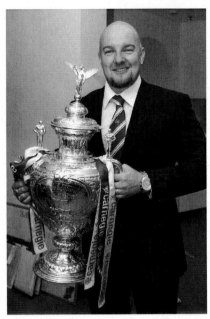

Mark Bitcon after another Challenge Cup win at Wembley.

'Before I came to Wigan as a child I was always more interested in football. I moved over here when I was 10 – my dad's job was a fireman – and we lived in Preston before that. There's no rugby league in Preston, it's all football, but I came to Wigan and went to St Mary and St John's, which is overlooking Central Park.

'I didn't know a lot about rugby league but after a week or two you're imbedded in it. In St Mary and St John's and then St John Fisher high school, I went to the two best schools to get engulfed in the culture of rugby league. It was a great era for the club when I moved over which was around 1989-90. It was the middle of that dynasty.

'Strangely, one of the guys I became best friends with, Damien Charnock, his auntie Mary Charnock worked at Central Park, so I ended up selling programmes and sitting on the wall. I probably didn't have that much interest in rugby but just wanted to hang out with my mates and everybody was involved in rugby league, by playing it, watching it or helping in some way.

'It's a great sport to play. Once it got a bit more serious and a bit more physical it wasn't for me, so I gravitated back to football and I played for Wigan junior Latics and had a great time with that, but then going to John Fisher there was no football team. At the time you either played rugby league or you didn't play school sport so I played for the school team for four or five years – reluctantly to be honest – when you've got a bit of speed you're thrown on the wing and I'd cross my fingers the ball wasn't going to come my way.

'Watching the game, I absolutely loved it. Going to Central Park was a job initially, but with Mary Charnock's association with the club over many years and being at St Mary and St John's it took on a different meaning. We would go down when the team were going to Wembley and see the team get on the coach when they left. We always used to get invited, walking down the path next to the Royal Oak and going into the car parked and on the bus.

'With players like Ellery Hanley and Shaun Edwards it was an unbelievable era. It was an unbelievable team. People talk about the All Blacks now and high performance in elite sport, but Wigan Rugby League were the centre of the universe in many respects, signing Martin Offiah after that – another massive signing and big news for the town, the club and rugby league.

'I got really lucky in that my experiences of Wigan Rugby League, as soon as I'd been in the town, were of an era where they were unbelievably the best team. The football team I supported before moving to Wigan was Liverpool because Liverpool were a team of success. Unless you're from that town or your parents support that team, you look for success and gravitate to that. I also used to go to Springfield Park and watch Wigan Athletic because I was into football.

'At the end of primary school and start of high school I was around Central Park. Mark Preston was the winger at the time, he was probably my favourite player back then and it was easy to see, even not knowing the sport, how good the likes of Ellery Hanley and Shaun Edwards were. You can't get away from it and I'd like to think that's still the case. And it's unbelievable for a town the size of Wigan to then get Premier League football, and the year we won the Challenge Cup and Wigan won the FA Cup within a month – unbelievable. It will never happen again.

'Manchester, Liverpool, there's no other town in the country that can say that and it's a unique thing. The values I learned through a PE teacher, Mr McLeod is something you take and going to St John Rigby College, John Ireland, another PE teacher influenced me. I'm always going to gravitate to PE teachers because it's what I do. They've absolutely helped me on my journey and I've been taught many life lessons from being taught by guys like that – iconic teachers and tutors who make you who you are. I've never been one of those who could have been this or could have been that. I was okay at quite a lot of things. I played a lot of tennis and Jeremy Bates opened the indoor centre at Wigan Tennis Centre and I loved doing that, then the golf boom came and I played golf with my dad and my brother. I was always interested and I was an all-rounder. I wouldn't say all-rounder in terms of excellence, but in terms of participation and being okay at quite a few things.

'I was brought up in Whitley and we used to play on Whitley Fields when the school was still there and Paul Deacon used to live in the next street, Paul Johnson was also nearby and we all used to meet up and play football. Deacs is just good at everything. He's the best golfer. I'd like to think I'd beat him at tennis and I remember running against him in town sports and he was just excellent at everything.

'When you realise, probably at 15 or 16, that you're not going to be an athlete but you want to be involved in sport, you look at maybe being a PE teacher. I went to John Rigby and was heavily shaped by John Ireland, Carrie Heap and Anne White in the PE department.

'Sports science was coming into the foreground and it was a subject that was getting taken seriously by a couple of institutions. Loughborough was one, Liverpool John Moores was the other. They are the two that are probably the birthplaces of that particular discipline. Now there's a pathway, strength and conditioning, it's the absolute norm. Then physios were NHS physios. Fitness might have been done by a sprint coach. It was very loose in those terms. Doctors were all part-time with a local GP helping out.

'There weren't any specialist qualifications directed to high performance sports, so in many respects it was a good time to get in because the competition wasn't massive, whereas now I get students all the time and there are hundreds of sports science courses up and down the country.

'There are post grad qualifications and people with PhDs and there are only so many jobs in performance sport. It's a lot more difficult to get into now than when I was starting. It comes from the realisation of what the next best thing is if you can't run out at Wembley and be Shaun Edwards or Ellery Hanley, and the next best thing is being able to prepare those players and still walking out at Wembley and doing your bit.

'There are some great memories from my career so far, such as walking out with the team at Stade de France for the 2007 rugby union World Cup quarter-final with Scotland. It was an unbelievable atmosphere and that was a moment where you think, "what I'm doing is pretty cool". It's the same when you walk out at Wembley for the first time with your team or at Old Trafford, or with the England team, which I've also been fortunate to do in rugby league.

'They are superb experiences. Players all have their memories and experiences, and things like that I'll always remember. The first time winning with Wigan, being part of Michael Maguire's staff in 2010, was another superb memory. The team hadn't had some success for a sustained period and we won the Grand Final in Michael's first year.

'Being part of bringing back some success to the club and working with England and Scotland in World Cups in two codes of rugby are definitely highlights – it's always an honour to work at an international level, whether you're from that country or not. You become very passionate about the culture and beliefs and the national identity that goes with the sport when you work for an international team. I wouldn't say any more that walking out at Wembley is a driving factor for me and that's not to be arrogant in any way. I think when you've done things a number of times then you think what's the next challenge.

'I'll be with Manchester City Academy hoping to develop the stars of the future for the international game and also for what is a massive organisation in the City group. They are leading the way with Pep Guardiola and his team at the minute and being part of that in an academy environment is something I'm looking forward to massively.

'At the core of everything I've done has been player development – improving people. If you're a teacher you're not in it for the money or because you like the subject – you might have a like for the subject and a passion for it – but the real passion is improving the student. It's letting them leave your company or the time you've spent with them a better person. I've come full circle with that. It started at an academy working with Shaun Edwards at Wasps in around 2001-2002. And wherever I've seemed to go there's always a Wigan connection. In my time in Scotland I worked with Alan Tait who is the defence coach. He was the unfortunate Leeds player Martin Offiah ran round to score that famous try at Wembley.

'Wigan was never far from where I've been and working at Gloucester my roommate was Denis Betts. But Wigan never leaves you and of course I ended-up coming back. Staff, players, athletes, I think Wigan has produced not only some top professional athletes but also some top coaches. Craig White in rugby union and Karen Atkinson who has England netball honours, including Commonwealth Games medals and netball World Championship medals, also went to St John Fisher. There are a lot of successful coaches as well as athletes.

'The rugby union guys in Owen Farrell and Chris Ashton are also well known, there's some great stories from this area that probably don't get the recognition they deserve when you consider not just what happens on the pitch, but the number of Wiganers working off it as well. For such a small town to contribute that much to elite sport is incredible.

'My brother is another, he has been at Manchester City as well and has been for a long time. But now I'm more in a reflective period, you probably think more about what you've achieved now than when you're doing it. You're with a group of staff and players in a bubble. The remit of professional sport when you're paid to do a job in performance is to do that, get the team to perform.

'There is the job side and the clinical side of "we need to achieve something here or else we're under pressure" but there is a romantic side, the sentimental side.

'There's no doubt that doing that with your home-town team, who you've had an association with and been involved with and is so ingrained in the town, then you do get those feelings. It puts it into perspective when you see fans after a Grand Final who are more delighted than you are. People live their lives through this club and if it goes well they have a good week at work, if it doesn't then it's not as good.

'I can testify to that because my wife is a big Wigan Warriors fan and if we don't have a good performance then I'm in for a tough week! You go to a family party and it's the first thing somebody asks you. It's been great to be part of that for the past nine years. It's great for Shaun Wane who is from the town and played at every level, coached at every level, and brought so many of these guys through, which is another remarkable story. I don't think you could point at another club who could have that.

'For Ian Lenagan, a Wigan born and bred guy, to put his faith in a group of Wiganers to run his club and Kris Radlinski as director, Shaun as head coach and me to run the performance side is something very special.

'The Shaun Edwards appointment looks like an unbelievable one because, again, he is steeped in that as a player and I'm sure he'll have those values. Mick Cassidy's coming back as head of youth so I'm sure the remit is to maintain that heavy Wigan influence. I think for this town and this team that is really important.

'Michael Maguire came in as an Australian in 2010 and very quickly adapted and embraced the culture of Wigan. We had a staff full of Wiganers who let him know what that first derby against Saints was going to be like and what was expected. I've never known a more passionate Australian for a Wigan/Saints derby. He knew how important that was. You can't get away from it and that's what culture is for me.

'To be a part of a small chapter of Wigan's history and that reconnection with the town after a long time working away with different teams has been special. My time here has been enjoyable, which is why I've stayed for nine years. You don't tend to stay for very long in professional sport but the staff, people, association with the town and the fans have been unbelievable. And the players have been too. It's easy to coach when the culture is so strong and the values they've learned are strong. Work ethic is the biggest one for me. Wiganers work hard and if you've got work ethic you'll get through it. That's what this town's all about.'

ANTHONY ATHERTON

Wigan Warriors Community innovation manager and former Wigan St Patrick's player with international honours

'It starts as a fan, you remember games, watching your favourite players and that almost being a reason you start to play. Through your professional life you see a different side, you see the roles and responsibilities the club has to its community, to its fans, to its players.

'I've coached as a volunteer for four years and worked at Wigan Warriors for eight months but worked with the club the last two or three years with programmes I've done when I worked for the RFL. It's been quite a long relationship that's changed and evolved on what I've been doing. From being born, it's just in you – it's what you do. You don't know any different.

'I don't remember this, but the first memory I've been told of it the 1985 Challenge Cup Final. Great game, super exciting, just short of my third birthday, but I slept all the way through the game. My family went down to Wembley for the day, 15-20 family members, and I started on one person's knee and just worked my way down and just slept all the way down. You don't remember it, but I've been told about it and seen pictures of it.

'I started playing at Ince St Williams when I was six, going into the under-7s. I remember quite vividly my first training session. The training session was something my dad's best friend Eddie Gallagher knew about and I was taken to Ince with my friend Robbie Gallagher. The Catholic club is still there, the little pitch we trained on is still there, and we were passed over this fence, and told "run over to that man, he's your coach, and say hello". Off you went. That coach was a man called Bernard Farrimond who my dad knew. He was very influential and then shortly after that another influential coach, Mick Parkinson – who has passed away, sadly – they coached me for my first few years and almost made you want to keep playing or there was something they were doing that made you want to go back. I don't know how you bottle it but there was something there from being chucked over a fence... you became addicted.

'So that's what I did on Saturday morning, then went to the chippy, then went to my grandma's. Then you did whatever you did in the afternoon, went watching St Pat's most likely as I got slightly older, and then you played on Sunday, went to grandma's and then you went to watch a game of rugby, went to gran's for tea.

'From nine o'clock Saturday morning to nine o'clock Sunday night it just went just rugby. Different chunks in different guises so that's how it worked. Playing the sport has always been kind of serious and you do go through that phase when you're really young, and I think every child will experience at some point, where you're going to play for Wigan, Great Britain, the full lot. But then as you start to get a little older you start to realise that not everybody does that and you start to weigh up the odds. There are lots of you and not many opportunities to do it.

'It was going back to Mick and Bernard and the enjoyment side of it, and the social aspect, so I don't think I could name a friend I've got that I haven't got through either playing or coaching. You've just ended up sat in a room with blokes with a common goal and you develop that group of friends which just evolves.

'Probably at about 14-15 where you've not been in town team squads or you've been to Lancashire trials and not progressed anywhere you play for a different reason. You kind of realised you weren't going to be a professional. You didn't fall out of love with the game but you realised if that's not why I'm here, I'm still getting my enjoyment, and what's next, so you do explore.

'I didn't get any rep honours till I was 22, almost 16 years of hard work. That was BARLA under-23s, coached by Jimmy Taylor, who funnily enough was my grandad's first apprentice, and it was another gentleman who was influential, Kevin Thompson, who had the conversation with me about playing for the under-23s squad.

'The people in that team you become friends with. It's good that relationship exists and if it didn't, and I didn't play, I think where would I be? It's just in you. It's the default thing you go to. You're rugby people first and good people at that. Yes, you're divided into your clubs when you play each other and you want your colours to win, that's never going to change, but you've got that common goal. We've all existed to play the game, be as good as we can be, and now we're helping and nurturing children in this town to do that same.

'To coach under-16s at Wigan Warriors is such a privilege. When Matty Peet [former Warriors head of youth] rang me, all of a sudden you're working with the best kids in the country. I coached Warriors first-team stars Tom Davies and Liam Marshall at under-18s at St Pat's too. But helping the next generation of Super League stars wasn't the main thing. You can learn some great things from losing. The majority of the time you lose because you've not done enough at that moment in time. If that helps players in their careers or lives always give their best at all times, they'll be more rounded people and be better people.

'Liam could do unbelievable things from nothing, great character, great personality. Tom was "work hard, work hard". Great person, pleasure to coach and it didn't surprise me they got an opportunity. They've been ready when opportunities presented themselves. It's a respectful sport. I was asked once if rugby league was a person, what does it look like? I described it as a scruffy old man who would wipe his feet on his way into your house and thank you for your tea and coffee. It's a bit rough and ready, it's not got money coming out of its ears, but it's traditional in its values and noble.

'You can tell when you're speaking to people if they've got a similar background and it stems from being in the sport from a period of their life. Moving to St Pat's as a teenager was one of the kind of things that changed the sport for me. A lot of players were being courted by professional clubs. I wasn't perhaps getting as much game time as I thought I should have and I almost went playing football.

'I was 14 or 15, and my dad had been involved at St Pat's and helped start that youth section with Derek Birchall and Gerry Fairhurst, among some other great people, and that was it, you were part of the best club in the country at what it does.

'I got called up to BARLA in maybe 2005. I'd played under-23s and then played in the Skanska Cup, where you played against combined services, students. We won that. It was in the middle of a bit of a spat between BARLA and the RFL. BARLA had their rep stuff and the RFL had Great Britain Amateurs, which became the Community Lions.

'There were a lot of good students that possibly missed out on rep honours because they weren't in community clubs at the time. They had a selection day at

Golbourne and I remember a sheet going round: tick if you don't want to be selected for Great Britain Amateurs. I didn't tick because I didn't want to be told who I could play for. It's my game, nobody's telling me I can and I can't. If I get picked, brilliant.

'I remember the phone call, I'd played alright and it was Jimmy Taylor asking me to come to France.

I then played in Australia in 2008 and BARLA called in the meantime saying I couldn't play for them anymore. There was a tour to South Africa and I didn't go on the back of that. But there was a change of guard and John Fieldhouse asked me and asked if I was still willing to play, and I said of course I was. I was back in and played another round of Skanska Cups.

'I got what I worked for because I eventually went to South Africa, France, Canada, Serbia, Italy to play.

'My dad told me to play, enjoy myself and play well, and if you get picked, you get picked. I played quite a bit of rep rugby. It was a fond memory. The pride when that letter drops and you have to ring your manager, it rewards the years of hard work.

'Coaching is a different side to it. It's a chance to give back to what and where I came from. The bulk of the giving back, not all of it, was done when I coached at St Pat's from 2005 to 2015. The nicest thing to see is the likes of Tom and Liam playing, which is bang on. But I look back at pictures of teams I've coached and there's 14 or 15 kids I've coached who have all played open age at St Pat's, so they've all got the enjoyment and the desire to keep on playing. It's great to go and see them, kids I've coached playing well and doing good things.

'Now it shifts a bit working at Wigan. It's more intense. It is about enjoyment to some degree but it's also about winning competitions and creating international players. It's about constantly striving for improvement. Your system has to be getting players to that next level like Sam Tomkins, George Williams, Liam Farrell, Sean O'Loughlin. They are international players and it's not about getting a quick debut and off you go.

'Sammy Kibula, Ollie Partington and James Worthington were in the under-16s when we were coaching them, so to see them having gone into the academy, which is great, and go into that system makes me proud. Being part of nurturing the best players in the country – what a privilege.

'One of the biggest influences on me as a person and a player was Dave Ruddy. He was at St Pat's 30 years. When you look at the list of players he's influenced it will be in the thousands, and when you talk about rugby league people he's the ultimate. He worked his socks off to make everything as good as he possibly can for the players, and once it's done he is a man with a sharp sense of humour and you can ring him up – right we're going out – and just chat about rugby, anything, life.

He was very supportive to me through a difficult spell when my dad died, which was one of the hardest things I've ever been through. You look at the group around you of people who will support you and it was surreal. There was something missing... but this support network around you. There will always be something missing, but to have security around you meant you weren't on your own through any of that.

'There must have been 150 people when we met up – I don't think I bought a drink for the next month. It was unbelievable. When you talk about rugby league people it comes together and they support you.

'But flip that, and I've been through some great times. In my time in rugby I've met my wife and had a child and I've seen a lot of things I think are the right thing to do. My son doesn't train yet, he's three, but on our Saturdays we're together and we watch a game of rugby. I thought my upbringing was great and I can't thank my parents enough. Now I'm making sure he experiences what I've had that were so good.

'To be involved in a sport which teaches him discipline, respect, manners. He gets it at home but that makes him a good person which is cool. I've not put my shirt up in St Pat's and I always said I'd do it when I finished playing, so I don't know if in the back of my mind I've actually finished playing. I think I have. I also did my time at Wigan rugby union when we switched to summer because I was not going shopping on a Saturday. It's just in you. It's in your blood and what you do.'

PART FOUR

LOOKING FORWARD
THE FUTURE OF WIGAN WARRIORS

ADRIAN LAM

Wigan debut: 10 February 2001, Challenge Cup round four away to St Helens (lost 22-8).
Last Wigan match: 8 October 2004, Super League play-off away to Leeds (lost 40-12).
Appearances: 119
Tries: 44
Goals: 1
Drop goals: 10
Points: 188
Head coach from 2019

When Adrian Lam takes over as head coach for the 2019 season, he'll be thinking of an old friend. Lam, a Challenge Cup winner with Wigan in 2002 and a player adored by fans, will be taking charge for a year, until Shaun Edwards's duties in rugby union with the Wales national team are complete, in an unusual arrangement but one which has gone down well with supporters.

It will be a year in which Lam will hope to boost his stock before looking for a permanent coaching role, but he thinks fate may have something to do with his year ahead in Wigan as he recalls a conversation with Terry Newton. 'I remember Terry saying to me, "You should come back here one day and coach because you'll make a great coach", said Lam on the day he was unveiled as Wigan's next coach. 'I said to him at the time, "I might just do that". And here we are.'

Adrian Lam will be Wigan's head coach in 2019.

Newton, a Wigan player between 2000 and 2005, died in 2010 and is remembered by fans and players as one of the most uncompromising players they have seen or played alongside. 'I want to find time to go and have a beer where he's buried and pay my respects and talk to him about this journey, because I think there's a bit of fate there,' said Lam. 'I had a particular thought about how to play and win games and I remember him coming up to me and saying, "You need to forget that and support me". So, I sat down with him over lunch and we spoke about how the English game was won, and from that moment I started playing my best football, purely on the back of those conversations. I think about him just about every day. We were very close and he was just about the best player I played with. His opinion on footy was important to me and so I coach similar to his thoughts.

Terry Newton passes the ball to Adrian Lam.

Despite Lam's last game for Wigan being back in 2004, he still gets stopped by fans of the club, even when he has been on the other side of the world. But he's happy to talk about his time at the club, and when Wigan toured Australia at the start of the 2018 season to play Hull FC in Wollongong before taking on South Sydney, there were plenty of opportunities for him to revisit happy memories. 'Some of my best times were playing here,' he said. 'With Wigan's tour Down Under earlier this year, I bumped into a lot of fans then – I'm all over the world and I bump into them! And I love talking about it, too, because I had some of the best times of my life at this club, at this town. I consider Andy Farrell, Kris Radlinski and Gary Connolly some of the best players to have played here, so to play alongside them was unbelievable.'

But his best highlight? Like so many players from the turn of this century, the obvious choice was when Wigan beat St Helens 21-12 to win the Challenge Cup at Murrayfield in 2002. 'The Challenge Cup in 2002 was the obvious highlight, but I have so many,' he said. 'I thanked Rads for recommending me for the [2019 coaching] role and he said, "I think you'll be great for the job". And I said, "You sure it's not just because you took the Lance Todd off me and this is you paying me back!" We had a running joke about it. I said, "Mate, I scored a try, set up a try and kicked a field goal – what did you do? Cut your foot!"'

SHAUN EDWARDS

Wigan debut: 6 November 1983, John Player Special Trophy round one at home to York (won 30-13).
Last Wigan match: 8 February 1997, Challenge Cup round four away at St Helens (lost 26-12).
Appearances: 467
Tries: 274
Goals: 23
Drop goals: 4
Points: 1146
Head coach from 2020

Countless kids in Wigan run around, living and breathing the dream they will one day play professional rugby in a Cherry and White shirt. From the moment they wake up until their orders to go to bed, each day involves a stint with an oval ball in the park or on the street – in the house, they are caught by parents sidestepping the kitchen bin while throwing a dummy with an empty pop bottle. Fewer than a handful of those kids realise this dream – and fewer still grasp the opportunity in the same way Shaun Edwards did.

Shaun Edwards will take over as Wigan Warriors head coach in 2020.

For what was believed to be a record fee of £35,000 for an amateur player, Edwards signed for Wigan at his parents' house at midnight on his 17th birthday, 17 October 1983. 'I was lucky enough to have interest from quite a few clubs and I actually got the biggest offer from St Helens,' he recalled. 'Dougie Laughton from Widnes was probably the first person to show any interest in me, and Widnes were probably the top rugby league team at the time – but I followed my heart and signed for Wigan.'

The son of Jack, an outstanding half-back for Warrington in the 50s and 60s, Edwards spent his early school years a stone's throw away from Central Park at St Mary's, turning out for the school team for matches held on the training pitch at the back of the Spion Kop stand. First crafting his trademark style at the age of seven, he played above his own age group until he captained Wigan schoolboys under-11s. It was a great thrill for me at the time. Schoolboy rugby was big back in those days.'

Shaun Edwards signs for Wigan RL at midnight on his 17th birthday in October 1983 at home in Springfield, watched by his dad Jackie, right, Maurice Lindsay, Jack Robinson, Tom Rathbone and coach Alex Murphy.

As people took notice, the young Edwards served the rest of his rugby league apprenticeship at two of the sport's most notorious nurseries, St John Fisher High School and Wigan St Patrick's, before turning pro.

Making his debut in November 1983 in a routine 30-13 win over York in the John Player Special Trophy, what was to come was beyond anyone's guess as he went on to claim 37 major honours in 467 appearances for the club over the next 14 years.

Not having to wait long for his first taste of a major final, he appeared at Wembley in the 19-6 loss to Widnes of 1984 – Wigan's first Wembley appearance since 1970. Taking up the story, Edwards said, 'We weren't a top team at the time – I think we were about a mid-table team really and I had been playing on the wing. Our full-back Steve Hampson broke his leg unfortunately – he had lots of bad luck concerning Wembley – so I had to play full back.

'It was only my third or fourth game at fullback and it was at Wembley! But Widnes were too good for us on the day. The board invested heavily in the team and we obviously went back the year after and beat Hull in what was a very memorable final.'

The 1985 final was a classic – the 28-24 win over Hull was Edwards's first and, playing at full-back again, he scored a try early in the second half. It also sparked a run on 13 consecutive seasons where the star would add a medal to his personal collection, though a return to Wembley only came in 1988 and with it a 43-game unbeaten Challenge Cup run that lasted eight years. Edwards was involved in every game. 'I was lucky with injuries. As the run continued there was more and more pressure on the players. You didn't want to be in the team that lost. Add that to a lot of incredibly competitive people and that's what created that dynasty I suppose.'

There were bumps and scrapes along the way, with Wigan notably squeezing past Halifax 19-18 in 1993 and seeing a Bobby Goulding drop-goal attempt bounce off the post at Central Park in 1995 in a 16-all draw. (Wigan annihilated their rivals in the reply the following Wednesday).

'Every year people think we coasted all the way through but we didn't,' Edwards explained. 'We had a lot of tough games along the way and nearly every campaign we had a game where we just scraped through. I remember once we drew with St Helens and beat them in the replay – another time we got a drop-goal in the last few minutes against Halifax, so there was always some ferocious battles along the way. But during those eight years we always got the silverware at the end of them. Just to be part of them was a great thrill for me, especially being a Wigan lad.'

Edwards's contribution to Wigan's incredible feat was recognised when he received the OBE in 1996. Along with his Challenge Cup medals, he was the only player to receive a medal for each of Wigan's seven consecutive Championship

Shaun Edwards leads the celebrations after Wigan's World Club Challenge win over Brisbane in 1994.

wins between 1989 and 1996, and he had played in all four of the club's World Club Challenge appearances up to that point, in 1987, 1991, 1992 and 1994.

On receiving the OBE he said, 'It was obviously good. I felt like I accepted it on behalf of the Wigan team really. It was me who got it because I suppose I was the one who had been in most finals and won most medals etc.'

Fans need no reminding the Cup run ended in 1996 with a defeat to Salford, then a second-tier side, after a routine thumping of Bramley in the previous round. Having seen the eight-year run through, Edwards offered his insight to that fateful day at The Willows. 'We had been playing for a very long time. I don't know if it was mental staleness of not,' he said. 'On the day, we turned the ball over too many times, we played against a well-drilled Salford team, who were deserving winners on the day. We made too many errors with the ball in hand, or completion rate was poor and we paid the price.'

But there was no time to dwell on what was the end of an era. The inaugural Super League season was around the corner, which would prove to be Edwards's last full-term at Central Park. As well as picking up his final domestic rugby league medal, the 1996 Premiership, Edwards took a glimpse into the sport which would provide his future living – rugby union.

Wigan played Bath in a match under league rules at Manchester City's Maine Road and repeated the exercise under union rules at Twickenham. In between,

Wigan shook the union world by winning the Middlesex Charity sevens, Edwards's first brush with union since being a dual-code England captain in his school days.

Predictably, the Riversides cruised to an 82-6 victory in the league encounter – the union match was a closer affair with a scoreline of 45-19 in Bath's favour, but Edwards thinks Bath's commitment to producing a good game to watch contributed to a closer score. 'I played in the rugby league game but I didn't play in the union game because I'd broke a couple of ribs. I'm pretty sure if Bath would have wanted to keep it very tight and play the rolling mauls and stuff like that then I think they would have won with a bigger margin. I think they wanted to show rugby union in a good light and they threw the ball around and that gave us some scraps of possession. I remember us scoring a couple of tries towards the end and one where we passed the ball inside our own goal line. I'm sure if Bath would have wanted to absolutely starve us of possession etc and not take the risks they could have, but they didn't because they wanted union to be shown as an entertaining game. I'm pretty sure we would not have got the chances we got and they would have beaten us, not as convincingly as we beat them at rugby league but by more than what the scoreline was.'

In 1997 Edwards became a father and being there for his son influenced his move from Wigan. The February saw the now legend play his last game for Wigan, a 26-12 Challenge Cup loss to St Helens at Knowsley Road, and move to London Broncos. Reflecting on the move he said, 'I wanted to play a part in my son's life. Financially it wasn't a good move for me. I was on much more money at Wigan than I was in London, but I suppose there was a point of view of people saying you're okay playing in a good Wigan side because you always had good players around you, so I suppose it was a challenge for me to go to London and play for one of the clubs, which wasn't seen to be one of the big Super League powers I suppose.'

Perhaps not a superpower, London finished second in Super League that year, beating Wigan twice in the process and getting the better of Canberra Raiders in the World Club Championship, a week after the Raiders had mercilessly taught the now Warriors a lesson by the tune of 50 points to 10.

The scrum-half briefly moved back north to play for the then champions Bradford Bulls in 1998, but the venture didn't last the season and he went back to the capital. 'I really wanted to go back to Wigan but the board hadn't been settled at the time so I ended up signing for Bradford,' he said. 'I was 31 at that stage and I got myself in really good condition in the off season, I trained especially hard but I realised I was really missing my son.

'I was just fortunate after those games Bradford were prepared to let me go back to London. They paid the same transfer fee so there was no money lost either way and London wanted me back. I went back and the rest of the season our form picked up a little bit and we finished about seventh that year – just outside the play-offs.'

A year later, Edwards also had a last dance at Wembley as London also reached the 1999 Challenge Cup Final – the last to be held there. 'When I look back at my career, the fact we came second in the league in my first season there, I'm very proud of that really and we also had a Wembley appearance. I don't know if they were giving tickets away or what, but we had some really good crowds too. We had 7,500, 8,000, 10,000 once when we played Bradford and Brisbane Broncos. It was a great season for the London Broncos.'

Like his first, Edwards's last Wembley appearance ended in defeat as Leeds won 52-16, but London put up much more of a fight than the final score suggested. 'You would look at the scoreline and think they got absolutely hammered, but we were actually winning the game with 20 minutes to go and we ended up with 12 players because we just got a lot of injuries on the day,' Edwards said. 'I had a broken thumb and I had an injection in it before the game but I could still feel the pain. It was still killing me during the game. We had a lot of people playing injured and it showed in the last 20 of the game.'

His last rugby league game was a 34-18 win over Huddersfield-Sheffield Giants in March 2000, bringing the curtain down on a magical career that brought 36 Great Britain Test appearances with his countless medals and accolades.

He was to join the coaching staff at London Wasps rugby union, where he would start to learn a new craft in the pursuit of more silverware. But on the horizon, his life was about to be ripped apart. 'From the moment my mum told me on that terrible morning, 9 February 2003, I knew my life would never be the same again.'

Losing anyone close leaves a permanent mark on people – regardless of age or circumstance – but Shaun Edwards's younger brother, Billy Joe, a promising star in the Wigan academy ranks, was only 20. The car accident that took his life and that of Craig Johnson, another Warriors youngster, gave no warning. 'It's a life changing event,' Edwards explained with disarming frankness. 'To lose a brother who was only 20 was very, very painful. That pain is with me all the time. You kind of get a little bit used to after a while, maybe a few years, but my life will never be as it was before, and you just have to accept that. The thing is, you just have to try and support your parents as much as possible without getting underneath their feet really.'

The year was supposed to be memorable for different reasons for the now rugby union coach – though such a loss is something one learns to live with rather than recover from. Three months later, London Wasps, the Zurich Premiership side that now had the services of Edwards as a coach, won the title in a 39-3 demolition of Gloucester in the final, which sparked a run of three successive titles for the club.

His coaching career began in 2001, and, despite being a legend at home and in rugby league, like being a kid playing above his age group all over again, Edwards had to prove himself. 'I had a year and a half out of the game trying to get a coaching job,' he recalled. 'I was frustrated and I couldn't really get the job that I wanted, then I went to Australia to spend some time with Wayne Bennett [the Australian supercoach who was in his 20-year stay at Brisbane at the time]. He was a great help to me, learning about coaching styles etc. He's a great guy and a guy I still speak to every now and again. I'm still grateful to Wayne for his advice, and when I came back I still didn't really have the offer I wanted and the club I would like to have joined in London was London Wasps.'

Armed with tutorship from one of the world's best at the craft, Edwards returned to take further steps towards his goal. 'There were a few people who helped me. Ellery Hanley was involved in rugby union at the time and he helped me with the technicalities. Clive Griffiths also helped me. He is a Grand Slam winning coach in union – I'm very grateful to those people. I met a guy from Wasps by chance, I was with Ellery, and he asked me what I was doing and I told him I wanted to become a coach. He told me to give him a ring in a couple of months' time when the season started and come to a session. He said we'll see how you do and take it from there, so I gave a session and they offered me a position. I was still very naive about a lot of things in rugby union, but there are certain things like teaching people how to pass properly, teaching people tackle techniques and various aspects of what I've learned from playing rugby league that crossed over to union. At first, I coached those kinds of things, but now I know a lot more about the game of rugby union and the technicalities of it.'

As well as a different game on the field, Edwards was working in a system very different to the conventional rugby league way of one head coach having control of the team. He explained, 'It's a bit different in rugby union. There was a director of rugby above me, one was Warren Gatland, who probably taught me more about the game of rugby union than anyone else, and then Ian McGeechan came in and our success continued under him. I worked under them as a head coach – all my work was put on the pitch.'

As well as another Premiership title in 2008, Edwards's time at Wasps produced two Heineken Cup successes in 2004 and 2007. The European competition is seen as the pinnacle of club rugby union, and Edwards draws comparisons between that and the sentimental value attached to rugby league's Challenge Cup. 'They were both at Twickenham, both 75,000 crowds, similar to going to Wembley,' he said. The Heineken Cup is similar to what going to Wembley is like – it's the Holy Grail if you like for club rugby in Europe.

'Wasps wasn't a big club in terms of numbers of fans watching etc, but we had a very talented squad who were, at the time, ahead of everybody in things like strength and conditioning and tactically as well; I think we were a little bit ahead of other teams at the time. That certainly helped us because it was only when I first came to union that we started having play-offs and that ability to peak at the end of the season like Wigan did last year is an art for a coach and his conditioning staff to achieve.

'Mark Bitcon was at Wasps and he learned a lot about how to peak at the end of the season and he's obviously put that knowledge into the Wigan team because they did so well last year.'

Like in his league career, Edwards's talent and hard work saw him appear on the international scene. In 2008, Wales claimed the Six Nations Championship in a year that saw Edwards enter the fray as defence coach. 'Warren Gatland got the post of Wales coach, someone I'd worked with a lot before and we'd been pretty successful. When Warren asked if I wanted to join up, he said I could do it part-time and I think because we'd been quite successful at Wasps and we had a very kind boss in Ian McGeechan. He allowed me to do it part time,' he said. 'The first Six Nations we entered went really, really well – we ended up winning it. I did both jobs for a number of years afterwards and just before the 2011 World Cup Wasps were in financial difficulty. I left there and went full-time with the Wales set up.'

And the international game has an effect on Edwards, and draws comparisons to how the competition has an effect on the Welsh population, just like the town's rugby league heroes capture the lives of Wiganers. 'It is a real buzz to be involved in a Six Nations. You go to great cities in Europe, Dublin, Edinburgh, and those cities come alive when there's a big game on, London, Paris, it is quite a big deal. It's great for the bars and cafes etc in the cities. Particularly in Wales, the whole country comes alive when the Six Nations is on.'

'Wales is very similar to Wigan. Except one's a country and the other one's a town. People love an oval-shaped ball game, are very knowledgeable about it and are working-class people who have a history of mining backgrounds as well – the people from South Wales are just like people from Wigan.'

Being away from Wigan hasn't numbed the pull of the place on Edwards, though, and the sporting achievements of the town's athletes means he never has to look far to find home. 2013 was particularly enjoyable for him, and he remembers the trip to Wembley for the FA Cup Final fondly. 'It was amazing,' he laughed. 'It was brilliant because I'm not the biggest soccer fan in the world, but Wigan Athletic playing in the FA Cup... I went with my best mate and his kid and it was almost like a school reunion, I was seeing so many people I'd not seen for 15 years. It was brilliant.

And to see Wigan Athletic win the FA Cup at Wembley. It was great when everyone was singing at the end. Dave Whelan has contributed in a lot of ways for the town, and I think it was always his dream to see Wigan Rugby League and Wigan Athletic do it in the same season, and he got his wish.'

He also got a buzz from seeing Warriors clinch a Super League and Challenge Cup double in 2013 after many pundits had written Shaun Wane's side off following a dip in form towards the end of the regular season. 'It was great. Over the course of the season there will be dips in form but they had hard lines the year before and I think the experience of peaking at the right time. The coaching staff and conditioning staff did a great job. Probably not putting too much pressure on when other people were complaining that they were losing games. As long as you make the play-offs that's the main thing and they proved that by peaking at the right time and getting the double.'

For a man who has enjoyed dizzying success in both of rugby's codes, favourite memories amongst fans will be argued until long after the next generation of stars. In 1990, after a guest stint in Australia, Edwards was awarded the Man of Steel award in a year that included a Test series against New Zealand and a cup final win over Warrington, which gave the now halfback a hard-man status thanks to him playing on with a fractured eye socket and depressed cheekbone.

'I'd been to Australia that year and had been in the Balmain team that lost in the Grand Final, but I was on the bench. I hadn't played that many games but I came back a much better player,' he said. 'I was lucky enough to get the man of the series against the Kiwis and I also played at Wembley with that injury so I think that all contributed.'

Despite the injury, which would be enough to make lesser men wretch, Edwards's teammates had no sympathy for him during the 36-14 win. 'Dean Bell was great because obviously when you have a bad injury it's pretty easy to feel sorry for yourself,' he said. 'The problem I had is I couldn't see out of my right eye at all so I was running around with my eye shut – almost like having a patch on my eye and trying to play. I didn't do as much as what was expected of me to be a player on the pitch so Dean said, "Either get stuck in or get off the pitch" and that's exactly what I needed. I didn't need too much compassion at that time. I needed someone to either say "play on or get off". That's exactly what he said to me and I got back in the game and contributed with what was a decent performance to help us win the cup for the third time in a row.'

But a personal highlight for Edwards came four years later when, against all odds, new coach Graeme West led Wigan to Australia to beat Brisbane in the World Club Challenge. Many tales of the trip have done the rounds; players partying, not thinking they had a chance – but Edwards set the record straight and credits a balance between focus and staying fresh with helping the Riversiders to a famous 20-14 win. 'You have to remember we played 44 games that season and right at the end of the season there was a change in the coaching staff,' he said. 'Under the first regime we were going to be travelling to different places, training here and there, and that's the last thing you need after 44 games non-stop. The lads needed a bit of rest and recuperation. West had the foresight to take us to the Gold Coast. We trained when we got there, then he gave us two and a half days off and freshened us up, and we ended up rewarding him by winning the game. If you notice, the British Lions, before the third test when they thumped Australia [in 2013], where were they before they game? The Gold Coast. At the end of a massively long season of slog you have to freshen players up – they are not machines. Gatland had the guts, was criticized heavily for it in the build-up, but they gave him the performance.'

Looking back, Edwards's life has thrust him into contrasting places in and out of rugby. The highs of winning trophies, royal honours and becoming a father have been knitted with the change of career pathway to be with his son during his playing career and the anguish of losing his brother.

On the pitch, the trend of dual-code stars means some will always ask Edwards if he wished he'd tried the 15-man code as a player, but his place at the centre of a team which would make a far-fetched movie script due to its success meant he was satisfied during his playing career. 'Lots of people ask me, do you wish you'd played union at an international level? And I always say not really, I was lucky with the career I had in rugby league and I was a small cog in what was a very successful Wigan wheel,' he said. 'I played in a team which probably even transcended its sport in terms of people being known throughout the country.'

More than 20 years on from his days guiding the Wigan players around the pitch from scrum half, Edwards will finally be back. Fans were thrilled to discover he was going to take over, once his duties as defence coach with Wales rugby union are finished, and while he has been in rugby union for the best part of two decades, he says he still understands the 13-man code well enough to do his job. 'I've took a risk to come here,' he admitted. 'The main reason I've done that is to challenge for trophies with Wigan. But it was time to have a crack at rugby league. Ian Lenagan offered me the opportunity and it just felt like the right time.

'There are tactical changes to the game, obviously. In the end, the game is still the same – there's big men in the middle, you need two tricky halfbacks and, on top of that, you need a tricky hooker who will understand the game. Plus, you need talented athletes on the outside to finish the tries off. The game was like that when my heroes played for Wigan in the 1950s, and it will be like that in another 40 years too, I think.'

But where there are clearly similarities in the rugby league Edwards left in 2000 to the game we watch today, some things are startlingly different to when he was lifting trophies as a standard part of his life as Wigan captain. 'I'm not going to compare the product,' he said. 'The only thing I'd say is that it's unrealistic to expect any coach or team to dominate the way Wigan did in the old days because there was no salary cap. As regards to the game, I still think it's very similar. I won't look back with rose-tinted glasses and say it was better in my day because that's a waste of time in my view. There are things which could potentially make the game more exciting, but there's no way I'd come back and start preaching about how to make it better. I'm back to help my team win games, it's as simple as that.'

Despite having a job to finish in rugby union, though, with Wales going on a World Cup charge in 2019, looking to do better than their quarter-final loss to South Africa in 2015, Edwards will be having an arms-length involvement at Wigan while they spend their season being looked after by Adrian Lam as head coach. 'I will try and be involved. I'm hoping to do some consultancy work with Ospreys outside of my international commitments, although when the internationals are on it's absolutely full-on, you're with Wales full-time,' he explained.

'Outside of that, what I did last year was some work with Cardiff Blues in a consultancy role, and I'll do that again with Ospreys – but later in the week, I'll be driving up to Wigan and watching training. I won't be doing any coaching, though, it will be all over to Adrian. We will speak on the phone regularly – but he's the boss during his period in charge.'

And how does Edwards expect Wigan to play under their new coach? 'I don't mind people taking risks,' he said. 'Watch the Wales defence in action, we're a risk-taking defence. I don't mind players throwing a cut-out pass, flying out for a big hit and things like that. As long as they've worked on it and practiced it in training and didn't just make it up on the fly. The key performance indicators in the game at the minute revolve around completion rates, look at Castleford last year, they played brilliant stuff but it came to the big game and they got blown away by Leeds. You need both styles, there's no doubt you need to create quick ball.'

Despite Edwards's roots and history with Wigan Rugby League, there was no question of him leaving Wales early to start his new post. He has been with the organisation since 2008, helping Wales to Grand Slams in 2008, 2012 and the Six Nations title in 2013, and feels he owes the Welsh his services for the World Cup. 'My commitment to the Welsh public meant I was going to stay. I was welcomed with real open arms there, and the support they've given me is absolutely unbelievable,' he said. 'They've accepted me as one of their own, and it'll be nice to finish off at the World Cup in 2019 with a bang. We should have been in the final in 2011 [lost 9-8 to

France in the semi-final], we got out of a real tough group [including England and Australia] in 2015.'

Having spent 17 years in professional rugby league, signing with Wigan in 1983 before leaving London Broncos in 2000, Edwards will have worked in rugby union longer by the time he returns to Wigan.

In that time, his success as a coach, first with Wasps as well as Wales and the British and Irish Lions, has marked him out as one of the most respected people in the 15-man code, but he picks two influences that have helped him to success for different reasons. 'Warren Gatland was the biggest influence – but Sir Ian McGeechan was very good too on the man-management side of things,' Edwards said. 'He came to Wasps and did something very intelligent, he realised we had a winning structure and he simply watched us, watched how we worked, learned from us and added some pearls of knowledge and I thought to myself, "that's a proper coach". What was amazing about Wasps is that we weren't a big club. There were only 6,000, fans but we had incredible players like Lawrence Dallaglio and Matt Dawson, and we did it against the odds. We were ahead of the rest; we were the first team to bring the blitz defence in, the first team not to kick the ball out and keep it in play rugby league-style. That was pleasing, because we did it against the odds.

'I was always very ambitious. I remember Lawrence Dallaglio's book saying I came in from league with the attitude that it was the same ball, the same posts and the same pitch – keep it simple. I've always thought it was a good way of coaching. That's the attitude I come back to rugby league with.'

And for those pointing to Edwards's time away from rugby league, and how that could pose a stumbling block, he has a simple response. He said, 'I was asked when I joined rugby union about not being involved in the sport for 18 years, since I captained England Schoolboys. They asked me then how I'd cope going into union, and I don't think I did too badly there.'

There might be a season-long wait, but when Edwards takes over the feeling will be as special for him as it will be for the supporters who remember him playing for the club at Central Park. Those who are too young to remember will be aware of Edwards and what his appointment at the club means. You don't have to go far in Wigan to see a reminder somewhere. A picture of a trophy presentation, fans who remember Edwards in action showing videos to the newest generation of Warriors fans, articles in books and the star dedicated to him on Wigan's walk of fame in the town centre.

But what will it be like for him when he's back at work in the town? How is he going to feel on the morning of the first St Helens derby when he's head coach? 'I'll wish I was still playing,' he smiled.

THE FINAL WORD

SHAUN WANE

Wigan debut: 3 January 1982, at home to Barrow (lost 18-15)
Last Wigan match: 19 August 1990, Charity Shield v Widnes (lost 24-8)
Appearances: 149
Tries: 11
Points: 43
Winner's medals: John Player Special Trophy: 1985-86, 1988-89
Lancashire Cup: 1985-86, 1987-88
League Champions: 1986-87, 1989-90
Regal Trophy: 1989-90
Challenge Cup: 1988
World Club Challenge: 1988
Premiership Trophy: 1987
Head coach from 2012 - 2018
League Leaders' Shield: 2012
Challenge Cup: 2013
Grand Final winner: 2013, 2016 and 2018
World Club Challenge winner: 2017

'I'll die a happy man, that I've done my dream job – the best job I could imagine ever on earth. I've done it and I've won things. I've won everything. I've walked out at Old Trafford and I've run on the field at the end at Old Trafford and hugged my captain, who has trusted my game plan for us to win. I've won a World Club Challenge in front of my own family. I've lived a dream, I've done some great things, and I've done it for my home-town club, who I've watched from being five years old. It's a dream for me.

Shaun Wane has won the Super League title twice as a head coach, in 2013 and 2015, and once as assistant coach in 2010.

Shaun Wane with the Challenge Cup in 2013.

The World Club Challenge was a special one in 2017. Winning it as a coach is more satisfying than as a player for me. I know there will be some who disagree with that, but, for me, I enjoyed doing it as a coach, but both are great memories.

'I've given 30 years to the club and hopefully I've given good service to the club, given them good players and done my bit. But it's time to move on.

'Throughout my coaching the main thing is I don't want just a player. I want to know and I want to be good in my mind that when they've finished playing they're financially good, they're not struggling for anything, they crack on and enjoy their lives. I try to develop them as people and try and carry on the good work their parents are doing. It's not just about playing for me. It's about having good people in the joint, having good players who are improving and are never satisfied. We have many of those players at Wigan.

'I've coached lads from being 14 to 30-odd years old. I've been there a long time so it's very satisfying seeing them as kids then seeing them get married and have their own kids. Going to weddings and christenings, it's very satisfying to me.

'All the schools I went to, we played rugby. My dad played amateur rugby so it was just when I could walk and go out with him we went to the rugby and that was it, that was the end. I loved it, I loved going on the field at the end of the game and asking for tie-ups and then when I was 16 my dream happened and I signed. I never thought I'd end up playing for the first team, ever. But I did and I had a decent career before going on to coach, so I've absolutely had a fantastic time.

'Before I signed I knew my form was going okay. I was playing for St Pat's a year older than I actually was, I played with Andy Platt, Mike Gregory and Joe Lydon, people like that, so I had a great amateur career and really enjoyed it. There were a few clubs speaking to me at the time, Widnes, Leeds, Warrington, but I was only ever going to sign for my home-town club and I always felt like I didn't belong. I didn't feel like I should've signed and wasn't good enough to sign, but I did and made my debut pretty quickly and my career kicked on.

'I had some good coaches at Wigan and I had some ordinary coaches, but I learned a lot and a lot of what not to do as well. As I finished playing I went out working for big companies like Tarmac and I had good managers and they shaped me into being the coach I am today. Some people would say not a good coach, some would say good, but the way I am has been shaped by past experiences, past jobs, past coaches and some things I've kept and some things I've stayed well away from.

'When I was young I got expelled from school. I did some terrible things and I was always in trouble. Every day, every week, without fail. The one saving factor for me was Wigan schools, under-11s, under-13s, 15s, 16s, people like Geoff Hurst and Mick Mullaney and Derek Birchall helped me. Some unbelievably good people and good coaches who kept me on the straight and narrow. I was out of control when I was a young kid, I was very, very wild and they steadied me. They had a big influence on me.

'I am moving on to become a high-performance coach with the Scotland national rugby union team. It's looking at certain details where I feel I can have an effect. Details in attack, details in defence. They already have good structures in place, good coaches, and if I can just add my bit and improve in a slight way then I've done my job.

'I'm a players' coach. I stick up for my players no matter what and I back them to the hilt. Privately, if I need to deliver some awkward conversations then I will, but I'll always back my players, stick up for my players. I have a very close relationship with all of them, and players that have been with me and left. It's been a fantastic 20-odd years and I've made some unbelievably good friendships, so I'll be going to Scotland and still be going to games at Wigan. I'll be keeping my eye on the young lads and the older players. Sam Powell, Liam Farrell, Sean O'Loughlin, people like that, and I'll be watching Catalans to see Micky McIlorum, Lewis Tierney and Sam Tomkins, I'll be keeping my eye on them.

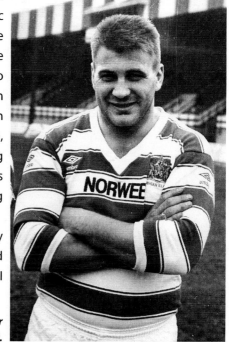

'Me and Lockers get on fantastically but we've had some very awkward conversations, I'll never back away. If I

Shaun Wane made 149 appearances for Wigan between 1982 and 1990.

think a player is under performing, he is getting told, no matter what relationship I've got with him. But I'll give him a way out, work with him myself on the field and that's how it works. I'm very honest, open, from player to me and me to the player. My way seems to have worked. I have a great relationship with the players, they seem to appreciate what I do and in a lot of ways I'm very, very sad it's come to an end, but it's the way it is and we just have to get on with it now.

'As for great memories, there are too many. I remember everybody writing us off in that year when we had injuries and we beat Warrington

Shaun Wane leads his side out for the 2016 Grand Final against Warrington.

at the end to win the 2016 Grand Final. I remember that being a win to prove everybody wrong because every single body in rugby league thought we couldn't do it and we were playing badly. We had games with 10 players out and we won the Grand Final. It was very close-knit that team.

'Winning the World Club Challenge at the DW Stadium in 2017 in front of my family with my grandson on the field, that was a great memory against a very good Cronulla team. Winning at Wembley has also been a highlight. I've just had so many great moments but apart from that, going to players' weddings, it's nice seeing them mature into family men who respect their wives. I like seeing them develop into good family men but when they get on a field change into somebody else, and that's the sort of individual I like.'

THANK YOU

Writing and compiling a book on the club I have supported all my life has been a privilege and is the realisation of an ambition I've held for as long as I can remember. It would not have been possible without the assistance of Wigan Warriors, and I'm grateful to the club for endorsing the book and allowing me to use the Warriors logo.

I would also like to thank each player, past and present, as well as the supporters who have given me their time to be interviewed. And I wish to thank those who have chosen to write their own stories about what Wigan Rugby League means to them. They are: Sean Lawless, Matt Macaulay, Jon Lyon, Darren Wrudd, Ben Reid, Bilko, Mark Illingworth, Greg Farrimond, Robert Kenyon, David Bailey, Gareth Davies and Dave Woods. A special mention to Bilko's website, cherryandwhite.co.uk, is also needed as this has been my one-stop shop to look up stats since I started writing.

Matthew Hennessey at Wigan Warriors has been generous with his time and assistance in helping me source interviews with players, and I would also like the thank the *Wigan Observer* and *Wigan Post* for allowing me use of their wonderful picture archive, which searching through has rekindled many happy memories. Bernard Platt has also been kind enough to help with use of his excellent photographs.

Phil Wilkinson and Janet Wilson have been generous with their support, and the opportunity to write this book would also not have been possible without them showing enough faith in me to take me on as a reporter in 2013.

At home, The Boss has been understanding and supportive when I have been shut away in the study to write and make phone calls, and her role in writing this book has been as valuable as the years of rugby league's influence, which has heavily shaped my life.

Thank you to Steve Caron at JMD Media for having faith in me and this project and helping me realise my ambition of seeing a book published. My parents' support from taking me to rugby matches to watch me develop into a mediocre player while getting soaked on freezing touchlines all those years ago will never be forgotten. This should also extend to every parent and coach who has done the same for the junior players in their lives. It's not an easy task but an essential one that often doesn't get the credit it deserves. Nor does the role my dad played on 27 April 2002 when just me and him went to create my happiest rugby memory at Murrayfield. There's not a day goes by I don't miss him dreadfully.